Cambridge IGCSE™ Physics Explained

About the author

Kaleem Akbar was born on the outskirts of Glasgow, Scotland in 1980. He graduated with a B.Sc. Honours degree in Optoelectronics and Laser Engineering from Heriot Watt University in 2002 and went on to do an M.Sc. at The University of St Andrews, before completing his PGDE (Post Graduate Diploma in Education) in Physics at Strathclyde University in Glasgow. He taught in Scotland before moving out to the Middle East and has taught Physics at IGCSE, AS and A2 level since September 2006. He wrote this book in response to his students' thirst for the essential details to achieve their full potential.

Cambridge IGCSE™ Physics Explained

Kaleem Akbar

Cambridge IGCSE™ Physics Explained
© Kaleem Akbar 2021

ISBN: 978-1-9996611-6-8

British Library Cataloguing in Publication Data
A catalogue record for this publication is available from
the British Library.

The example questions and answers contained in this book have
been written by the author.

Cambridge Assessment International Education bears no
responsibility for the example answers.

**IGCSE™ is the registered trademark of Cambridge
Assessment International Education.**

**Published 2021 by
REID EDUCATIONAL PRESS
Ayr, United Kingdom**

www.igcsephysics.com/cambridge

Acknowledgements

The author would like to thank the following professionals who have helped to make this book possible:

Lynda Anderson-Coe for editing the Physics content
Craig Walton for creating the illustrations
Shahad Al Qattan for designing the front cover

A special thanks to my wife **Toni Reid** for her unflappable support and to my good friend **Alistair Rae** for his counsel.

Thanks are also due to the countless students who have provided their invaluable feedback and recommendations for improving my original notes over the years.

Important information for students

The Cambridge IGCSE™ Physics 0625 and Cambridge IGCSE™ (9-1) 0972 syllabuses

The syllabuses contain **Core** and **Supplement** material. Core material should be regarded as basic material that all students must know for achieving a grade C on syllabus 0625 and a grade 5 on syllabus 0972. Supplement (or extended) material is more demanding material which will allow the student to achieve a higher grade.

Features in the book

Symbols

This book uses symbols to allow you to understand which material is Core and which is Supplement.

❑ Core material
○ Supplement material

Examples

The book contains examples of the types of calculations you may have to perform. All questions and answers have been written by the author.

Top Tip

Top Tip boxes contain useful advice and guidance that will help you to work to the best of your abilities.

Note

Note boxes summarise or highlight some important ideas.

N.B. is used at the beginning of some sentences. It is an abbreviation for a Latin expression and means 'note well'. It indicates that the sentence is particularly important.

Units

The SI system of units is the world's most widely used system of measurement. SI is an abbreviation for le Système International d'Unités.

The system has seven base units including the kilogram (kg), metre (m) and second (s).

There are other derived units including the metre per second (m/s), as well as recognised multipliers such as mega (M), kilo (k), centi (c) and milli (m), as well as G (giga), μ (micro) and n (nano) in the supplement syllabus.

All of the units used in this book are part of the SI system.

How to use this book

- You can show that you have learned the statements and explanations in each section with a tick in the checklist on page xii next to each topic or next to each square or circle bullet in the main text.
- A column has been left on the outside of each page so that you can make additional notes.
- Highlighter pen can also be used to emphasise important statements throughout this book.
- At the back of the book you will find **additional support material** with a list of all the **equations** expressed in different formats, including the triangular format. Simply cover up the quantity you want to calculate and the triangle will show whether the other quantities have to be multiplied or divided.
- There is a **glossary of terms** at the back of the book. A glossary is a brief dictionary that will help you to understand any words or phrases you're not sure of.
- The **glossary of examination terms** will help you to understand how you should answer examination questions.

Cambridge IGCSE Physics

The course

This book has been designed to cover all of the learning outcomes for the latest Cambridge IGCSE™ Physics 0625 and Cambridge IGCSE™ Physics (9-1) 0972 syllabuses for examinations from 2023 onwards. You should be aware that the syllabuses can vary slightly from year to year.

Examination structure

All candidates are expected to take three separate examination papers as outlined below.

Candidates who have studied the Core syllabus content will take **Papers 1, 3 and either 5 or 6.** The maximum grade that can be achieved from these papers is C for syllabus 0625 and 5 for syllabus 0972.

Candidates who have studied the Core and Supplement syllabus content will take **Papers 2, 4 and either 5 or 6**. The maximum grade that can be achieved from these papers is A* for syllabus 0625 and 9 for syllabus 0972.

Papers 1 and 2 are multiple-choice papers. These papers:

- take 45 minutes to complete
- consist of 40 items of the four-choice type
- test assessment objectives AO1 (Knowledge with understanding) and AO2 (Handling information and problem solving)
- are weighted at 30% of the final total mark.

Papers 3 and 4 are written papers. These papers:

- take 1 hour 15 minutes to complete
- consist of short-answer and structured questions
- test assessment objectives AO1 and AO2
- are weighted at 50% of the final total mark.

Candidates will take **either** Paper 5 or Paper 6, in which they will not be required to use knowledge outside the Core syllabus content.

Paper 5 is a practical test. The paper:

- takes 1 hour 15 minutes to complete
- tests skills in assessment objective AO3 (Experimental skills and investigations)
- is weighted at 20% of the final total mark.

Paper 6 is an alternative to the practical paper. The paper:

- takes 1 hour to complete
- tests skills in assessment objective AO3
- is weighted at 20% of the final total mark.

Good examination habits

- Make sure you are fully equipped for your examination; ensure you have pens, pencils, a pencil sharpener, a ruler, a rubber, a calculator, a protractor and compasses.
- Draw all diagrams in pencil.
- Draw graphs in pencil; ensure the drawn line is not thicker than the grid lines on the graph paper. Make sure that any best fit line is drawn in one sweeping movement using a ruler for a straight line and free hand for a curve. When drawing a curve, ensure that your wrist is on the inside of the curve. (If necessary, rotate the question paper.) Plot plus signs (+), crosses (×) or encircled dots (Ⓞ) rather than dots (·) on your graph.
- Always fully show your working for numerical questions to demonstrate your understanding. Remember to include units for calculated quantities in your answers to numerical questions.
- Ensure that you re-read the questions and not just your answers when you have completed your examination. You may find you have the right answer but for an entirely different question.
- Working through past examination questions is an important part of your preparation.

Contents

Additional support material

Revision checklist

			Tick box once revised. (The more times you revise each topic the better.)				
			1	2	3	4	5
Motion, forces and energy	1.1	Physical quantities and measurement techniques					
	1.2	Motion					
	1.3	Mass and weight					
	1.4	Density					
	1.5	Forces					
	1.6	Momentum					
	1.7	Energy, work and power					
	1.8	Pressure					
Thermal physics	2.1	Kinetic particle model of matter					
	2.2	Thermal properties and temperature					
	2.3	Transfer of thermal energy					
Waves	3.1	General properties of waves					
	3.2	Light					
	3.3	Electromagnetic spectrum					
	3.4	Sound					
Electricity and magnetism	4.1	Simple phenomena of magnetism					
	4.2	Electrical quantities					
	4.3	Electric circuits					
	4.4	Electrical safety					
	4.5	Electromagnetic effects					
Nuclear physics	5.1	The nuclear model of the atom					
	5.2	Radioactivity					
Space physics	6.1	Earth and the Solar System					
	6.2	Stars and the Universe					

"Everything should be made as simple as possible, but not simpler."

Attributed to Albert Einstein 1879 – 1955

Unit 1   Motion, forces and energy

Section 1.1   Physical quantities and measurement techniques

❏   When making measurements, physicists use different instruments, such as rulers to measure length, measuring cylinders to measure volume and stopwatches to measure time.

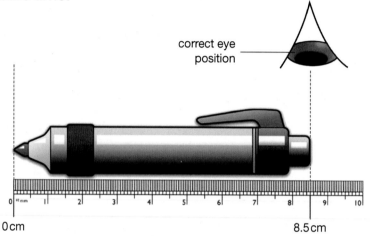

correct eye position

0 cm   8.5 cm

❏   A ruler is used to measure length. When using a ruler, be careful to avoid **parallax** error.

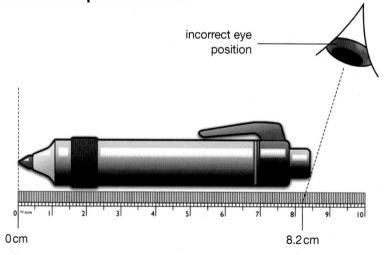

incorrect eye position

0 cm   8.2 cm

Note

Parallax causes an object to appear shorter or longer depending on how you view it. An object must be viewed at right angles to the scale to measure its length correctly.

❏   In the diagrams opposite the pencil is placed so that one end is on the zero of the metre rule, and the length is 8.5cm. Always check that the metre rule is not damaged or worn, and that the scale does start at zero, otherwise you would be introducing an error into your measurement. If the metre rule is damaged, you could place the end of the pencil at the 1.0cm mark for example. The other end would then be at 9.5cm and the length would be: 9.5−1.0 = 8.5cm.

❏   A measuring cylinder is used to measure volume. Volume must be measured to the bottom of the **meniscus** (the bottom of the curved surface of liquid).

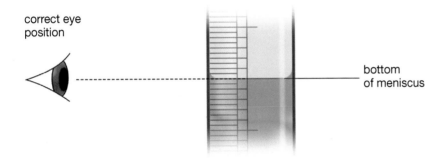

correct eye position

bottom of meniscus

❏   When using a measuring cylinder, again be careful to avoid parallax error.

❏   If the volume is not measured at right angles to the meniscus, parallax error causes incorrect high or low measurements.

❏   To get a more **accurate** value for small measurements, measure several units together.

If you have, say 50 sheets of paper, it is possible to measure the thickness of all 50 sheets and then calculate the thickness of one sheet by dividing by 50.

Similarly, if you measure the height of a column of 20 coins you can calculate the thickness of one coin by dividing the height of the column by 20.

Repeat the process several times (at least three times from different places) and calculate an average of your readings.

❏   Measuring the **period** of one pendulum swing can be very difficult, especially if the arc of the swing is small. The time it would take you to react would affect the measurement.

❏   By measuring the time taken for many (10 or 20) complete swings (oscillations), the period can be calculated by dividing the total time taken by the number of swings.

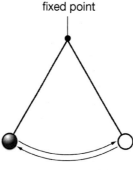

fixed point

one complete swing
(all the way to the right
and back to the left)

$$\text{period} = \frac{\text{total time}}{\text{number of swings}}$$

❏   Time can be measured with an analogue stopwatch or clock as shown above. These are mechanical devices as they operate from a coiled spring, which operates a series of gear wheels as it unwinds.

❏   A digital stopwatch can measure time to 0.01 of a second and so gives a **more precise** reading than using a mechanical stopwatch with a sweep second hand. It could still be **inaccurate** because of the reaction time of the person using it.

❏   The digital stopwatch on the opposite page shows a time of 3 minutes and 43.00 seconds.

❏ Digital timers are often used in connection with electronic circuits and can be switched on and off by sensors. They can therefore measure time intervals with high accuracy as well as high precision.

Top Tip

Repeating measurements, identifying and removing any results that are obviously wrong, and calculating an **average** or **mean value** is likely to improve the **accuracy** of an experiment.

❏ Some quantities have magnitude (size) only and are called **scalar** quantities. **Vector** quantities have magnitude and direction. You will learn more about those later.

Section 1.2   Motion

❑   **Speed** is a measure of how fast something is moving or the distance travelled per unit of time.

❑   **Average speed** is the speed measured over a relatively long period of time.

$$\text{average speed} = \frac{\text{total distance travelled}}{\text{total time taken}}$$

❑   **Instantaneous speed** is the speed measured over an extremely short period of time.

❑   **Speed** has the symbol v or sometimes u, and its unit is the **metre per second** (m/s).

❑   **Distance** has the symbol s, and its unit is the **metre** (m).

❑   **Time** has the symbol t, and its unit is the **second** (s).

❑   These quantities are related by the equation:

$$v = \frac{s}{t}$$

v = speed (m/s)
s = distance (m)
t = time (s)

❑   *Example*
A car travels at 20 m/s for 1 minute and 10 seconds.
Calculate how far it travels.

Answer

Step 1   List all the information in symbol form and change into appropriate and consistent SI units if required.

$v = 20$ m/s
$t = 1$ minute and 10 seconds $= 70$ s
$s = ?$

Step 2   Use and rearrange the correct equation.

$$v = \frac{s}{t} \quad \Rightarrow \quad s = vt$$

Step 3   Calculate the answer by putting the numbers into the equation.

$$s = vt = 20 \times 70 = 1400\,m = 1.4\,km$$

ALWAYS REMEMBER TO STATE THE UNIT FOR CALCULATED QUANTITIES.

○   A **scalar** quantity has **magnitude** (size) only.
A **vector** quantity has **magnitude** (size) and **direction**.

○   **Speed** is a scalar quantity because it has magnitude (size) only and can be described as the distance covered per unit time.

○   **Velocity** is a vector quantity because it has magnitude and direction. It can be described as the speed in a given direction.

○   The table below gives examples of scalars and vectors:

Scalar	Vector
speed	velocity
time	acceleration
distance	displacement
energy	force
mass	weight
power	momentum
temperature	electric field strength
density	gravitational field strength

Distance–time graphs

❑   Stationary
        (Not moving, at rest)

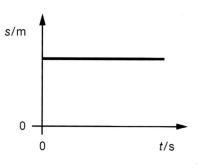

❑   Constant speed
        (No acceleration)

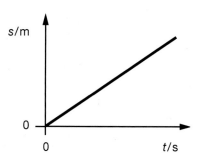

❑   Increasing speed
        (Acceleration)

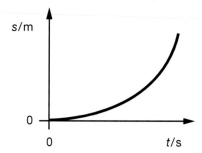

❑   Decreasing speed
        (Deceleration)

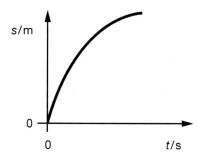

○   The speed can be calculated from the **gradient** (slope) of a
        distance–time graph.

> **Note**
>
>
>
> In mathematics the gradient is given by:
>
> $$m = \frac{\Delta y}{\Delta x}$$
>
> m = gradient
> Δy = change in y
> Δx = change in x
>
> For a distance–time graph:
>
> $$\text{gradient} = \frac{\text{distance travelled}}{\text{time taken}} = \textbf{speed}$$

Speed–time graphs

❏ **Constant speed**
Steady (uniform) speed
No acceleration
At rest if $v = 0$

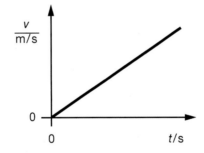

❏ **Constant acceleration**
Speeding up

❏ **Constant deceleration**
Slowing down
Negative acceleration
Decreasing speed

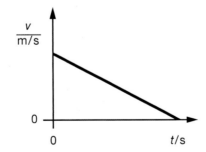

○ **Changing acceleration**
Increasing acceleration
(Gradient of curve increases)

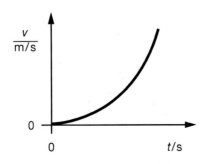

○ Changing acceleration
Decreasing acceleration
(Gradient of curve decreases)
Not decreasing speed

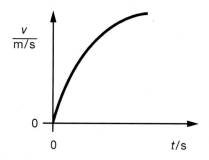

○ Changing deceleration
Decreasing deceleration
(Gradient of curve decreases)
Decreasing speed

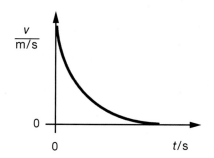

○ Acceleration has the symbol *a*, and it is the rate of change of velocity (how quickly an object becomes faster or slower). Its unit is the **metre per second squared** (m/s²).

$$a = \frac{\Delta v}{\Delta t} = \frac{v - u}{t}$$

a = acceleration (m/s²)
Δ*v* = change in velocity (m/s)
Δ*t* = time taken for change in velocity (s)
v = final velocity (m/s)
u = initial velocity (m/s)
t = time (s)

N.B. The symbol 'Δ' (Greek letter delta) means 'change in'.

The information from a **speed–time graph** can be used to calculate various values.

○ The **acceleration** – which is calculated by dividing the change in velocity by the time taken, i.e. the gradient.

❑ The **distance travelled** – which is equal to the **area under** the speed–time graph.

○ The **maximum acceleration** – which can be found by choosing the part of the graph with the steepest gradient (steepest slope) and then calculating the gradient.

Note

In mathematics the gradient is given by:

$$m = \frac{\Delta y}{\Delta x}$$

m = gradient
Δy = change in y
Δx = change in x

For a distance–time graph:

$$\text{gradient} = \frac{\text{distance travelled}}{\text{time taken}} = \text{speed}$$

❏ **Example 1**

The distance–time graph below shows the distance travelled by a car from $t = 0$.

(a)   Describe the motion during stages AB, BC and CD.

(b)   Calculate the speed during the three stages of the journey.

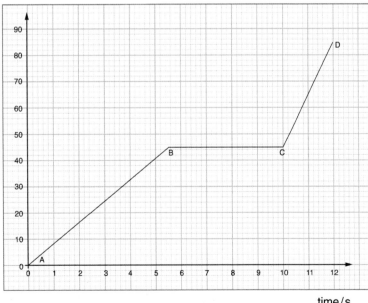

Answer

(a)   Stage AB: constant speed

Stage BC: stationary

Stage CD: constant speed (but a greater speed than in stage AB)

(b)   speed AB = gradient = $\dfrac{45-0}{5.5-0}$ = 8.2 m/s (to 2 sig. figs)

speed BC = 0 m/s

speed CD = gradient = $\dfrac{85-45}{12.0-10.0}$ = 20 m/s

ALWAYS REMEMBER TO STATE THE UNIT FOR CALCULATED QUANTITIES.

Example 2

The speed–time graph below represents a motorbike going on a very short journey from the rider's house (A) to a local store (F). Using the graph:

❑   (a)   describe the motion during the stages of the journey AB, BC, CD, DE and EF

○   (b)   calculate the acceleration during the five stages of the journey

❑   (c)   determine the maximum speed during the journey

❑   (d)   calculate the total distance travelled.

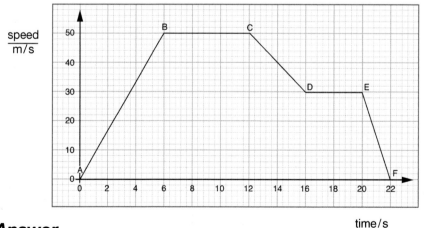

Answer

(a)   Stage AB: constant acceleration

Stage BC: constant speed

Stage CD: constant deceleration

Stage DE: constant speed

Stage EF: constant deceleration

(b)   AB: $a = \dfrac{v - u}{t} = \dfrac{50 - 0}{6.0} = 8.3 \, \text{m/s}^2$ (to 2 sig. figs)

CD: $a = \dfrac{v - u}{t} = \dfrac{30 - 50}{4.0} = -5.0 \, \text{m/s}^2$

EF: $a = \dfrac{v - u}{t} = \dfrac{0 - 30}{2.0} = -15 \, \text{m/s}^2$

For BC and DE $a = 0$

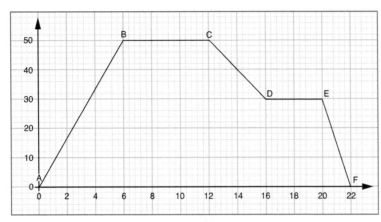

(c)   Maximum speed $= 50 \, \text{m/s}$

(d)   Distance travelled $=$ area under the graph

AB: $\dfrac{1}{2}(6.0 \times 50) = 150 \, \text{m}$

BC: $(6.0 \times 50) = 300 \, \text{m}$

CD: $\dfrac{1}{2}[4.0 \times (50 - 30)] + (4.0 \times 30) = 40 + 120 = 160 \, \text{m}$

DE: $(4.0 \times 30) = 120 \, \text{m}$

EF: $\dfrac{1}{2}(2.0 \times 30) = 30 \, \text{m}$

Total distance $= 150 + 300 + 160 + 120 + 30 = 760 \, \text{m}$

ALWAYS REMEMBER TO STATE THE UNIT FOR CALCULATED QUANTITIES.

○   The acceleration equation can be rearranged as:

$$v = u + at$$

v = final velocity (m/s)
u = initial velocity (m/s)
a = acceleration (m/s^2)
t = time (s)

○   When the **initial velocity u** is zero, the equation can be more simply expressed as $v = at$.

○   ***Example***

A toy car accelerates from rest at 10 cm/s^2 for 18 s.
Calculate the final velocity.

Answer

Step 1   List all the information in symbol form and change into appropriate and consistent SI units if required.

u = 0 because the toy car **starts from rest**
a = 10 cm/s^2 = 0.10 m/s^2
t = 18 s
v = ?

Step 2   Use the correct equation.

$v = u + at$
$v = at$ because $u = 0$

Step 3   Calculate the answer by putting the numbers into the equation.

$v = at$
   $= 0.10 \times 18 = 1.8$ m/s

**ALWAYS REMEMBER TO STATE THE UNIT FOR
CALCULATED QUANTITIES.**

In an examination situation you will often be required to think further using pre-existing knowledge.

Example

A quad bike decelerates uniformly from 3.5m/s to 1.0m/s in 10s. Calculate the distance travelled by the bike.

There are two ways to solve this problem.

Answer

○   Method 1 – Calculation

Step 1   List all the information in symbol form and change into appropriate and consistent SI units if required.

$u = 3.5\text{m/s}$
$v = 1.0\text{m/s}$
$t = 10\text{s}$
$s = ?$

Step 2   Use the correct equation.
Because the deceleration is uniform:

$$\textbf{distance} = \textbf{average speed} \times \textbf{time} = \left(\frac{u+v}{2}\right)t$$

Step 3   Calculate the answer by putting the numbers into the equation.

$$s = \left(\frac{u+v}{2}\right)t = \left(\frac{3.5+1.0}{2}\right) \times 10 = 22.5$$
$$= 23\text{m (to 2 sig. figs)}$$

ALWAYS REMEMBER TO STATE THE UNIT FOR CALCULATED QUANTITIES.

❑   <u>Method 2 – Using a graph</u>

Step 1   Sketch a speed–time graph using the information given.

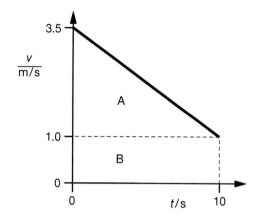

Step 2   Calculate the area under the graph. This is equal to the distance travelled.

$$\text{Area A} = \frac{1}{2} \left[(3.5 - 1.0) \times 10 \right] = 12.5\,\text{m}$$

$$\text{Area B} = 1.0 \times 10 = 10\,\text{m}$$

$$\text{Area A} + \text{Area B} = 12.5 + 10 = 22.5$$
$$= 23\,\text{m (to 2 sig. figs)}$$

ALWAYS REMEMBER TO STATE THE UNIT FOR CALCULATED QUANTITIES.

Section 1.3   Mass and weight

❑   Weight has the symbol **W** and it is a gravitational force. Its unit is the **newton** (N).

❑   Force and hence weight can be measured using a force meter, also known as a spring balance or newton meter.

❑   The **weight** of an object is defined as the force due to gravity acting on an object's mass.

❑   The **mass** of an object is a measure of the amount of matter in the object and can be measured using a mass balance.

❑   Mass has the symbol **m**, and its unit is the **kilogram** (kg).

◯   Mass is a property that resists change in motion. The greater the mass the more difficult it is to set an object in motion, to stop it or to change its direction.

❑   The mass of an object does not change as the strength of gravity changes. The weight, however, does change as the strength of gravity changes.

❑   The **gravitational field strength** is the force (weight) per unit mass; it has the symbol **g**, and its unit is the **newton per kilogram** (N/kg).

$$g = \frac{W}{m}$$

g = gravitational field strength (N/kg)
W = weight (N)
m = mass (kg)

❑ The relationship between weight, mass and gravitational field strength can be expressed as:

$$W = mg$$

W = weight (N)
m = mass (kg)
g = gravitational field strength (N/kg)

❑ On Earth the gravitational field strength is approximately 9.8 N/kg.

❑ Because g is a constant near to Earth, the weight of an object is proportional to its mass.

❑ If mass doubles, weight doubles. It follows that weights may be compared using a mass balance.

❑ **Example**
On Earth a man has a mass of 85 kg. Calculate his weight.

Answer

Step 1 List all the information in symbol form and change into appropriate and consistent SI units if required.

m = 85 kg
g = 9.8 N/kg
W = ?

Step 2 Use the correct equation.

$W = mg$

Step 3 Calculate the answer by putting the numbers into the equation.

$W = mg = 85 \times 9.8 = 833 = 830\,N$ (to 2 sig. figs)

ALWAYS REMEMBER TO STATE THE UNIT FOR CALCULATED QUANTITIES.

Top Tip

The **mass** of an object remains the **same** whether it is on Venus, Mars or Earth or anywhere else. This is because the **amount of matter** in the object stays the **same**. The **weight changes** because the **gravitational field strength** changes on different planets.

❑ The diagram below shows how the mass remains constant whether an astronaut is on the Moon or on Earth. Only the weight changes due to the different gravitational field strengths.

Earth
mass = 150 kg
gravitational field
strength = 9.8 N/kg
weight = 150 × 9.8 = 1470 N
= 1500 N (to 2 sig. figs)

Moon
mass = 150 kg
gravitational field
strength = 1.6 N/kg
weight = 150 × 1.6 = 240 N

Acceleration of free fall

❑   When an object is dropped from a height and falls to the ground, the force acting on it that causes it to fall is the force due to **gravity**.

❑   The acceleration of free fall (acceleration due to gravity) is approximately constant for objects near to the Earth (ignoring any air resistance).

❑   The acceleration of free fall is numerically equal to the gravitational field strength.

   N.B. *g* on Earth is sometimes taken as $10\,N/kg$ or $10\,m/s^2$ to simplify calculations, experiments or explanations.

○   Any **object falling** under gravity accelerates at approximately $9.8\,m/s^2$ near the surface of the Earth.
   This is known as the **acceleration of free fall**. If there is no **air resistance** then the object continues to speed up by $9.8\,m/s$ every second. It will **accelerate**.

○   If there is sufficient air resistance, then the object's acceleration starts at $9.8\,m/s^2$ and then **decreases to zero**, at which time its velocity becomes **constant**. This velocity is called **terminal velocity**.

   N.B. Any object **thrown upwards decelerates** at $9.8\,m/s^2$ (ignoring air resistance).

○   A student drops two objects of different masses from the leaning tower as shown opposite. The objects accelerate at $9.8\,m/s^2$ and hit the ground at the same time provided air resistance is negligible.

○   If the student had dropped a feather at the same time as one of the objects shown, it would have been more affected by air resistance and would have quickly reached terminal velocity.

○   When a parachutist jumps from a small aircraft he begins to fall to the ground as a result of the force due to gravity (his weight). At first his acceleration is $9.8\,\text{m/s}^2$.

○ The graph opposite shows how his velocity varies with time during his descent.

○ As he accelerates, air resistance opposes his motion and decreases his acceleration. At A the gradient of the graph is decreasing. The faster he travels, the greater the air resistance. In other words, the air resistance increases as he falls.

○ Eventually he reaches terminal velocity at B when the air resistance is equal to the force due to gravity. Because the two forces are in opposite directions there is no resultant (net) force (see page 31).

○ This terminal velocity is too high for him to land safely.

○ When he opens his parachute the air resistance increases greatly because of the very large surface area of the parachute.

○ The air resistance is greater than the force due to gravity. He continues to fall but decelerates rapidly, as shown at point C.

○ As he slows down, the air resistance decreases until once again he reaches terminal velocity at D, when the air resistance equals the force due to gravity. This terminal velocity is much lower and allows him to land safely.

○ When he lands, the ground exerts an upward force on him and he comes to rest.

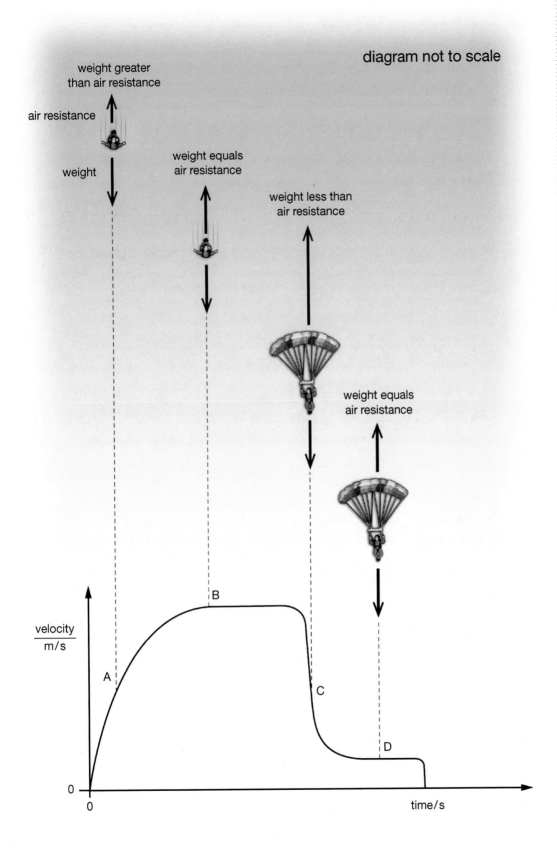

diagram not to scale

weight greater
than air resistance

air resistance

weight

weight equals
air resistance

weight less than
air resistance

weight equals
air resistance

velocity
m/s

B

A

C

D

0

0

time/s

Section 1.4   Density

❏   Density is defined as the **mass per unit volume** (how much mass is packed into a unit volume).

❏   Density is measured in kg/m³. (Another common unit is g/cm³.)

   The symbol for density is **ρ**, which is the letter rho from the Greek alphabet.

❏   Mass has the symbol **m**, and its unit is the **kilogram** (kg).

❏   Volume has the symbol **V**, and its unit is the **metre cubed** (m³).

❏   These quantities are related by the equation:

$$\rho = \frac{m}{V}$$

ρ = density (kg/m³)
m = mass (kg)
V = volume (m³)

❏   Generally, the density of a material when it is a solid is greater than its density when it is liquid. The density of a liquid is greater than that of a gas.

❏   Water is an exception because the density of the solid, ice, is lower than that of water. Ice floats in water because it is less dense.

❏   Lead is more dense than water and sinks. Some wood is less dense than water and floats.

❏   A liquid of lower density floats on top of a liquid of higher density, e.g. oil floats on water, provided the liquids do not mix.

❏   A ship made of steel floats on sea water because it contains other materials and a lot of air. Its average density is less than the density of sea water. If it carries a lot of cargo it floats lower in the water than if it carries less cargo.

Note

Each substance has its own density; one bar of gold has the **same density** as 100 bars of gold.

❑ Consider the following diagram representing gas particles in a box. All the particles have the same mass.

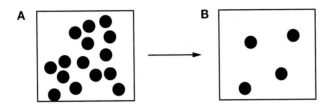

Boxes A and B have the same volume but a different number of particles. Box A has higher density as it has more particles.

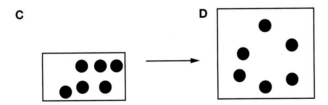

Box C is half the volume of box D with the same number of particles; hence box C has the higher density. The density of a gas depends on the number of particles (the mass) and the volume.

❑   The table below gives the densities of some common materials.

Material	Density kg/m³
air	1.3
oil	750–950
ice	920
wood	350–1100
water	1000
sea water	1030
rubber	900–1500
aluminium	2700
diamond	3520
steel	7750–8050
lead	11300
gold	19300

Determining density

❑   **Determining the density of a regularly shaped object**

1.   Use a mass balance to measure the mass **m** of the object.

2.   Use a ruler to measure the dimensions of the object and then calculate its volume **V**.

3.   Then use the following equation to calculate density:

$$\rho = \frac{m}{V}$$

> **Note**
>
>
> If you are using a force meter (newton meter) instead of a mass balance then you are measuring the weight **W**. Calculate the mass from the weight value using the equation:
>
> $$m = \frac{W}{g}$$ where **g** is the gravitational field strength (9.8 N/kg).

❏   *Example*

The block of wood has a mass of 80g. Calculate its density.

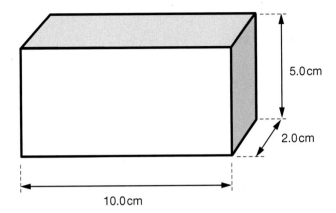

5.0cm

2.0cm

10.0cm

Answer

Step 1   List all the information in symbol form and change into appropriate and consistent SI units if required.

l = 10.0cm
w = 2.0cm
h = 5.0cm
m = 80g
ρ = ?

Step 2   Use the correct equations.

$$V = l \times w \times h \ \text{ and } \ \rho = \frac{m}{V}$$

Step 3   Calculate the answer by putting the numbers into the equations.

$$V = l \times w \times h = 10.0 \times 2.0 \times 5.0 = 100\,\text{cm}^3$$

$$\rho = \frac{m}{V} = \frac{80}{100} = 0.80\,\text{g/cm}^3$$

ALWAYS REMEMBER TO STATE THE UNIT FOR CALCULATED QUANTITIES.

Both kg/m^3 and g/cm^3 are acceptable units.

❏ **Determining the density of a liquid**

1. The mass *m* of the liquid can be measured using a mass balance. To find the mass of the liquid we subtract the mass of the empty measuring cylinder from the mass of the liquid and the measuring cylinder.

2. The volume *V* can be read directly from the measuring cylinder.

3. Then use the following equation to calculate density:

$$\rho = \frac{m}{V}$$

❏ *Example*

Use the information in the diagram below to calculate the density of water.

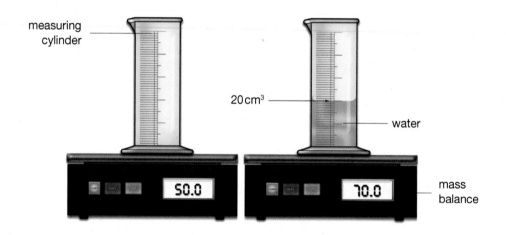

Answer

Step 1   List all the information in symbol form and change into appropriate and consistent SI units if required.

$m = 70 - 50 = 20\,g$
$V = 20\,cm^3$
$\rho = ?$

It is acceptable to use g and cm^3 for density calculations.

Step 2   Use the correct equation.

$$\rho = \frac{m}{V}$$

Step 3   Calculate the answer by putting the numbers into the equation.

$$\rho = \frac{m}{V} = \frac{20}{20} = 1.0 \, \text{g/cm}^3$$

ALWAYS REMEMBER TO STATE THE UNIT FOR CALCULATED QUANTITIES.

❏   **Determining the density of an irregularly shaped object**

In the procedure below we use the **displacement** of water method to determine the volume **V**.

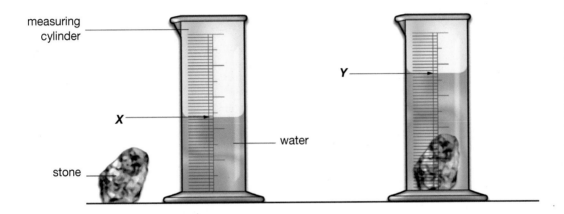

1.   Measure the mass **m** of the irregularly shaped object, in this case a stone, using a mass balance.

2.   Partially fill a measuring cylinder with a known volume **X** of water.

3.   Immerse the stone into the water.

4.   Measure the new volume **Y**.

5.   The volume of the stone is **Y−X**.

6.   Use the following equation to calculate the density

$$\rho = \frac{m}{V}$$

Remember: Always measure from the bottom of the **meniscus** when using a measuring cylinder to measure the volume of water.

❑   ***Example***

An irregularly shaped piece of steel has a mass of 102 g. The steel is immersed in the water as shown. Using the information from the diagram, calculate the density of steel.

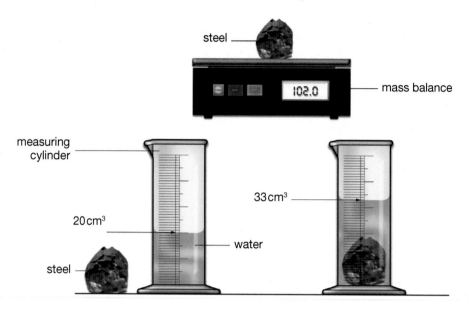

Answer

Step 1   List all the information in symbol form and change into appropriate and consistent SI units if required.

$m = 102\,g$

$V = 33 - 20 = 13\,cm^3$

$\rho = ?$

Step 2   Calculate the density by putting the numbers into the equation.

$$\rho = \frac{m}{V} = \frac{102}{13} = 7.85 = 7.9\,g/cm^3 \text{ (to 2 sig. figs)}$$

ALWAYS REMEMBER TO STATE THE UNIT FOR CALCULATED QUANTITIES.

Top Tip

If an irregularly shaped object floats on water, use a pin or a sharp pencil to poke it down below the surface so you can find its volume. Be careful not to push the pin or pencil into the water otherwise you will be measuring its volume as well as that of the irregular object.

Section 1.5   Forces

Effects of forces

❑   A **force** is a pull, push, twist, stretch, squeeze, tug or shove. We can observe the effects of forces but cannot see the actual forces themselves.

❑   Forces can:
-    change the speed of an object
-    change the direction of movement of an object
-    change the shape of an object
-    change the size of an object.

○   Force has magnitude and direction, so it is a vector.

Changing the speed of an object

❑   If the forces acting in opposite directions are equal, the forces are said to be **balanced**. The sum of the forces is zero in such cases. (In the following diagram all the values of **F** are the same.)

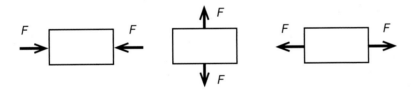

❑   When there are **no forces** acting, or the forces acting on an object are **balanced**, the object may be **stationary**.

❑   When an object is moving at a **constant** speed in a straight line, there is no **resultant force**. The forces on it are equal and in opposite directions.

❑   If the forces on an object are not balanced there is a **resultant force** that causes the object to speed up, slow down or change direction, depending on the direction of the resultant force. The resultant force is the **overall unbalanced force**.

○   **Resultant force** is the vector sum of all the forces on an object.

This leads to the following laws:

❏   <u>**Newton's 1st Law**</u> states that an object remains **at rest** or **moves** at a **steady speed** in a **straight line** unless acted on by a **resultant** or **unbalanced force**.

○   <u>**Newton's 2nd Law**</u> states that an object **accelerates** in the direction of a **resultant** or **unbalanced force**.

$$F = ma$$

F = resultant force (N)
m = mass (kg)
a = acceleration (m/s^2)

❏   Resultant force has the symbol F, and its unit is the **newton** (N).

❏   Mass has the symbol m, and is a measure of the amount of matter in an object. Its unit is the **kilogram** (kg).

○   Acceleration has the symbol a, and it is the rate of change of velocity (how quickly an object becomes faster or slower). Its unit is the **metre per second squared** (m/s^2).

❏   When the resultant force applied to an object is constant and the **mass** of the object **increases**, the **acceleration decreases**.

❏   When the mass of an object is constant and the **resultant force** applied to the object **increases**, the **acceleration increases**.

○   The two equations for acceleration in the Cambridge IGCSE Physics syllabus are:

$$a = \frac{F}{m} \qquad\qquad a = \frac{\Delta v}{\Delta t} = \frac{v - u}{t}$$

Changing the direction of motion of an object

Circular motion

○   If an object is moving in a **circle**, or along the **arc** of a circle,
    there must be a **force** acting on it to continually change its
    direction.

○   The force, which always acts **towards the centre** of the circle,
    is given the name **centripetal force**. It acts **perpendicularly** (at
    right angles) to the direction of motion of the object at any
    given instant.

○   In circular motion, a force always acts towards the centre. This
    ensures that the object **accelerates** towards the centre but
    does not move towards the centre. Objects A and B are
    examples of objects experiencing centripetal force.

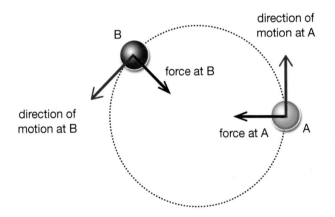

○   If the force for a given mass and radius is increased, the speed
    increases.

○   If the force for a given mass and speed is increased, the radius
    decreases.

○   If the mass is increased it requires a greater force to keep the
    speed and radius constant.

○   Satellites orbiting the Earth, the Earth orbiting the Sun, a tennis
    ball attached to a string and moving in a circle, are all examples
    where **centripetal forces** are present.

Adding and subtracting to calculate resultant forces

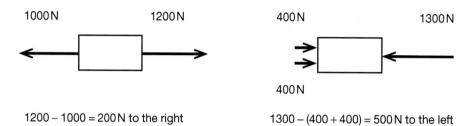

1000N   1200N   400N   1300N

400N

1200 − 1000 = 200N to the right   1300 − (400 + 400) = 500N to the left

○   Force is a vector, so it always has a direction.

❑   If forces are acting in opposite directions they should be subtracted. If forces are acting in the same direction they should be added.

❑   The same principles are used for forces acting vertically upwards and downwards, e.g. the forces on a falling object.

○   ***Example***

A jet ski accelerates at 2.0m/s² and has a resultant force of 540N in the direction of motion. Calculate the mass of the jet ski. (Ignore the mass of the rider.)

Answer

Step 1   List all the information in symbol form and change into appropriate and consistent SI units if required.

$$F = 540N$$
$$a = 2.0m/s^2$$
$$m = ?$$

Step 2   Use and rearrange the correct equation.

$$F = ma \quad \Rightarrow \quad m = \frac{F}{a}$$

Step 3   Calculate the answer by putting the numbers into the equation.

$$m = \frac{F}{a} = \frac{540}{2.0} = 270\,kg$$

ALWAYS REMEMBER TO STATE THE UNIT FOR CALCULATED QUANTITIES.

The resultant of two vectors at right angles to each other

○   Force, velocity and acceleration are **vector** quantities.

   Remember: A vector has **magnitude (size)** and **direction**.

○   Speed and mass are **scalar** quantities.

   Remember: A scalar quantity has **magnitude (size)** only.

○   We have learned how to add and subtract forces acting in the same or opposite direction. To find the resultant force when two vectors are at right angles we can draw a scale diagram.

Consider a girl who sets out to cross a river in a canoe travelling due east at 4.0 m/s. There is a current in the river of 3.0 m/s due north. To find out what will happen, we replace the two velocities with a single resultant velocity **R** that shows the direction in which the girl actually travels and her speed.

○   To find **R** we draw a scale diagram with the velocities in the correct direction, using a suitable scale, such as 1.0 cm : 1.0 m/s.

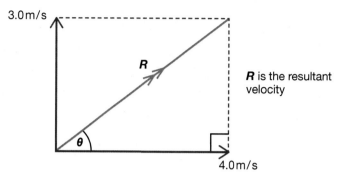

diagram for illustration purposes only, not to scale

○   The velocity of the girl is due east and the velocity of the river is due north. The angle between them is 90°.

The resultant velocity is obtained by completing the parallelogram with dashed lines. An arrow that represents the resultant velocity **R** is then drawn in. It is the diagonal line across the parallelogram from where the velocities originated. Measure the length of this arrow using a ruler and find the size of **R** using the scale of the diagram. You should find it is 5 cm, representing a velocity of 5 m/s.

Measure the angle, **θ**. You should find it is 37°, indicating that the canoe travels at 37° north of east.

○   Alternatively, we can calculate the value of **R** and its direction from the geometry of a triangle.

Applying Pythagoras' theorem and $\tan \boldsymbol{\theta} = \dfrac{\text{opposite}}{\text{adjacent}}$

$$\boldsymbol{R}^2 = 3^2 + 4^2 = 25$$
$$\boldsymbol{R} = \sqrt{25}$$
$$\boldsymbol{R} = 5 \text{ m/s}$$
$$\tan \boldsymbol{\theta} = \frac{3}{4}$$
$$\boldsymbol{\theta} = 36.9° = 37° \text{ (to 2 sig. figs)}$$

The girl travels at 5 m/s in a direction 37° north of east.

Friction

❑ The force of friction **opposes the motion** of an object.
Air resistance (drag) is a form of friction. Similarly, drag is the resistance a swimmer experiences as he tries to move through water. Drag can be reduced by streamlining, which provides a smooth surface over which the fluid can flow more easily.

❑ Friction causes heating, e.g. when one material is pushed across the surface of another.

❑ Friction can be useful in certain situations and not very useful in others.

❑ Friction is **useful** in the following situations and can be **increased** by:
- a skydiver opening a parachute allowing him/her to slow down quickly due to increased air resistance.
- pressing the brake pedals in a car, slowing it down quickly.

❑ Friction is **not useful** in the following situations and can be **decreased** by:
- skiers putting wax on their skis to make them smooth
- making objects **streamlined**, allowing them to travel faster by cutting through the air
- oiling engines to allow the parts to move easily.

○   ***Example***

A Formula One car has a mass of 900 kg (including the driver). When the engine exerts a driving force of 9000 N, the opposing frictional force is 800 N. Calculate the acceleration.

Answer

Step 1   Draw a diagram showing the forces acting on the object and their directions.

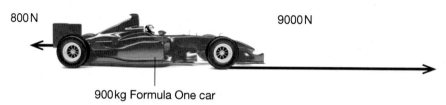

800 N   9000 N

900 kg Formula One car

Step 2   Calculate the **resultant** (**unbalanced**) force.

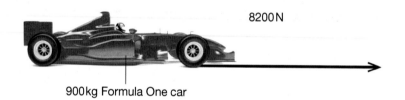

8200 N

900 kg Formula One car

$$F = 9000 - 800 = 8200\,N$$

Step 3   List all the information in symbol form and change into appropriate and consistent SI units if required.

$F = 8200\,N$
$m = 900\,kg$
$a = ?$

Step 4   Use and rearrange the correct equation.

$$F = ma \qquad \Rightarrow \qquad a = \frac{F}{m}$$

Step 5   Calculate the answer by putting the numbers into the equation.

$$a = \frac{F}{m} = \frac{8200}{900} = 9.11 = 9.1\,m/s^2 \text{ (to 2 sig. figs)}$$

**ALWAYS REMEMBER TO STATE THE UNIT FOR
CALCULATED QUANTITIES.**

Changing the shape of an object

Hooke's Law

○   Hooke's Law states that the **extension x** of a spring is **directly proportional** to the **force F** applied. A consequence of this is that if the force is doubled, the extension is doubled.

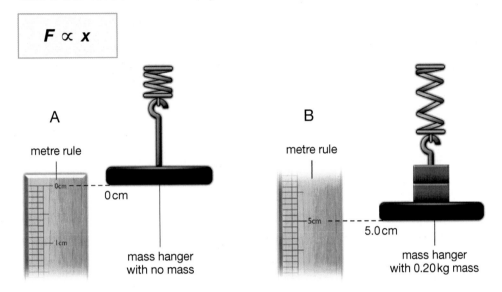

$$F \propto x$$

❑   The following experiment investigates Hooke's Law using a spring.

1.   Assemble the apparatus as shown in diagram A. (In a laboratory environment a clamp stand, metre rule, spring, mass hanger and some slotted masses would be needed.)

2.   Note and record the reading on the scale of the rule next to the bottom of the mass hanger without adding any masses. In diagram A this is 0 cm.

3.   Add one slotted mass (the weight or load of a 100 g mass is 1.0 N) to the hanger and measure the extension on the scale.

   N.B. g is 10 N/kg in this instance to simplify this experiment.

   The extension is measured by:

   extension = new length − original length

4. Repeat step 3, adding one mass at a time and record the corresponding extension reading.
    (Diagram B shows two 100g masses added. In this case the extension would equal the length of the spring with the 2.0N load minus the length of the spring with no load which is 5.0 – 0 = 5.0cm.)

5. Prepare a table of your results for load (calculated from the mass readings) and extension.

6. Plot a graph of extension against load. Your graph should be a straight line passing through the origin. This shows that the extension is directly proportional to the load (weight or force).

❑   The spring should return to its original length if you remove the masses. This means the spring is elastic.

○   If you continued to add masses your graph would look like the one below. The **limit of proportionality** is shown and is where the straight line ends.

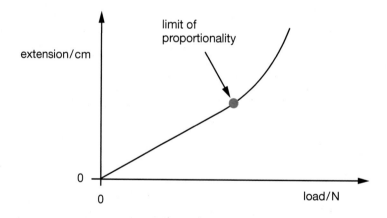

Note

If any two quantities are **directly proportional**, when they are plotted against each other on a graph, the graph has two characteristics.
-   It passes through the **origin**.
-   It is a **straight line**.

For Hooke's Law, if the load (force) is doubled then the extension doubles up to the limit of proportionality. In other words, the gradient of the extension–load graph is the same up until this point.

❑   Force has the symbol **F** and its unit is the **newton** (N).

❑   Extension of a spring has the symbol **x** and is measured in mm, cm or m.

○   The stiffness of the spring, known as the **spring constant**, has the symbol **k** and is measured in N/mm, N/cm or N/m.

○   The **spring constant k** is the force per unit extension and can be calculated by using the equation:

$$k = \frac{F}{x}$$

○   The force required to extend a spring can be found by rearranging the above equation:

$$F = kx$$

F = force (N)
k = spring constant (N/m)
x = extension (m)

○   The limit of proportionality is an important point.

-   If the spring is stretched only up to this point, the extension is directly proportional to the load (weight) applied. The spring obeys Hooke's Law.

-   If the spring is stretched beyond this point, it no longer extends proportionally to the load (weight) applied. The spring doesn't obey Hooke's Law.

Note

The **limit of proportionality** is the point beyond which the spring extension **is not directly proportional** to the load. Up to this limit the extension increases by a set amount for every newton of force applied. Above this limit the increase in extension per newton is greater.

○   ***Example***

A spring is stretched by 0.030m when a load of 3.0N is added. The limit of proportionality is not reached. Calculate:

(a)   the spring constant of the spring

(b)   the load required to stretch the spring by 0.080m.

Answer

(a)   **Step 1**   List all the information in symbol form and change into appropriate and consistent SI units if required.

$F = 3.0\,N$
$x = 0.030\,m$
$k = ?$

Step 2   Use and rearrange the correct equation.

$$F = kx \quad \Rightarrow \quad k = \frac{F}{x}$$

Step 3   Calculate the answer by putting the numbers into the equation.

$$k = \frac{F}{x} = \frac{3.0}{0.030} = 100\,N/m$$

(b)   **Step 1**   List all the information in symbol form and change into appropriate and consistent SI units if required.

$k = 100\,N/m$ (answer to part (a))
$x = 0.080\,m$
$F = ?$

Step 2   Use the correct equation.

$$F = kx$$

Step 3   Calculate the answer by putting the numbers into the equation.

$$F = kx = 100 \times 0.080 = 8.0\,N$$

ALWAYS REMEMBER TO STATE THE UNIT FOR CALCULATED QUANTITIES.

Turning effect of forces

❑   A **moment** is a measure of the **turning effect** of a force.

❑   The turning effect depends on two things:

-   the **magnitude** of the force applied
-   the **perpendicular distance** of the force from the **pivot**.

❑   Moment may be given the symbol *M*, and its unit is the **newton metre** (Nm).

❑   Force has the symbol *F*, and its unit is the **newton** (N).

❑   Distance has the symbol *d*, and its unit is the **metre** (m).

❑   These quantities are related by the equation:

$M = Fd$	M = moment (Nm) F = force (N) d = perpendicular distance from the pivot (m)

❑   The moment is greater if either *F* or *d* is increased. For example, you can use a longer spanner to make it easier to undo a tight nut, or you can apply more force on the original spanner.

❑   Examples where moments are important include:

-   door handles
-   see-saws (or teeter-totters)
-   cranes
-   levers.

Note

Doors are difficult to open or close if you pull or push near the pivot (the hinges); the further from the pivot you try to open or close the door, the easier it is. **The longer the distance from the pivot, the smaller the force required.**

❑   A pivot is an object around which rotational movement takes place.

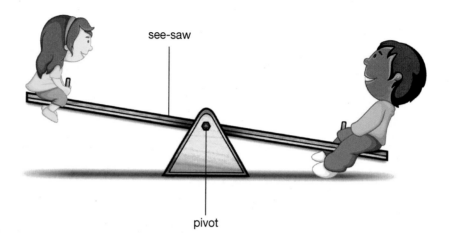

❑   The **principle of moments** states that for a beam to be balanced about a pivot, the sum of the clockwise moments **equals** the sum of the anti-clockwise moments.

sum of clockwise moments = sum of anti-clockwise moments
$$F_2 d_2 = F_1 d_1$$

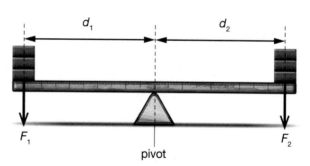

F_1 causes an anti-clockwise turning effect
F_2 causes a clockwise turning effect

❑   When there is no resultant force and no resultant moment (turning effect), a system is in **equilibrium (balanced)**.

❏   The following experiment demonstrates the principle of moments.

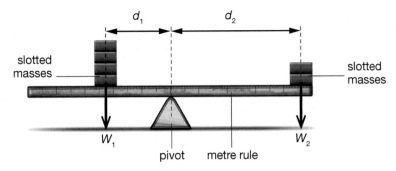

A typical experimental arrangement is shown above.

Apparatus:

- one triangular prism to act as the pivot

- one metre rule

- slotted masses, 100g each (of weight 1.0N each).

    N.B. *g* is 10N/kg in this instance to simplify this experiment.

1.   Balance the metre rule on the pivot at the 50.0cm mark of the rule.

2.   Add different masses (of weights) W_1 and W_2 at different distances d_1 and d_2 from the pivot. Carefully adjust the distances d_1 and d_2 until the metre rule balances horizontally.

3.   Record the values of W_1, W_2, d_1 and d_2.

4.   Repeat steps 2 and 3 several times, with different values for W_1, W_2, d_1 and d_2.

5.   For each set of results, calculate the moment of a force $W_1 \times d_1$ and $W_2 \times d_2$. You will see that $W_1 d_1 = W_2 d_2$. The metre rule is balanced when the clockwise moment equals the anti-clockwise moment, thus demonstrating the principle of moments. There is no net turning effect when a body is in equilibrium.

    Remember: Weight is a force, so we use *W* instead of *F* in this case.

The values below are a sample set of results showing that the anti-clockwise moment = the clockwise moment.

W_1/N	d_1/m	W_2/N	d_2/m	$W_1 \times d_1$/Nm	$W_2 \times d_2$/Nm
1.0	0.50	2.0	0.25	0.50	0.50
2.0	0.30	3.0	0.20	0.60	0.60

Note

If there is no net moment and no net force, a system is said to be in equilibrium.

○ **Example 1**

The diagram below shows an experimental set-up for investigating the moment (turning effect) of a force. The metre rule shown is balanced and therefore in equilibrium.

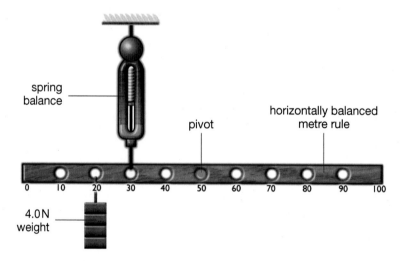

(a)   State two conditions for the metre rule to be in equilibrium.

(b)   Show that the reading on the spring balance is 6.0 N.

(c)   The weight of the rule is 1.7 N. Calculate the force exerted by the pivot on the metre rule.

Answer

(a)   1.   sum of clockwise moments
                        = sum of anti-clockwise moments
        i.e. there is no net moment on a body in equilibrium.

        2.   upward force = downward force
        i.e. there is no net force on a body in equilibrium.

(b) W_1 is 4.0N and it is 30cm (0.30m) from the pivot.
        W_2 is the reading on the spring balance, which is
        20cm (0.20m) from the pivot.

$$W_1 d_1 = W_2 d_2$$

$$4.0 \times 0.30 = W_2 \times 0.20$$

$$W_2 = \frac{4.0 \times 0.30}{0.20}$$

$$W_2 = 6.0N$$

(c)   upward force = downward force

        The upward force is 6.0N (reading on the spring balance).

        The downward force is
        4.0N + 1.7N (weight + weight of rule) = 5.7N

        Therefore a 0.30N downward force is required to
        balance the other forces, and so this is the force exerted
        by the pivot on the metre rule.

ALWAYS REMEMBER TO STATE THE UNIT FOR CALCULATED QUANTITIES.

○ **Example 2**

The diagram shows a metre rule in equilibrium. Calculate the unknown weight **F**.

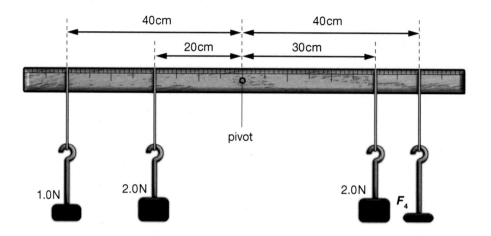

Answer

clockwise moments $= F_3d_3 + F_4d_4$

$= (2.0 \times 0.30) + (F_4 \times 0.40) = 0.60 + 0.40\,F_4$

Anti-clockwise moments $= F_1d_1 + F_2d_2$

$= (1.0 \times 0.40) + (2.0 \times 0.20) = 0.80\,\text{Nm}$

As the ruler is in equilibrium
sum of clockwise moments = sum of anti-clockwise moments

$$0.60 + 0.40F_4 = 0.80$$

$$0.40F_4 = 0.20$$

$$F_4 = 0.50\,\text{N}$$

ALWAYS REMEMBER TO STATE THE UNIT FOR CALCULATED QUANTITIES

Note

Not all calculations will be split into steps as shown in previous examples. In this calculation, knowledge is required of all steps. However, it is often important to convert units into SI units i.e. cm have been converted to m.

Centre of gravity

❑ The centre of gravity of an object is the point through which all the weight appears to be acting.

❑ This is a useful simplification as we can assume that the force of **gravity** only acts on a **single point**.

❑ This means a single arrow can represent the weight **W** of an object, as shown in the diagram of the tower below.

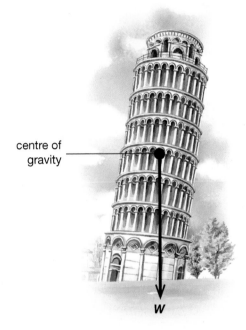

centre of gravity

W

❑ Although the tower is leaning, it does not topple because the line of action of its weight falls within the base (see page 51).

❑ The centre of gravity for objects with a regular shape is in the centre. Drawing dashed lines from various points through the middle of the shape can easily help find the centre of gravity as shown below.

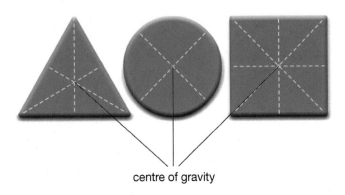

centre of gravity

❏   The following experiment describes how to find the centre of gravity of an **irregular** plane shape such as a piece of card.

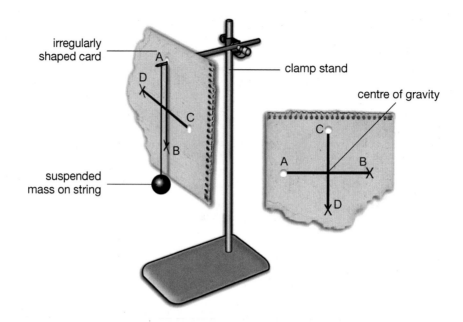

1.   Hang (suspend) the card from a rod held in a clamp stand from hole A.

2.   Suspend a mass on a string from the same rod.

3.   Put a cross towards the bottom of the card directly behind the string (e.g at point B).

4.   Remove the card and draw a line to mark the position of the string (e.g. from A to B). The centre of gravity is somewhere along the line of the string.

5.   Repeat steps 1 to 4 with the card hanging from different positions (e.g. from hole C). The centre of gravity is where the lines cross.

Top Tip

The centre of gravity is the point through which all the weight appears to act. A ruler balances perfectly when its centre is placed directly over a pivot. Otherwise it tips over.

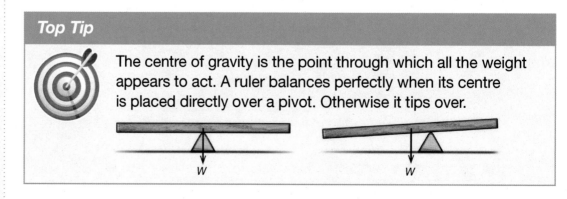

❏   The idea of centre of gravity is useful when predicting whether or not an object topples (falls) over.

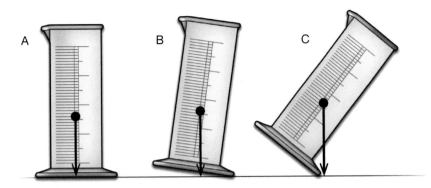

Consider measuring cylinders A, B and C.

- Measuring cylinders A and B do not topple over as the line of action of their weight falls within the base.

- Cylinder A is said to be in **stable equilibrium** as there is no resultant moment.

- Although cylinder B does not topple over, it is not in equilibrium. If it is released it will move back to the upright position.

- Cylinder C topples over as its line of action of its weight falls outside the base.

❏   A balanced object that is easy to topple over is said to be in **unstable equilibrium**, e.g. an inverted cone balanced on its point. When it is balanced the line of action of its weight acts through the point of the cone. A slight movement causes the line of action of its weight to fall outside the point and the cone topples.

Note

Racing cars travel at very high speeds and need to be very stable. They have a small height, which gives them **a low centre of gravity**. A racing car is also wide so that if it starts to tip, the line of action of its weight stays within the base and it rights itself.

In general:
wide and short = stable (low centre of gravity)
tall and thin = less stable (high centre of gravity)

Section 1.6   Momentum

○   **Linear momentum** is defined as the product of the mass and velocity.

○   **Momentum** is a vector quantity; it has size and direction. The momentum of an object changes if either the mass or the velocity changes, and this includes changing direction.

❑   Mass has the symbol m, and its unit is the **kilogram** (kg).

❑   Velocity has the symbol v, and its unit is the **metre per second** (m/s).

○   Momentum has the symbol p, and its unit is the **kilogram metre per second** (kgm/s).

○   These quantities are related by the equation:

$$p = mv$$

p = momentum (kgm/s)
m = mass (kg)
v = velocity (m/s)

○   Any mass that is moving has momentum.

-    An oil tanker (large boat) has a large momentum even when it is moving slowly because it has a very large mass.

-    A speedboat has a small momentum in comparison to the oil tanker because, although it can move much faster, it has a much smaller mass.

○   Momentum is the tendency of an object to keep moving in the same direction.

-    The same force acting for the same time produces a greater effect on the direction of motion of the speedboat.

○   *Example*

Calculate the momentum of a car with a mass of 1000 kg travelling due east at 25 m/s. Assume east is the positive direction.

Answer

Step 1   List all the information in symbol form and change into appropriate and consistent SI units if required.

$m = 1000$ kg
$v = 25$ m/s
$p = ?$

Step 2   Use the correct equation.

$p = mv$

Step 3   Calculate the answer by putting the numbers into the equation.

$p = mv = 1000 \times 25 = 25\,000$ kg m/s

Momentum is a vector quantity and so the answer should read: The momentum is 25 000 kg m/s due east.

ALWAYS REMEMBER TO STATE THE UNIT FOR CALCULATED QUANTITIES.

○   If we had a similar car travelling at the same speed due west we would say its momentum was −25 000 kg m/s because it is travelling in the opposite direction.

Newton's 2nd Law and momentum

○ We have previously learned (page 32) that according to Newton's 2nd Law:

$$F = ma$$

    F = force (N)
    m = mass (kg)
    a = acceleration (m/s²)

○ The acceleration can be calculated by using:

$$a = \frac{v - u}{t}$$

    a = acceleration (m/s²)
    v = final velocity (m/s)
    u = initial velocity (m/s)
    t = time (s)

○ The acceleration equation can be substituted into $F = ma$ to give:

$$F = \frac{m(v - u)}{t} = \frac{mv - mu}{t}$$

○ Since $p = mv$ then, in this case, mv is the final momentum and mu is the initial momentum. Therefore

$$force = \frac{change\ in\ momentum}{time}$$

$$F = \frac{\Delta p}{\Delta t} = \frac{\Delta (mv)}{\Delta t}$$

○ Rearranging this equation gives

$$F\Delta t = \Delta(mv)$$

○ We call $F\Delta t$ the **impulse**, i.e. the change in momentum when a force acts on a body for an interval of time. The unit of impulse is the newton second (Ns).

○   ## *Example*

A model train of mass 4.0 kg travels along a straight track. Its velocity increases from 2.0 m/s to 9.0 m/s in 5.0 s. Calculate the average force acting on the train.

Answer

Step 1   List all the information in symbol form and change into appropriate and consistent SI units if required.

m = 4.0 kg
u = 2.0 m/s
v = 9.0 m/s
t = 5.0 s
F = ?

Step 2   Use the correct equation.

$$F = ma = \frac{mv - mu}{t}$$

Step 3   Calculate the answer by putting the numbers into the equation.

$$F = \frac{(4.0 \times 9.0) - (4.0 \times 2.0)}{5.0} = 5.6\,N$$

ALWAYS REMEMBER TO STATE THE UNIT FOR CALCULATED QUANTITIES.

> **Note**
>
> It is common practice to denote an object moving from left to right as having a positive velocity and momentum, and an object moving from right to left as having negative velocity and momentum.

Conservation of momentum

○   The **principle of conservation of momentum** states that the total momentum of objects before they collide is equal to their total momentum after the collision provided no external forces act on the objects.

momentum before collision = momentum after collision

This principle allows us to predict how an object moves after a collision. A golf club striking a ball, a meteor crashing into a planet and two cars crashing into one another are all examples of collisions.

A lorry of mass m_1 travelling at a velocity of u_1 collides with a car of mass m_2 travelling at a velocity of u_2. After the collision, their velocities are v_1 and v_2, respectively, as shown below.

$$m_1u_1 + m_2u_2 = m_1v_1 + m_2v_2$$

Before collision

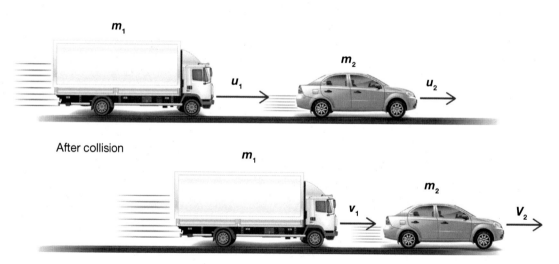

After collision

○   ### *Example* 1

A rubber ball A of mass 1.0 kg moving to the right at a velocity
of 4.0 m/s collides with another rubber ball B of mass 1.0 kg,
which is stationary. Ball A is stationary after the collision.
Calculate the velocity of ball B after the collision.

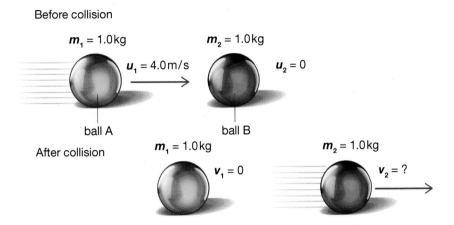

Answer

Step 1   List all the information in symbol form and
change into appropriate and consistent SI
units if required.

Before collision: After collision:

$m_1 = 1.0$ kg $m_1 = 1.0$ kg

$u_1 = +4.0$ m/s $v_1 = 0$

$m_2 = 1.0$ kg $m_2 = 1.0$ kg

$u_2 = 0$ $v_2 = ?$

Step 2   Use the correct equation.
momentum before = momentum after

$$m_1 u_1 + m_2 u_2 = m_1 v_1 + m_2 v_2$$

Step 3   Calculate the answer by putting the
numbers into the equation.

momentum before:

$$m_1 u_1 + m_2 u_2 = (1.0 \times 4.0) + (1.0 \times 0) = 4.0 \, \text{kg m/s}$$

momentum after:

$$m_1 v_1 + m_2 v_2 = (1.0 \times 0) + (1.0 \times v_2)$$

momentum before = momentum after

$$4.0 = v_2$$

Ball B moves to the right at 4.0m/s.

ALWAYS REMEMBER TO STATE THE UNIT FOR CALCULATED QUANTITIES.

○ ***Example* 2**

A toy car of mass 1.0kg moving to the right at a velocity of 1.0m/s collides with and sticks to a second toy car of mass 1.5kg moving at a velocity of 2.0m/s to the left. Calculate the velocity of the combined cars after the collision.

Before collision

$m_1 = 1.0$kg $u_1 = 1.0$m/s $u_2 = 2.0$m/s $m_2 = 1.5$kg

After collision

$v = ?$ $m_1 + m_2 = 2.5$kg

Answer

Step 1   List all the information in symbol form and change into appropriate and consistent SI units if required.

Before collision: After collision:

$m_1 = 1.0$kg

$u_1 = +1.0$m/s $m_1 + m_2 = 2.5$kg

$m_2 = 1.5$kg $v = ?$

$u_2 = -2.0$m/s

Since the toy cars stick together, the masses are combined after the collision.

Step 2   In all collisions with no external forces, momentum is conserved (see page 56). Use the correct equation.

momentum before = momentum after

$$m_1 u_1 + m_2 u_2 = (m_1 + m_2)v$$

Step 3   Calculate the answer by putting the numbers into the equation.

$$(1.0 \times 1.0) + (1.5 \times -2.0) = 2.5v$$
$$-2.0 = 2.5v$$
$$v = -0.80 \, \text{m/s}$$

The cars move to the left at 0.80 m/s.

ALWAYS REMEMBER TO STATE THE UNIT FOR CALCULATED QUANTITIES.

Section 1.7   Energy, work and power

Energy

❑   Energy **cannot** be **created** or **destroyed**; it may change from one form to another. We say that energy is **conserved**. In other words:

total energy into system = total energy out of system

❑   The unit of all forms of energy is the **joule** (J).

❑   There are various stores of energy.

Kinetic: movement energy

Potential: stored energy

Elastic (or strain): stored (i.e. potential) energy when an elastic material is stretched or squashed

Gravitational potential: energy stored due to height

Internal (thermal): vibration/movement energy of particles (atoms and molecules), i.e. heat

Radiation: energy carried as electromagnetic waves, e.g. light

Electrical: energy transferred by charges, e.g. current

Electrostatic: potential energy of separated charges

Chemical: energy stored in fuels such as petrol and food

Sound: energy transferred as pressure waves through materials

Nuclear: energy stored inside the nucleus of an atom

❑   Some examples of **conservation of energy transfers** are:

1.   A bus accelerating along a horizontal road
       chemical ➡ kinetic + thermal + sound

2.   A go-cart braking after travelling at a constant speed
       kinetic ➡ thermal

3.   A bicycle freewheeling downhill and speeding up
       gravitational potential ➡ kinetic + thermal

4.   A catapult slinging a stone
       elastic (potential) ➡ kinetic + thermal + sound

5.   An electric lamp

      electrical ➡ radiation (including light) + thermal

❏   In all changes, some energy is always transferred as thermal energy (often due to **friction**) and is often wasted.

Kinetic energy

❏   Kinetic energy is the energy associated with **movement** and is abbreviated as **k.e.** (symbol E_k), and its unit is the **joule** (J).

❏   Mass has the symbol **m**, and its unit is the **kilogram** (kg).

❏   Both **speed** and **velocity** have the symbol **v**, and their unit is the **metre per second** (m/s). When speed or velocity increases, **k.e.** increases.

○   These quantities are related by the equation

$$E_k = \frac{1}{2}mv^2$$

    E_k = kinetic energy (J)
    m = mass (kg)
    v = velocity (m/s)

To calculate the speed when you know the kinetic energy and mass, rearrange the above equation to give:

$$v = \sqrt{\frac{2E_k}{m}}$$

Remember: The **size** of the velocity **v** is equal to the speed of the object.

Top Tip

When a car travels at a **constant speed**, its **kinetic energy remains constant** as its speed **v** is not changing. Although its **k.e.** is not changing, the car still needs fuel (chemical energy) to keep moving at a constant speed because it is doing work against frictional forces.

○ **_Example_**

A toy car has a mass of 5.0 kg and travels at 60 cm/s. Calculate the kinetic energy of the car.

Answer

Step 1   List all the information in symbol form and change into appropriate and consistent SI units if required.

$$v = 60\,cm/s = 0.60\,m/s$$
$$m = 5.0\,kg$$
$$E_k = ?$$

Step 2   Use the correct equation.

$$E_k = \frac{1}{2}\,mv^2$$

Step 3   Calculate the answer by putting the numbers into the equation.

$$E_k = \frac{1}{2}\,mv^2 = \frac{1}{2} \times 5.0 \times 0.60^2 = 0.90\,J \text{ (to 2 sig. figs)}$$

(**Remember**: It is only speed that is squared.)

ALWAYS REMEMBER TO STATE THE UNIT FOR CALCULATED QUANTITIES.

Gravitational potential energy

❑   When an object is **lifted**, the work done against gravity is transformed into gravitational potential energy. It is abbreviated as **g.p.e.** or just **p.e.** (symbol E_p), and its unit is the **joule** (J).

○   The change in gravitational potential energy is equal to the work done by or against gravity.

Remember: We use the symbol '**Δ**' to indicate 'change in'.

○ The change in gravitational potential energy **g.p.e.** can be expressed by the following equation.

$$\Delta E_p = mg\Delta h$$

ΔE_p = change in gravitational potential energy (J)
m = mass (kg)
g = gravitational field strength (N/kg)
Δh = change in height (m)

❑ Energy is conserved. If we know the energy of an object at any one point, then calculating the energy at any other point is possible ignoring energy dissipated as thermal energy.

○ *Example*

A boy of mass 75 kg dives from a diving board 8.0 m above the surface of the water.

(a)   Calculate his gravitational potential energy at A (above that at the water's surface, B) just before he dives.

(b)   Find his kinetic energy at B just before he hits the water.

(c)   Determine his speed at B.

(d)   State the energy changes that occur after he enters the water.

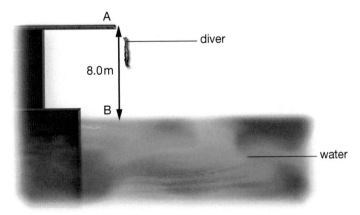

Answer

(a)   **Step 1**   List all the information in symbol form and change into appropriate and consistent SI units if required.

$m = 75\,\text{kg}$
$\Delta h = 8.0\,\text{m}$
$g = 9.8\,\text{N/kg}$

Step 2   Use the correct equation.

$$\Delta E_p = mg\Delta h$$

Step 3   Calculate the answer by putting the
numbers into the equation.

$$\Delta E_p = 75 \times 9.8 \times 8.0 = 5880\,J$$

(b)   As he falls, his gravitational potential energy is converted to
kinetic energy, since energy is conserved.

$$\Delta E_k = \Delta E_p = 5880\,J$$

(c)   **Step 2**   Use and rearrange the correct equation.

$$E_k = \frac{1}{2}mv^2 \implies v = \sqrt{\frac{2E_k}{m}}$$

Step 3   Calculate the answer by putting
the numbers into the equation.

$$v = \sqrt{\frac{2E_k}{m}} = \sqrt{\frac{2 \times 5880}{75}} = 13\ m/s\ \text{(to 2 sig. figs)}$$

**ALWAYS REMEMBER TO STATE THE UNIT FOR
CALCULATED QUANTITIES.**

(d)   When the boy enters the water, he slows down so he loses
kinetic energy, but he causes the water to move so it gains
kinetic energy. Some water will splash out and gain
gravitational potential energy. You will hear the splash, so
some of the energy transfers to sound energy and some is
wasted when it transfers to thermal energy in the water as a
result of friction/drag acting on the boy.

Top Tip

When an object falls freely in a vacuum under gravity its
gravitational potential energy (**g.p.e.**) decreases (since it is
getting lower) and its kinetic energy (**k.e.**) increases (since it is
getting faster). The **total energy** (g.p.e. + k.e.) stays the **same**
since energy is conserved.

If a runner runs up a hill at constant speed, her **k.e.** remains the same because the speed is **constant**, and her **g.p.e.** increases because she is getting **higher**. Her stored **chemical** energy decreases as she runs and some of the energy transfers to thermal energy. The **total energy** remains the **same** since energy is not lost: it just transfers from one store to another.

○   When an object falls, the equations for the change in **gravitational potential energy** and the final **kinetic energy** are related as shown below:

$$\Delta E_p = \Delta E_k$$

$$mg\Delta h = \frac{1}{2}mv^2 \text{ where } \Delta h \text{ is the change in height}$$

The mass **m** can be cancelled from both sides:

$$g\Delta h = \frac{1}{2}v^2$$

This can be rewritten as: $v = \sqrt{2g\Delta h}$

○   The speed or the change in height can be calculated provided we know one of them, as we know that the **gravitational field strength** on Earth is 9.8 N/kg. Consequently we can calculate the final speed or the initial height without knowing the mass.

You could be asked to find the speed of an object dropped from a height. The key here is to understand that the gravitational potential energy (**g.p.e.**) at the **top** is equal to the kinetic energy (**k.e.**) at the **bottom** just before it hits the ground.

At the top
The object has no **k.e.** since it is initially at rest (stationary). It has maximum **g.p.e.** since it is high up.

Near the bottom
When the object is at the bottom, it has maximum **k.e.** since it gets faster as it falls. All its **g.p.e.** has been transferred to **k.e.**

○   ***Example***

A boy drops a golf ball from rest off a cliff, which is 90 m high.

(a)   Calculate how fast the ball is travelling just before it hits the ground.

(b)   The speed is actually smaller in reality than that calculated. Explain why the actual speed is smaller than the value calculated in (a).

Answer

(a)   **Step 1**   List all the information in symbol form and change into appropriate and consistent SI units if required.

$$\Delta h = 90 \text{m}$$
$$g = 9.8 \text{N/kg} = 9.8 \text{m/s}^2$$
$$v = ?$$

Step 2   Use the correct equation.

$$v = \sqrt{2g\Delta h}$$

Step 3   Calculate the answer by putting the numbers into the equation.

$$v = \sqrt{2g\Delta h} = \sqrt{2 \times 9.8 \times 90} = 42 \text{m/s}$$

ALWAYS REMEMBER TO STATE THE UNIT FOR CALCULATED QUANTITIES.

(b)   The calculation ignores air resistance and assumes that **no energy** is transferred to the surroundings and that **all the gravitational potential energy is transferred into kinetic energy**. In fact, some of the energy is dissipated as thermal energy.

○ Some energy is **always** transferred as thermal energy; therefore the speed is always lower than the one calculated, as in the example on the opposite page.

○ In any process the energy tends to **dissipate** (spread) into the surroundings. When a pendulum bob is pulled to one side it is given gravitational potential energy because it is given height. When it is released this begins to transfer to kinetic energy, and then, as it swings past the centre of oscillation, it begins to transfer back to gravitational potential energy. As time progresses the swings become smaller; some of the gravitational potential/kinetic energy is being wasted as thermal energy through friction partly due to air resistance. This energy is not recoverable.

○ Energy transfers are often multi-stage. Consider a hydroelectric power station (see the diagram at the bottom of page 75).

- The water is stored in a dam at a higher level than the turbines of a generator. It has gravitational potential energy.

- The water travels through tunnels or pipes to the turbines and its gravitational potential energy transfers to kinetic energy as it loses height.

- As the water causes the turbines to move the kinetic energy of the water transfers to kinetic energy of the turbines.

- The movement of the turbines is transferred to the generator and electricity is produced. The kinetic energy of the turbines is transferred to electrical energy.

- The electrical energy is transferred via power lines to the consumer. It can then be used in many ways.

Remember: The total energy remains the same although some energy is dissipated or 'lost' to the surroundings in each transfer.

○   When the power station is first switched on.

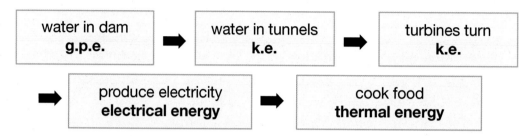

| water in dam **g.p.e.** | water in tunnels **k.e.** | turbines turn **k.e.** |

| produce electricity **electrical energy** | cook food **thermal energy** |

○   A **Sankey diagram** is a useful visual representation showing energy input and output.

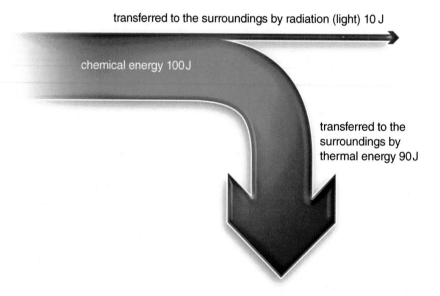

transferred to the surroundings by radiation (light) 10 J

chemical energy 100 J

transferred to the surroundings by thermal energy 90 J

The diagram above represents the energy of a light bulb with an efficiency of 10%, i.e. of the 100 J input only 10 J of the output is transferred by radiation (light). The rest is 'wasted' as thermal energy.

When drawing a Sankey diagram, make sure that the thickness of the arrows represents the relative amounts of energy.

○   Sankey diagrams can also be used to represent more complex examples of energy transfer.

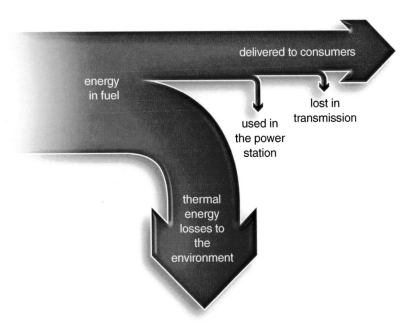

The diagram above shows how the energy of the fuel in a power station is used. Only about one-third of the input energy is delivered to consumers.

❑ **Efficiency** is often used to describe how good a device is at transferring energy from one store to another.

It is better for a car engine to be 70% rather than 50% efficient. This means the engine is transferring seven tenths of the chemical energy from the fuel into **useful** energy. The other 30% or three tenths is probably **dissipated** as thermal energy, amongst others. (Note that in cold countries some of this 30% would be **useful energy** rather than wasted as it would keep us warm in the car.)

❑ **Useful** energy can be described as the type of energy we want from a device or what it's built (designed) to do. For example, a television set gives out light, thermal energy and sound energy. We want to see and hear the television, so light and sound are useful forms of energy. We do not need the thermal energy; therefore it is sometimes described as wasted energy.

○   Efficiency is defined as:

$$\text{efficiency} = \frac{\text{useful energy output}}{\text{total energy input}} \times 100\%$$

For example, 100 J of electrical energy from a battery is transferred into 100 J of energy in a torch. If 15 J comes out as light then the other 85 J are wasted as thermal energy, and the efficiency of the torch is 15%. If 10 J comes out as light then 90 J are wasted as thermal energy, and the efficiency of the torch in this case is 10%. **100 J** of **input energy** is **always** converted into **100 J** of **output energy**.

Top Tip
Remember: **total energy into system = total energy out of system**

Work

❑   **Work** is done when a force is exerted through a distance. More work is done when:

-     the **force** is **larger**

-     the **distance** moved is **greater**.

❑   The **work done** is a measure of the amount of energy transferred by the force; it has the symbol **W**, and like all forms of energy, its unit is the **joule** (J).

○   Work done is related to the **force** and the **distance moved in the direction of the force** by the formula:

$W = Fd = \Delta E$

W = work done (J)
F = force (N)
d = distance moved by the force (m)
ΔE = energy transferred (J)

○   ***Example***

A 20N force pushes a toy tractor and 50J of energy is transferred to the tractor. Calculate the distance moved.

Answer

Step 1   List all the information in symbol form and change into appropriate and consistent SI units if required.

$F = 20\,N$

$W = \Delta E$ = energy transferred = $50\,J$

$d = ?$

Step 2   Use and rearrange the correct equation.

$$W = Fd \quad \Rightarrow \quad d = \frac{W}{F}$$

Step 3   Calculate the answer by putting the numbers into the equation.

$$d = \frac{W}{F} = \frac{50}{20} = 2.5\,m$$

ALWAYS REMEMBER TO STATE THE UNIT FOR CALCULATED QUANTITIES.

Energy resources

○   Energy cannot be created or destroyed; it can be **transferred** from one store into another. Transfers are never 100% efficient and the useful output energy is is less than the input.

○   Radiation from the **Sun** is our main source of energy. The exceptions are geothermal energy, nuclear energy and tidal energy. The Sun's energy comes from nuclear fusion.

○   **Fossil fuels** (**coal**, **oil** and **gas**) are currently the main source of energy used worldwide. The **chemical energy** in fossil fuels can be used to produce electricity.

○ Fossil fuels are the very highly compressed remains of dead plants and animals that lived many millions of years ago. Fossil fuel reserves will eventually run out. They are a **finite** or **non-renewable** resource.

Energy sources are **renewable** or **non-renewable**:

Renewable	Non-renewable
waves	oil
solar	coal
tidal	gas
wind	uranium (nuclear fission)
hydroelectric	hydrogen (nuclear fusion)
geothermal	

Nuclear fission and nuclear fusion

❑ **Nuclear fission**, which occurs in nuclear power plants, is the process in which large nuclei like uranium **split** into smaller ones, releasing a huge quantity of energy.

○ **Nuclear fusion**, which occurs in the Sun, is the process in which two small nuclei **combine** to form a larger one, again releasing an enormous amount of energy. In the Sun fusion occurs when hydrogen atoms combine to form helium (see page 242).

○ Research is currently being done to find out how nuclear fusion can be carried out in a controlled way to produce electrical energy. There are many difficulties to overcome before fusion reactors can produce electrical energy on a large scale, but nuclear fusion could solve the world's energy needs.

Generation of electricity from fossil and nuclear fuels

❏ **Chemical** energy from fuel is converted to **electrical** energy. There are essentially four main steps to generating electricity in a power station when using fossil fuels (coal, oil and gas) or nuclear fuel. After generation the electrical energy is transmitted all over the country (see page 235).

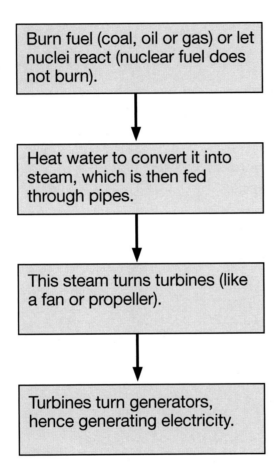

Burn fuel (coal, oil or gas) or let nuclei react (nuclear fuel does not burn).

↓

Heat water to convert it into steam, which is then fed through pipes.

↓

This steam turns turbines (like a fan or propeller).

↓

Turbines turn generators, hence generating electricity.

Generation of electricity from renewable sources

❏ ***Solar energy – makes use of energy from the Sun***
Solar cells, known as photovoltaic (PV) cells, convert light energy directly into electricity.

sunlight

❏ ***Wind energy – uses wind to turn turbines***
Wind energy turns the turbine blades in a wind turbine. The turbines rotate the generator. The generator transfers the kinetic energy of the wind to electrical energy.

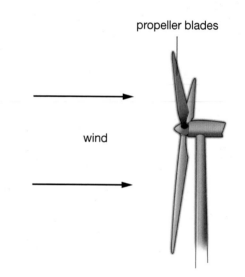

propeller blades

wind

❏ ***Wave energy – makes use of ocean waves to turn turbines***
Generators are driven by the transverse (up and down) motion of the wave. The kinetic energy of the wave motion causes water to rise and fall in the air chamber. The air above the water causes the turbine to turn and electricity is produced by the generator.

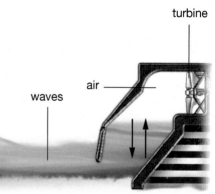

turbine

air

waves

❏ *Tidal energy – makes use of incoming and outgoing tides*

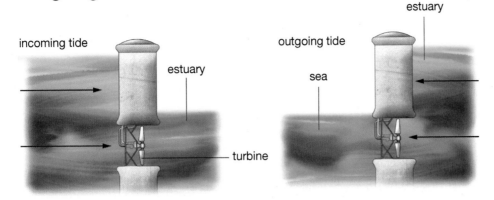

Tidal energy causes the water to move. As it does so it turns the turbines and electricity is generated. The gravitational potential energy and kinetic energy of the water transfers to electrical energy.

❏ *Geothermal energy – uses heat energy from the Earth's core*

Water is fed down through pipes several kilometres underground, passing through hot rocks. These rocks heat the water until it turns into very hot steam. The steam is fed back up to ground level and is used to turn turbines and generate electricity.

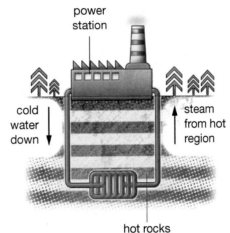

❏ *Hydroelectric energy – uses a dam to trap water*

A dam is built to trap water, sometimes in a valley where there is an existing lake. Water is allowed to flow through tunnels in the dam, to turn turbines and thus drive the generators that produce electricity.

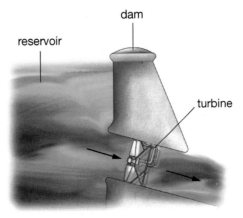

Other useful forms of energy obtained from these sources

❑ Electricity is a very useful form of energy for modern life. But the same natural energy sources have long provided us with other types of useful energy.

- Chemical energy from fuels such as wood or coal is transferred to thermal energy by combustion (burning).

- Stored chemical potential energy in petrol can be used to move engines and vehicles (kinetic energy).

- Geothermal energy can be used to heat homes using a series of pumps and pipes.

- Solar energy can be used directly as thermal and light energy. Solar water-heating panels can be fixed on roofs to capture this efficiently.

- Wind and watermills have been used for centuries, for example for pumping water, grinding flour and crushing rocks.

Advantages of non-renewable sources

❑ These fuels are far more energy dense than renewable sources and thus, in many countries, they allow production of larger amounts of energy in comparison to renewable sources. They are also relatively easy to transport and can be stored ready for use.

Disadvantages of non-renewable sources

❑ Fossil fuels are becoming increasingly expensive to mine (coal) and drill for (oil), as reserves are running out (being **depleted**). They cause **global warming** due to high carbon dioxide (CO_2) emissions when they are burnt. Some also produce sulfur dioxide (SO_2), which causes **acid rain**.

Nuclear power stations are expensive to build and any radiation leak or explosion may have a devastating effect on the immediate population and environment, as well as the population and environment at large.

Advantages of renewable sources

❑ They are all regarded as clean (producing little or no pollution) and will not run out. The fuel itself is cheap or free.

Disadvantages of renewable sources

❑   Generally all renewable energy sources have high initial installation costs and the supply may not be constant.

❑   *Solar energy*

-   When the sun doesn't shine (e.g. at night) no electricity is produced.
-   Dirty solar panels are inefficient.
-   To install panels is an expensive process.
-   The panels take up large areas.

❑   *Wind energy*

-   When the wind doesn't blow no electricity is produced.
-   Wind farms can destroy the natural beauty of a landscape and are noisy.
-   Offshore wind farms are expensive to build and need to be avoided by boats.

❑   *Wave energy*

-   Waves vary in size and therefore produce varying quantities (amounts) of energy. When the sea is calm, no electricity is produced.
-   Installation is expensive and challenging.
-   Boats would have to be careful and be aware of the location of the turbines to prevent accidents.

❑   *Tidal energy*

-   Many countries do not have suitable locations.
-   Might affect local marine life and destroy habitats.

❑   *Geothermal energy*

-   There are few locations that are suitable.
-   It is often necessary to drill very deep and this makes the energy very expensive to obtain.

❑   *Hydroelectric energy*

-   The local environment may be destroyed because water needs to be stored behind a dam, the land behind it flooding.
-   Dams are expensive to build.

Power

❑ If a man pushes a weight through a distance, he does work. His power is related to how quickly he does that work; the faster he does it the more power he has.

❑ A car does work when its engine exerts a driving force and it moves through a distance. Cars with more powerful engines can do work quicker than less powerful ones. They can usually travel faster.

❑ **Power** is the rate of doing work. It has the symbol **P**, and its unit is the **watt** (W); one watt is defined as **one joule per second**:

$1\,W = 1\,J/s$

A 100 W lamp uses 100 J of energy every second.

○ Power is related to energy (work done) and time by the equation:

$$P = \frac{W}{t} = \frac{\Delta E}{t}$$

P = power (W)
W = work done (J)
ΔE = energy transferred (J)
t = time (s)

○ It follows that **efficiency** can also be expressed by the following equation:

$$\text{efficiency} = \frac{\text{useful power output}}{\text{total power input}} \times 100\,\%$$

Note

The **time taken** to do something **does not** have an effect on the **work done**. The time taken **does** have an effect on the **power**.

○   *Example*

An athlete exerts an average force of 30N in the direction of her motion while running. She runs a distance of 1.6km in 5.0 minutes. Calculate her power expended as a result of the 30N force.

Answer

Step 1   List all the information in symbol form and change into appropriate and consistent SI units if required.

$$F = 30N$$
$$d = 1.6km = 1600m$$
$$t = 5.0 \text{ minutes} = 5.0 \times 60 = 300s$$
$$P = ?$$

Step 2   Choose the correct equations.

$$W = Fd \qquad\qquad P = \frac{W}{t}$$

Step 3   Calculate the answer by putting the numbers into the equations.

$$W = Fd = 30 \times 1600 = 48000J$$

$$P = \frac{W}{t} = \frac{48000}{300} = 160W$$

ALWAYS REMEMBER TO STATE THE UNIT FOR CALCULATED QUANTITIES.

Top Tip

In some calculations, **two** equations have to be used to find the answer as shown above.

Section 1.8 Pressure

❏ Pressure is defined as the **force per unit area**.

❏ Pressure has the symbol **p**, and its unit is the **pascal** (Pa).

❏ Pressure, force and area are related by the equation:

$$p = \frac{F}{A}$$

p = pressure (Pa) or (N/m²)
F = force (N)
A = area (m²)

❏ 1 Pa is equivalent to 1 N/m² (**newton per metre squared**).

❏ Pressure can be increased by **increasing the force** on a constant area.

❏ Pressure can be increased by **decreasing the area** for a constant force.

❏ A girl weighing 500 N and wearing high heels with an area of 2 cm² in contact with the floor can make indentations on a wooden floor, because the pressure she exerts is 2 500 000 Pa.

An elephant weighing 40 000 N and standing on all four feet, a total area of 0.4 m², would exert a pressure of only 100 000 Pa.

❏ A sharp knife cuts bread more easily than a blunt knife. This is because the sharp knife has a much smaller surface area in contact with the bread than a blunt knife. When you push down on the knife (exert a force) the sharp knife exerts greater pressure on the bread and it cuts easily.

○ **Example**

A rectangular block has a mass of 250g and dimensions 5.0cm × 12.0cm × 2.0cm. Calculate the maximum pressure that can be exerted on the surface due to the block.

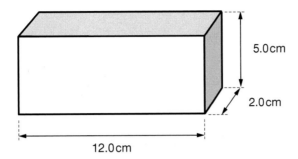

5.0cm

2.0cm

12.0cm

Answer

Step 1   List all the information in symbol form and change into appropriate and consistent SI units if required. The question asks for the maximum pressure. The maximum pressure is exerted when the block rests on the smallest area.

m = 250g = 0.25kg

A = 5.0 × 2.0 = 10cm² = 10 × 10⁻⁴m²
$= 1.0 \times 10^{-3} m^2$

p = ?

Remember: Take care when changing the units of area:

$1 cm^2 = 1 \times 10^{-4} m^2$

Step 2   Choose the correct equations.

$$F = \text{weight} = W = mg \qquad p = \frac{F}{A}$$

Step 3   Calculate the answer by putting the numbers into the equations.

$$w = mg = 0.25 \times 9.8 = 2.45 N$$

$$p = \frac{F}{A} = \frac{2.45}{1.0 \times 10^{-3}} = 2450 = 2500 Pa \text{ (to 2 sig. figs)}$$

ALWAYS REMEMBER TO STATE THE UNIT FOR CALCULATED QUANTITIES.

More practical examples of pressure

❑ Snow shoes shaped like tennis rackets are used in very cold places so that people don't sink into the snow. The **large area** of the snow shoe **decreases** the **pressure** on the snow.

snow shoes

❑ Camels have **large feet** to **decrease** the **pressure** they exert on the ground so that they do not sink into the sand.

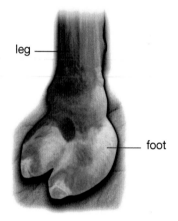

leg

foot

❑ Pushing a drawing pin into soft wood is easy as the point has a **very small area** so there is a **very large pressure**.

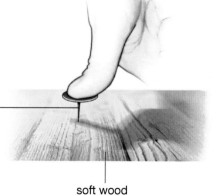

drawing pin

soft wood

❑   The air around us exerts a pressure. This pressure is called **atmospheric pressure**.

❑   Atmospheric pressure has the following properties.

- Its effect **acts equally in all directions**.
- It **decreases** as altitude (height above sea level) increases because the air molecules become further apart (the air is less dense).
- It **increases** as altitude decreases because air molecules become closer together (the air is more dense). At **sea level**, it is approximately equal to 100 000 Pa (100 kPa).

❑   Liquids also exert pressure. Pressure has the following properties in **liquids**.

- The pressure acts **equally in all directions**; it pushes on every surface that the liquid is in contact with.
- The pressure increases with **increasing depth** due to the weight of the column of liquid (height h) above the measurement point.
- The pressure also depends on the density of the liquid; the greater the **density**, the greater the pressure at a given depth.

❑   The pressure of a liquid varies directly with the height h and the density ρ (rho) of the liquid. As a result the pressure is greater at the bottom of a 10 cm tall measuring cylinder full of water than the pressure due to 10 cm of oil in an identical cylinder because the water is more **dense**.
To achieve the same pressure with oil you would need a taller cylinder to increase the height h.

○ In a liquid, change in pressure, density, gravitational field strength and difference in height/depth are related by the equation:

$$\Delta p = \rho g \Delta h$$

Δp = change in pressure (Pa or N/m^2)
ρ = density (kg/m^3)
g = gravitational field strength (N/kg)
Δh = difference in height/depth (m)

Remember: density $= \dfrac{\text{mass}}{\text{volume}}$ $\rho = \dfrac{m}{V}$

By rearranging the equation we see that the difference in height/depth depends on pressure, density and gravitational field strength:

$$\Delta h = \frac{\Delta p}{\rho g}$$

○ ***Example***

A diver is 18m below the surface of water of density 1000 kg/m^3. Calculate the pressure the water exerts on him.

Step 1   List all the information in symbol form and change into appropriate and consistent SI units if required.

g = 9.8 N/kg
Δh = 18 m
ρ = 1000 kg/m^3
Δp = ?

Step 2   Use the correct equation.

$\Delta p = \rho g \Delta h$

Step 3   Calculate the answer by putting the numbers into the equation.

$\Delta p = \rho g \Delta h = 1000 \times 9.8 \times 18 = 1.8 \times 10^5 \, \text{Pa}$

(to 2 sig. figs)

ALWAYS REMEMBER TO STATE THE UNIT FOR CALCULATED QUANTITIES.

Top Tip

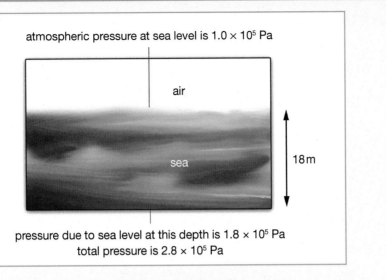

atmospheric pressure at sea level is 1.0×10^5 Pa

air

sea

18 m

pressure due to sea level at this depth is 1.8×10^5 Pa
total pressure is 2.8×10^5 Pa

The **total** pressure on the diver is 280 000 Pa (2.8×10^5 Pa) rather than 180 000 Pa (1.8×10^5 Pa) because atmospheric pressure of 100 000 Pa (1.0×10^5 Pa) has to be added to the pressure caused by sea water.

Unit 2 Thermal physics

Section 2.1   Kinetic particle model of matter

States of matter

❑   The three states of matter are:

1.   solid

2.   liquid

3.   gas.

❑   Substances can change state when they are heated or cooled. For example, when ice is heated it eventually changes into water; we call this change of state **melting**.

❑   When pure water is heated to 100°C, it **boils** and becomes steam; we call this change of state **boiling**.

❑   And when steam is cooled to 100°C, it **condenses** into water, and when water is cooled to 0°C, it **solidifies** into ice.

Particle model

❑   The kinetic particle model of matter explains the behaviour of solids, liquids and gases in terms of how they are **arranged** and the **movement** of the particles from which they are made.

◯   All matter is made up of 118 substances called **elements**. An **atom** is considered to be the basic building block of ordinary matter, e.g. the smallest possible amount of an element. Atoms are composed (made up) of smaller particles called protons, neutrons and electrons (see page 169). Atoms can become electrically charged when they lose or gain electrons; this is known as ionisation (see pages 171-2).
Electrically neutral atoms can group together to form **molecules**.

O   Atoms, molecules, ions, protons, neutrons and electrons are referred to as particles.

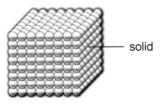

solid

❑   **Properties of a solid**

- The particles are fixed **close together** in a regular lattice pattern, for example arranged in neat rows.
- The particles **vibrate** around a fixed position but do not move from place to place.
- Solids have a **fixed shape**.
- Solids have a **fixed volume** (provided the temperature and pressure remain constant).

O   There are very **strong forces of attraction** between particles because they are close together. (Individual particles cannot break free from the lattice.)

O   Solids cannot be squashed or compressed easily because the particles are close together and it takes a very large force to push them closer.

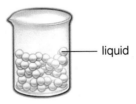

liquid

❑   **Properties of a liquid**

- The particles are still close together but have no fixed arrangement.
- The particles are **free to move** and tend to **slip and slide** past each other.

- Liquids do not have a fixed shape; they **take the shape** of the bottom of the container they are in.

- Liquids have a **fixed volume** (provided the temperature and pressure remain constant).

○ There are slightly **weaker forces of attraction** between particles.

○ Liquids cannot be squashed or compressed as the particles are close together.

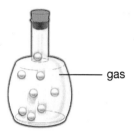

—— gas

❑ **Properties of a gas**

- The particles are very much further apart than in liquids.
- The particles **move very fast** in **random directions**.
- The particles are constantly **colliding** with each other and the walls of the container.
- Gases have **no fixed shape** or **volume**; they fill any container in which they are placed.

○ Gases can be squashed or **compressed** because the particles are far apart.

○ There are **negligible** forces of attraction between particles.

Note

The **temperature of a substance** is a measure of the **kinetic energy** of its particles. The **faster** the particles move or vibrate, the greater the temperature and the **hotter** the substance. The **slower** the particles move or vibrate, the **colder** the substance.

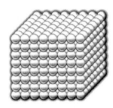  

The table below lists the main properties of solids, liquids and gases.

Solid	Liquid	Gas
very slightly compressible	incompressible	can be compressed
fixed shape	takes on the shape of the bottom of the container	fills the container, taking on its shape
fixed volume	fixed volume	no fixed volume
static	can flow	can flow
particles very closely packed	particles disordered and closely packed	particles far apart
very strong forces of attraction between particles	strong forces of attraction between particles	almost no forces of attraction between particles

Note

Particles in the solid state have the least energy and particles in the gaseous state have the most energy.

Remember: When it comes to states of matter:

think movement – think energy.

Brownian motion

❑   The Brownian motion experiment uses a microscope to view very small smoke particles in a transparent air cell. It shows the smoke particles moving randomly. This is evidence of free-moving air particles.

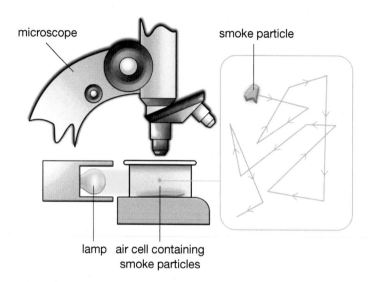

microscope   smoke particle

lamp   air cell containing
       smoke particles

❑   According to the kinetic particle theory, a gas such as air is made up of an extremely large number of tiny, invisible particles that have relatively large spaces between them and are constantly moving randomly.

❑   These particles have no effect on each other except when they collide. The particles bounce off each other without losing kinetic energy.

❑   The smoke particles in the air cell are constantly bombarded from all sides by the air particles. The larger smoke particles can be seen to move in **random straight lines** in a zig-zag pattern (see diagram above).

○   This random movement is due to **collisions** between the **very light** but **fast-moving air molecules**, which are too small to be seen, and the **smoke particles**, which are larger and can be seen.

○ Air consists mainly of nitrogen molecules, N_2, and oxygen molecules, O_2. A smoke particle is a solid lump of mainly carbon atoms.

Gases and the absolute scale of temperature

Pressure caused by gases

○ All **moving particles** have **kinetic energy** and **momentum**.

○ **Gas** particles have **large** energies (because they are moving very fast). The particles in a gas do not all have the same energy; some have more than others. The **average** kinetic energy is related to the **temperature** of the gas.

❑ **Increasing** the **temperature** of a gas increases the **average kinetic energy** of particles within that gas and they move **faster**.

❑ The gas particles exert a **force** on the walls of a container when they collide with it. This force on the container is called gas pressure. Increasing the temperature of a gas increases the average kinetic energy of the particles and the force they exert.

○ The **pressure** exerted by the gas particles is **the force per unit area**. The total pressure of the gas is the effect of the sum of all the collisions with the wall.

○ When the particles collide with the walls of the container they change direction and bounce back. This means that the velocity (a vector quantity) has changed. If the velocity changes, the momentum changes, and force is related to a change of momentum (see page 54).

○ The force is **larger** if the particles are moving **faster** (because the change in momentum is greater) or if there are **more particles** colliding with the walls **per second**.

❑ A **higher temperature** causes **more** collisions in a given time and causes the collisions to be **harder** because the particles are moving faster. Consequently, a higher temperature causes a **larger pressure**.

Pressure changes in a gas

❑   Important variables that can vary for a gas are:

1.   pressure
2.   volume
3.   temperature
4.   mass.

Boyle's Law

❑   Boyle's Law explains how the pressure and volume are related when the **temperature is kept constant**.

❑   If the piston of a bicycle pump with a sealed end is pushed in at constant temperature, then the further you push it in, the harder it gets to push.

❑   This is because the **pressure** inside the container (pump) **increases as the volume decreases**.

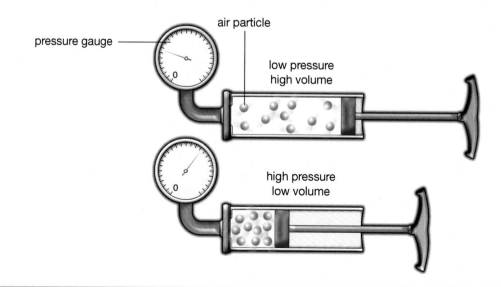

❑   The pressure increases because the gas particles are squeezed
     into a smaller space. Therefore there are more collisions per
     second amongst the particles and with the container walls. The
     more frequent collisions cause a larger force on the walls and
     hence a larger pressure. The collisions do not get harder
     because the temperature does not change; it is the frequency
     of collisions that is responsible for the change in pressure.

Top Tip

**When the volume of a fixed mass of gas is decreased at
a constant temperature, the pressure increases.**
This is because the particles are squeezed into a smaller space
and therefore **collide more often** with the walls of the container
and so the pressure increases. They **do not** move faster.

○   Boyle's Law states that:

**For a fixed mass of gas at constant temperature, the
pressure is inversely proportional to the volume.**

○   This means that for a fixed mass of gas at constant temperature,
     the **pressure** multiplied by the **volume** is **constant**.

pV = constant

○   In other words, when **the pressure increases, the volume
     decreases** and vice versa, as shown in the graph below.
     Notice that the line does not touch either axis.

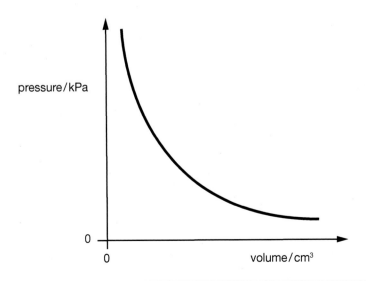

○ Pressure and volume are related by the equation:

$$p_1 V_1 = p_2 V_2$$

p_1 = initial pressure (Pa or N/m²)
V_1 = initial volume (m³)
p_2 = final pressure (Pa or N/m²)
V_2 = final volume (m³)

○ **Example**

A pump contains 0.300 m³ of air at atmospheric pressure. The air is compressed slowly, the temperature of the air does not change. Calculate the pressure when the volume of the air is compressed to 0.125 m³.

Remember: Atmospheric pressure is 100 kPa.

Answer

Step 1   List all the information in symbol form and change into appropriate and consistent SI units if required.

p_1 = 100 kPa = 100 000 Pa
V_1 = 0.300 m³
V_2 = 0.125 m³
p_2 = ?

Step 2   Use and rearrange the correct equation.

$$p_1 V_1 = p_2 V_2 \quad \Rightarrow \quad p_2 = \frac{p_1 V_1}{V_2}$$

Step 3   Calculate the answer by putting the numbers into the equation.

$$p_2 = \frac{p_1 V_1}{V_2} = \frac{100\,000 \times 0.300}{0.125} = 240\,000 \text{ Pa}$$

**ALWAYS REMEMBER TO STATE THE UNIT FOR
CALCULATED QUANTITIES.**

When a gas is in a cylinder of constant cross-sectional area, the volume is proportional to the length of the cylinder occupied by the gas. In this case, the equation

$$p_1 V_1 = p_2 V_2$$

can be replaced by

$$p_1 l_1 = p_2 l_2$$

where

p_1 = initial pressure (Pa or N/m²) l_1 = initial length (m)

p_2 = final pressure (Pa or N/m²) l_2 = final length (m)

Increasing the temperature of a gas

❑   The pressure of a **fixed volume** of gas is related to its temperature. As the temperature increases, so does the pressure.

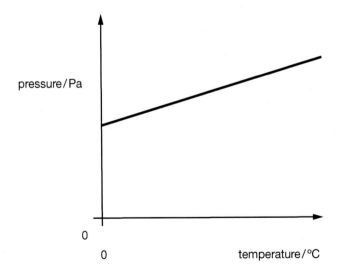

❑   When the temperature of a gas is increased the **internal energy** of its particles **increases**. The average speed of the particles increases because the average kinetic energy of the particles increases.

❑   The pressure of the gas is determined by the force of the particles colliding with the walls of the container and the area over which that force acts.

❑   As the temperature increases, the force increases and so the **pressure of a gas increases with temperature**.

❑   As the volume of the container is kept constant, more particles hit the walls of the container every second and they are also travelling faster hitting the walls harder, so pressure is increased.

Top Tip

When the temperature of a fixed mass of gas is increased at constant volume, its pressure increases. This is because the kinetic energy and therefore average speed of the particles increases and so the force exerted on the walls of the container is greater.

Decreasing the temperature of a gas

❑   When the temperature of a gas is decreased the average kinetic energy of the particles decreases. The temperature at which particles can be considered to be stationary is called **absolute zero**. This corresponds to a temperature of –273°C.

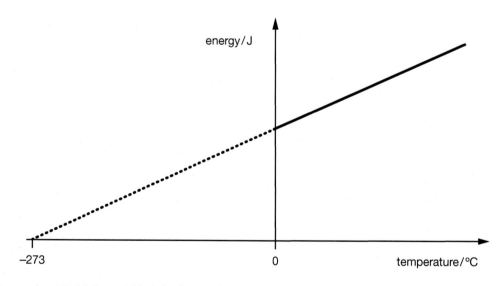

❑   In 1848 Lord Kelvin introduced a new scale of temperature called the Kelvin scale or the absolute scale. The unit of the scale is the kelvin K and one kelvin is the same size as one degree Celsius. The zero of the Kelvin scale is absolute zero, the lowest possible temperature.

Remember: The unit of the scale is not degrees kelvin, it is kelvin.

❑   We can convert from kelvins to degrees Celsius, and vice versa, using the following equation:

T (in K) = θ (in °C) + 273

○   ***Example***

Express the following temperatures in kelvins:

(a)   0°C

(b)   20°C

(c)   100°C.

Answer

Step 1   List all the information in symbol form and change into appropriate and consistent SI units if required.

θ = 0°C

θ = 20°C

θ = 100°C.

Step 2   Calculate the answer by putting the numbers into the equation .

(a) T (in K) = θ (in °C) + 273

T = 0 + 273 = 273K

(b) T (in K) = θ (in °C) + 273

T = 20 + 273 = 293K

(c) T (in K) = θ (in °C) + 273

T = 100 + 273 = 373K

ALWAYS REMEMBER TO STATE THE UNIT FOR CALCULATED QUANTITIES.

Top Tip

To convert from degree Celsius to kelvin:
temperature in °C + 273 = temperature in K

To convert from kelvin to degree Celsius:
temperature in K − 273 = temperature in °C

Section 2.2   Thermal properties and temperature

Thermal expansion of solids, liquids and gases

❑   **Thermal expansion** is the **increase in volume** of a solid, liquid or gas that is caused by **heating**.

○   For the same temperature increase **gases** expand the most, then **liquids** and then **solids**.

Remember: The particle separation in liquids is very slightly greater than in solids. The particle separation in gases is much greater than in solids or liquids.

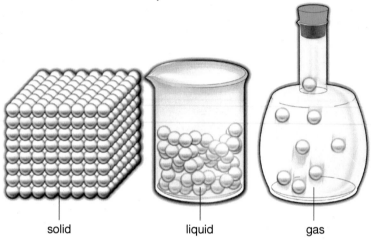

solid   liquid   gas

Expansion in solids

❑   When a solid substance is heated its particles vibrate more. This causes the particles to move slightly further apart and therefore the substance **expands** in all directions.

❑   When the substance is cooled its particles vibrate less. This causes the particles to move closer together and therefore the substance **contracts** in all directions.

Note

The particles themselves **do not** expand individually; they move further apart collectively.

A substance expands when its particles move further apart in all directions due to an increase in their kinetic energy.

Applications and consequences

There are several applications and consequences of expansion in solids. Some examples are given below.

❑ *Applications – the bimetallic strip*

Bimetallic strips are made up of two metals such as brass and steel joined side by side. Brass expands more than steel when heated and contracts more when cooled down. This causes the strips to bend as shown below.

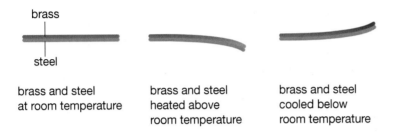

brass

steel

brass and steel
at room temperature

brass and steel
heated above
room temperature

brass and steel
cooled below
room temperature

The bimetallic strip is found in many devices such as fire alarms, electrical thermostats and old-fashioned car indicator lights.

❑ *Consequences – overhead cables and bridges*

Overhead power cables like those shown below are left slack in the summer. This is because the cables contract in winter. If they became too tight, they could snap.

Metal joints as seen below can be found in many of the world's bridges. They allow room for thermal expansion and contraction.

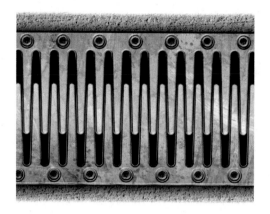

Expansion in liquids

❑   Most **liquids expand** when they get hotter. They expand **more than solids** but **less than gases**.

◯   When a liquid is heated the kinetic energy of the particles increases and their separation increases. The particles in liquids have weaker forces of attraction compared to solids, so liquids expand more than solids when heated.

❑   Water is an exception; it behaves differently.

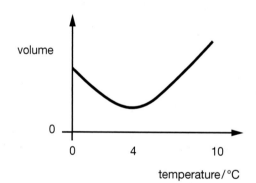

-   As the temperature decreases from 10°C to 4°C the volume decreases and density increases. The density of water is greatest at 4°C.

-   As the temperature decreases from 4°C to 0°C the volume increases and the density decreases.

-   At 0°C water freezes and turns to ice. Unusually water expands when it freezes; hence ice is less dense than water. This is why ice floats in water.

-   Most other substances are denser when they are in the solid state.

❑   A liquid-in-glass thermometer is a device that uses the expansion of a liquid to measure temperature. The liquid is contained in a glass bulb, and, as the temperature rises, the liquid expands along a narrow capillary tube.

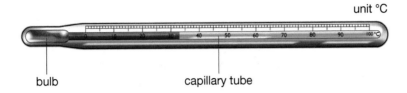

bulb   capillary tube

❑   There are several types of thermometer including the **mercury-in-glass** or the **alcohol-in-glass** thermometer, shown in the diagram above. The liquid expands uniformly as the temperature rises, and the scale alongside the capillary tube is calibrated to give the temperature.

Expansion in gases

○   The particles in gases are far apart and have negligible forces of attraction, so gases expand the most.

○   In the diagram below the 10N weight keeps the pressure constant, but allows the volume to vary. As the temperature increases the volume increases.

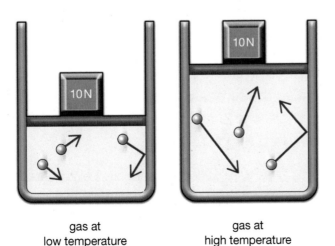

gas at   gas at
low temperature   high temperature

When the temperature of a gas is increased at constant pressure (shown in the diagram on previous page), **the volume increases.**

This is because the gas particles have more **kinetic energy** and therefore they move **further apart**.

Remember: We do not need to allow a gas to expand if it gets hotter. A gas can be put inside a sealed container, so that it has a fixed volume.

❑   If a gas is heated in a sealed container its pressure increases (see page 95). If it increases too much there is an **explosion**.

Specific heat capacity

❑   **Heat** is a form of energy (**thermal energy**) and its unit is the **joule** (J). When substances **absorb** thermal energy, their temperature usually rises.

❑   This rise in temperature shows that the **internal energy** of the substance is increasing.

○   An increase in temperature of an object increases the average kinetic energy of all the particles (atoms, molecules ions and electrons) in the object.

○   **Specific heat capacity** (s.h.c.) is the amount of thermal energy needed to raise the temperature of **1kg** of a substance by **1°C**. It has the symbol *c* and its unit is the **joule per kilogram degree Celsius**, J/(kg°C).

$$c = \frac{\Delta E}{m\Delta\theta}$$

c = specific heat capacity (J/(kg°C))
ΔE = thermal energy transferred (J)
m = mass (kg)
Δθ = change in temperature (°C)

Top Tip

On a summer's day in a hot country, the sand on a beach is very hot to step on; it is cold to step on at night. Sand has a **low specific heat capacity** and so it heats up and cools down quickly.

Example

The specific heat capacity of water is 4200 J/(kg °C). Calculate the temperature change when 150 kJ of energy is given to 3.0 kg of water.

Answer

Step 1   List all the information in symbol form and change into appropriate and consistent SI units if required.

$$\Delta E = 150 \text{kJ} = 150\,000\,\text{J}$$
$$c = 4200\,\text{J/(kg °C)}$$
$$m = 3.0\,\text{kg}$$
$$\Delta \theta = ?$$

Step 2   Use and rearrange the correct equation.

$$c = \frac{\Delta E}{m \Delta \theta} \quad \Rightarrow \quad \Delta \theta = \frac{\Delta E}{cm}$$

Step 3   Calculate the answer by putting the numbers into the equation.

$$\Delta \theta = \frac{\Delta E}{cm} = \frac{150\,000}{4200 \times 3.0} = 11.9 = 12\,°C \text{ (to 2 sig. figs)}$$

ALWAYS REMEMBER TO STATE THE UNIT FOR CALCULATED QUANTITIES.

Note

The change in temperature $\Delta \theta$ would be numerically equal to ΔT. In the example above, the change of 12 °C would be equal to a change of 12 K

Determining specific heat capacity of a solid

○   Remember that specific heat capacity is defined as the thermal energy needed to raise the temperature of 1 kg of a substance by 1 °C.

○   The following experiment describes how to determine the specific heat capacity of a metal.

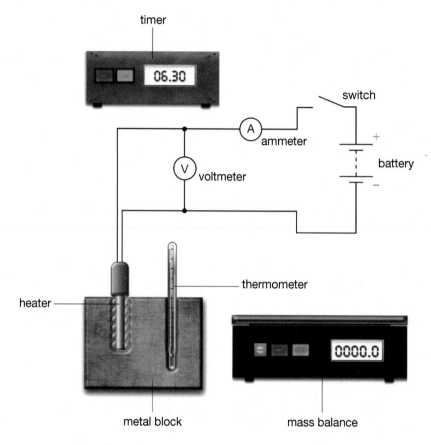

1.   Place the metal block on the mass balance; record its mass **m**.

2.   Set up the experiment as shown.

3.   Record the initial temperature $\theta_{initial}$ of the block.

4.   Switch the apparatus on, start the timer, and record the current and voltage readings.

5.   After a time **t** switch off the power supply and record the final temperature θ_{final} of the block.

6.   In the diagram the digital timer reads 6 minutes 30 seconds. This must be converted to seconds, i.e. 390 seconds.

Calculations to be made

1. Energy supplied by heater:

    $\Delta E = Pt$ where electrical power $P = IV$ (see *Top Tip* below)

    So, on substitution, $\Delta E = IVt$

2. The change in temperature:

    $\Delta \theta = \theta_{final} - \theta_{initial}$

3. The specific heat capacity of the metal block:

    $$c = \frac{\Delta E}{m\Delta \theta}$$

Top Tip

Energy supplied can be found using:

energy = power × time or $\Delta E = Pt$

The unit of energy is the joule (J), the unit of power is the watt (W) and the unit of time is the second (s).

As **electrical power = IV**, then $\Delta E = IVt$

The unit of energy is the joule (J), the unit of current is the ampere (A), the unit of voltage is the volt (V) and the unit of time is the second (s).

Determining specific heat capacity of a liquid

○   The following experiment describes how to determine the specific heat capacity of water.

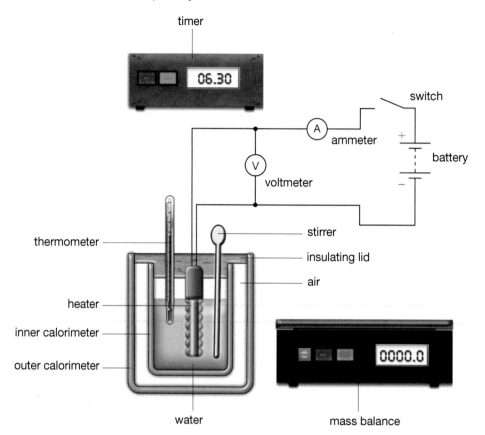

1.   Place the empty inner calorimeter on the mass balance; record its **mass m_1**.

    N.B. A calorimeter is a container usually made of copper used when measuring specific heat capacity.

2.   Add sufficient water to cover the heater when placed in the calorimeter. Place the calorimeter and water on the mass balance; record its **mass m_2**.

3.   Calculate the mass of the water, **m** by subtracting **m_1** from **m_2**.

4.   Set up the experiment as shown.

5.   Record the initial temperature **$\theta_{initial}$** of the water.

6.   Switch on, start the timer, and record the current and voltage readings.

7.   Stir the water during heating.

8. After a time t, switch off the power supply and record the final temperature θ_{final} of the water.

9. Convert the time to seconds.

Calculations to be made

1. Energy supplied by heater:

$\Delta E = Pt$ where electrical power $P = IV$

So, on substitution, $\Delta E = IVt$

2. The change in temperature:

$\Delta \theta = \theta_{final} - \theta_{initial}$

$$c = \frac{\Delta E}{m \Delta \theta}$$

Improvements to the experiments

On occasion you may be asked to suggest improvements for practical experiments. In the previous two experiments we are trying to find how thermal energy affects the metal block/water, therefore we want to make sure **minimal thermal energy is dissipated to the surroundings**.

The experiment could have been improved by:

1. adding lagging (insulation) on the sides, top and underneath the block. In the calorimeter experiment, the trapped air acts as an insulator

2. repeating the experiment to take an average.

Assumptions in the experiment and sources of error

We assume that all the thermal energy supplied is used to heat the metal block/water. Some energy, however, is dissipated to the surroundings including to the calorimeter containing the water.

Calculating thermal energy dissipated to the surroundings

○   Very often in calculations we assume that no thermal energy is dissipated to the surroundings and that all input energy is transformed into useful output energy. Provided that the insulation is sufficiently effective, the thermal energy that is lost to the surroundings is very small and can often be ignored.

○   The example below shows how to calculate thermal energy dissipated to the surroundings, when this is not negligible.
Remember: Energy is conserved:
energy into system = energy out of system

Useful equations are:

$\Delta E = Pt$
$\Delta E = IVt$

ΔE = thermal energy transferred (J)
P = power (W)
I = current (A)
V = voltage (V)
t = time (s)

○   ***Example***
A 1.0 kW immersion heater takes 15 minutes to raise the temperature of 1.0 kg of water by 70 °C. The specific heat capacity of water is 4200 J/(kg °C). Calculate the thermal energy that is dissipated to the surroundings.

Answer
Step 1   List all the information in symbol form and change into appropriate and consistent SI units if required.

P = 1.0 kW = 1000 W
t = 15 minutes = 15 × 60 = 900 s
c = 4200 J/(kg °C)
m = 1.0 kg
$\Delta\theta$ = 70 °C
thermal energy dissipated = ?

Step 2   Choose the correct equations.

$\Delta E = Pt$
$\Delta E = cm\Delta\theta$

Step 3   Calculate the answer by putting the numbers into the equations.

Thermal energy given to the water by heater:

$$E_{in} = Pt = 1000 \times 900 = 900\,000\,J$$

Energy used to raise temperature of water (the rest is dissipated):

$$E_{out} = cm\Delta\theta = 4200 \times 1.0 \times 70 = 294\,000\,J$$

Energy dissipated to surroundings:

$$\Delta E = E_{in} - E_{out} = 900\,000 - 294\,000$$
$$= 606\,000\,J$$
$$= 610\,000\,J \text{ (to 2 sig. figs)}$$

ALWAYS REMEMBER TO STATE THE UNIT FOR CALCULATED QUANTITIES.

Top Tip

Very often the specific heat value obtained in calculations using experimental results is higher than the actual value; this is because thermal energy is **dissipated to the surroundings**.

Note

If 1 kg of lead is given the same amount of thermal energy as 1 kg of copper then the temperature rise of the lead is about **three times greater** than that of copper. Lead's specific heat capacity is about **three times smaller** than copper's.

Melting, boiling and evaporation

❏ The three states of matter are **solid**, **liquid** and **gas**.

❏ The **changes of state** that can take place are:

boiling   – a liquid changing to a gas
condensation – a gas changing to a liquid
solidification – a liquid changing to a solid
melting   – a solid changing to a liquid.

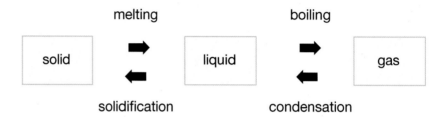

❏ Energy must be **provided** for melting or boiling. Energy is **given out** during solidification or condensation.

❏ The temperature of a substance remains **constant** whilst **changing state** at its melting point or boiling point. The temperature remains the same until the change of state is complete.

❏ The **melting point** is the temperature at which a solid turns into a liquid. The melting point of pure ice is 0 °C at standard atmospheric pressure (the average pressure of the air at sea level on the Earth).

❏ The **boiling point** is the temperature at which a liquid turns into a gas. The boiling point of pure water is 100 °C at standard atmospheric pressure.

❏ When melting or boiling, all the supplied energy is being used to **weaken** or **break** the bonds between particles.

❏ When condensation occurs the particles slow down and the bonds are **strengthened** or **formed**. These bonds bring the particles closer together and the substance becomes liquid.

❏   When solidification occurs the temperature drops and fewer particles have enough kinetic energy to overcome neighbouring attractions. The particles can only vibrate, the substance gains a shape of its own and becomes a solid.

❏   The amount of energy needed to change the state of a substance depends only on the **mass** and the **type of substance**. Different substances require different amounts of energy when boiling or melting.

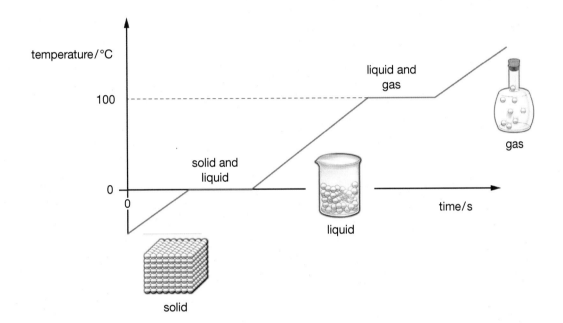

○   The graph above shows how the temperature changes with time when ice is heated.

-   Whilst the ice is solid, its temperature increases as thermal energy is supplied.
-   When the ice reaches 0°C the temperature remains constant as all the supplied thermal energy is used to change state from solid (ice) to liquid (water).
-   The water changes temperature from 0°C to 100°C as thermal energy continues to be supplied.
-   At 100°C the temperature remains constant as the water is turned to steam.

Evaporation

❑   Evaporation involves a change of state from liquid to vapour. (A vapour is a substance in its gaseous state below its boiling point – see page 110.) Evaporation is the reason why wet clothes dry on a washing line, or a saucer of water eventually dries up.

❑   Evaporation is the **escape** of the most **energetic particles** from the **surface** of a liquid. Not all particles in a liquid have the same energy. It is those particles that are moving the fastest (i.e. those with the greatest kinetic energy) and are at the surface that can escape.

❑   If the more energetic particles leave the liquid, it follows that the average energy of the remaining particles of the liquid falls and so its temperature falls. Evaporation **leads to the cooling** of the liquid.

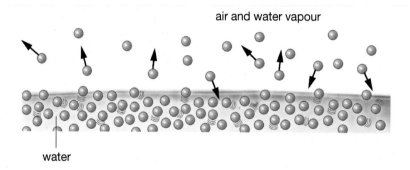

air and water vapour

water

○   Some vapour particles return to the surface of the liquid unless they are removed by draught or wind.

Factors affecting the rate of evaporation

○   A **higher temperature increases** the average kinetic energy of the liquid particles; therefore many more particles have a chance of escaping from the surface.

○   A **larger surface area** allows more particles to be closer to the surface, which increases the rate of evaporation. (This is like making an entrance to a school wider, allowing more people to get into the school at one time.)

○   Draught or wind can take away those particles that have escaped the liquid's surface, so that these particles cannot return to the liquid's surface.

○   In a humid atmosphere there are already a lot of water particles in the air. These particles can join the liquid water without difficulty. Consequently, when water evaporates into a humid atmosphere, some water particles return to the liquid's surface as fast as others escape. (An analogy that is useful here is that you are digging a hole and someone else is filling it in behind you.)

Cooling effect of evaporation

○   Rapid (fast) evaporation has a noticeable cooling effect on objects in contact with the liquid.

-   As the liquid evaporates, it takes away **thermal energy** from an object. (Human sweating is an example of this.)

-   Evaporation has a cooling effect because particles with the greatest kinetic energy escape; consequently the particles left behind have less kinetic energy and therefore the temperature falls. The liquid then draws thermal energy from a body with which it is in contact.

Boiling and evaporation

○   Boiling (see page 110) is also a change of state from liquid to vapour (vaporisation). But boiling and evaporation differ in the following ways.

-   Boiling occurs **throughout** the liquid, whereas evaporation only occurs at the **surface** of the liquid.

-   Boiling only occurs at **one temperature** (100°C for water at standard atmospheric pressure), whereas evaporation occurs at **all temperatures**.

-   Boiling requires a supply of energy for the liquid to reach the required temperature, whereas evaporation occurs at all temperatures, utilising the internal energy of the liquid.

-   Boiling is usually a rapid process. Evaporation is usually a slow process but can be speeded up by the presence of a draught over the surface of the liquid and an increased surface area in contact with the air.

Section 2.3 Transfer of thermal energy

❏   The three principal methods of thermal energy transfer are:

1. conduction
2. convection
3. radiation.

Conduction

○   Particles **gain energy** when heated. In a solid the particles cannot change positions but they vibrate, and this transfers thermal energy through the solid from particle to particle as they collide. In addition metals are particularly good conductors because they have **free-moving (de-localised) electrons**. The vibrating particles hit electrons and send them through the metal. This causes energy to be transferred quickly.

○   The thermal conductivity of a material is dependent on how quickly thermal energy is transferred from the hotter end to the colder end of a material. Materials that can transfer thermal energy quickly are good thermal conductors, while materials that transfer thermal energy slowly are bad thermal conductors.

○   Not all solids are good conductors of thermal energy but generally they conduct thermal energy better than thermal insulators. An insulator is a material that does not easily allow the transfer of thermal energy. Polystyrene is an example of a solid that is a thermal insulator.

○   Liquids and gases are bad conductors of thermal energy because the particles are further apart and collisions are less likely.

Convection

❑ A liquid or gas **expands** as it is heated and it becomes **less dense**; this causes the hot fluid (liquid or gas) to **rise** and the cooler fluid above it to **fall** in a circular fashion. The rising of the hot gas or liquid sets up a **convection current**.

Remember: It is **NOT** heat that rises; it is the molecules of hot liquid or gas that rise.

Radiation

❑ Energy in the form of **infrared radiation** (part of the electromagnetic spectrum) travels in all directions from any **hot body**. This is how thermal energy is transferred through a vacuum, such as from the Sun through space to Earth, i.e. thermal energy transfer by radiation does not require a medium.

○ The amount of thermal energy radiated from a body depends on its temperature; a very hot body radiates more thermal energy than a cool body. A body with a large surface area radiates more than a body of small surface area at the same temperature.

○ All bodies emit and absorb radiation at the same time. If a body emits more than it absorbs it cools down. If it absorbs more than it emits it warms up. If it emits thermal energy at the same rate as it absorbs it, it stays at a constant temperature.

○ The temperature of the Earth is affected by factors such as the greenhouse gases (water vapour, methane and carbon dioxide) in the atmosphere, as they control the balance of radiation it absorbs and emits.

❑ Because infrared radiation is an electromagnetic wave it can be reflected. This means that a highly polished surface reflects thermal radiation away, e.g. a polished metal plate behind the element of an electric fire reflects the thermal energy into the room.

Conduction is the transfer of energy by vibrating particles in **solids**. Some good conductors such as metals also have free-moving electrons to carry the energy.

Convection is the transfer of energy by **hot gas or liquid rising** and **cold gas or liquid falling**.

Radiation is the transfer of energy as an electromagnetic wave. Radiation is the only way thermal energy can travel through a vacuum.

Experiments demonstrating thermal energy transfer

❑   *Conduction*

1.   Select four strips of different material of equal dimensions.

2.   Attach a drawing pin to the end of each strip, using the same amount of petroleum jelly or candle wax for each strip.

3.   Heat the other ends of the strips equally.

4.   The strip that allows the pin to drop first is the best conductor, and so on.

5.   Glass is a bad conductor, so the drawing pin stays attached longer.

❑   *Convection*

1.   Fill the glass tube container (see diagram) with cold water.

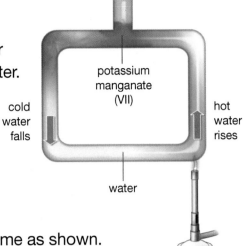

2.   Carefully drop a few crystals of potassium manganate (VII) into the container through the hole at the top.

3.   Heat gently with a small flame as shown.

4.   The purplish pink colour moves in a circular anti-clockwise path until all the water becomes coloured. Hot water rises and cold water falls.

○   *Radiation*

1.   The diagram below shows two aluminium plates placed an equal distance from an electric heater. One of the plates is painted matt black and the other has a shiny polished surface. A cork is attached to the back of each plate with wax.

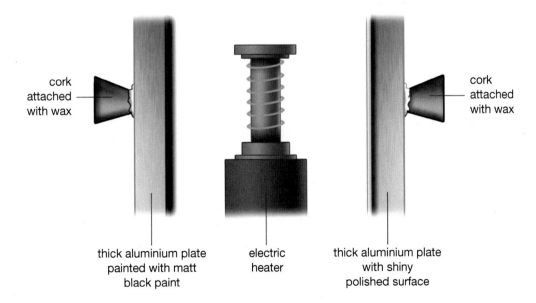

cork attached with wax

thick aluminium plate painted with matt black paint

electric heater

thick aluminium plate with shiny polished surface

cork attached with wax

2.   The cork attached to the matt black plate will drop off first, indicating that the matt black surface is a better **absorber** of thermal radiation than the shiny polished surface. Shiny surfaces are good reflectors of thermal radiation and so they are poor absorbers.

○ The hollow metal cube shown below is known as Leslie's cube. It has one shiny white surface, one dull white surface, one shiny black surface and one dull black surface.

rubber stopper

1. Fill the cube with hot water and seal it with a stopper. All four sides of the cube are at the same temperature, because they are all in contact with the hot water.

2. Place four thermometers or infrared detectors a small distance from each of the surfaces. These detect how much thermal energy is radiated from each surface. Make sure the detectors are **equal** distances from the cube to ensure the experiment is fair.

3. The detector or thermometer at the dull black side has the highest reading, the shiny white side has the lowest reading. Therefore the dull black surface is the best emitter (i.e. the best surface for radiating thermal energy), and the shiny white surface is the worst emitter.

❑ The table below gives a summary of the behaviour of surfaces from the previous two experiments.

	Best surface	Worst surface
Radiant thermal energy absorbers	dull black	shiny white
Radiant thermal energy reflectors	shiny white	dull black
Radiant thermal energy emitters	dull black	shiny white

Consequences of thermal energy transfer

❏   Some everyday examples of thermal energy transfer are given below.

- We feel the thermal energy radiated by the Sun, electric fires and electric lamps when our skin absorbs the radiation.

- White clothes are often worn in sunny weather because they reflect infrared radiation better.

- Highly polished teapots are not good radiators and so keep their contents warmer for longer than black teapots.

- White buildings keep cooler in warm weather than dark ones because they reflect the radiation from the Sun.

- If you heat a metal saucepan of water on top of the cooker, the thermal energy transfers to the water by conduction. You can see the water moving as convection currents begin to transfer the thermal energy through the water.

- The handle of a saucepan is often made of a poor conductor of thermal energy such as wood or plastic so that very little thermal energy is conducted to your hand and it is not burnt when lifting the pan.

- A cup of hot liquid stays warmer in a polystyrene cup than in a metal one. In fact the process of cooling of a liquid is quite complex, but the biggest difference here is that the polystyrene is a poor conductor of thermal energy and the metal is a good conductor so it is better at transferring the thermal energy to the surroundings.

Top Tip

Any hot object cools down more quickly if the temperature **difference** between the object and its surroundings is greater. For example, a cup of hot chocolate cools down more quickly if the surrounding room is much colder than the drink. A smaller difference in temperature results in a longer cooling time.

Other applications and consequences of thermal energy transfer

Reducing thermal energy loss from the home

❏ When a house is heated in cold weather, there is thermal energy transfer from the inside of the house to the surroundings. The diagram shows typical values for the proportions of the total energy lost through different parts of a house. (Of course, the energy is not really 'lost'; it escapes from the house into the environment.)

Thermal energy transfer often involves all three types of transfer, conduction, convection and radiation.

Thermal energy loss at any given time depends on the difference in temperature between the inside and outside of the house. As the temperature difference increases, the rate of thermal energy loss increases.

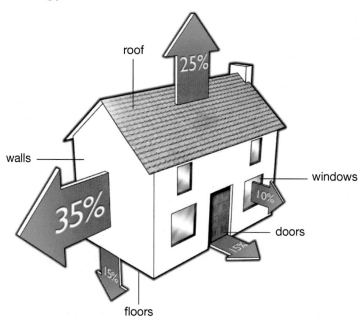

❏ **Loft insulation** – Fibreglass reduces thermal energy loss by conduction as it is a good insulator. Fibreglass also prevents thermal energy loss by convection currents as the fibres trap the air and stop it rising.

- ❏ **Double glazing** – Air trapped between the sheets of glass reduces convection and conduction. Radiation passes through unless the glass has a special reflective coating.

- ❏ **Floor insulation** – Carpets stop thermal energy loss by conduction as the carpet fibres trap air. Air is a very good insulator.

- ❏ **Wall insulation** – Cavity walls (two layers of bricks with a gap between) can be filled with foam to prevent convection currents in the cavity as well as conduction through the walls.

The domestic radiator

- ❏ A radiator is really misnamed. It radiates some thermal energy so, if you stand close enough, you can feel the infrared radiation being emitted by the surface of the radiator.

  However, most of the thermal energy is taken away by the hot air that rises from the radiator.

  Colder air from the room flows in to replace this hot air, and a **convection** current is formed as shown below.

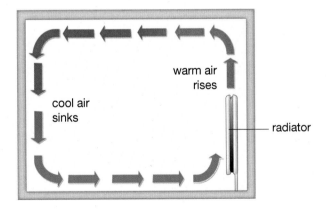

The vacuum flask

- ❏ A vacuum flask reduces conduction, convection and radiation. When a flask contains a hot liquid, the vacuum between the silvered surfaces (see the diagram opposite) stops energy transfer by conduction and convection.

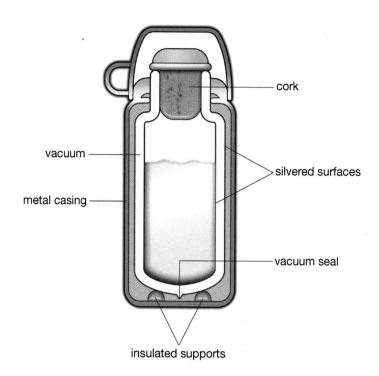

cork

vacuum

silvered surfaces

metal casing

vacuum seal

insulated supports

Silvered surfaces reduce thermal energy loss by infrared radiation, by reflecting the radiation back inside the flask to keep the liquid warm.

The cork at the top and the insulated supports at the bottom reduce thermal energy loss by conduction. The cork at the top also reduces thermal energy loss by convection and evaporation.

How a car radiator cools the engine

○   A car radiator contains a liquid known as a coolant, and the liquid is pumped via a series of pipes to various parts of the engine. The coolant in the pipes near the engine becomes warm by conduction as the engine warms when in use.

○   The coolant is pumped to the radiator. The walls of the radiator are heated by conduction from the warm coolant, and they in turn conduct thermal energy to the air surrounding the radiator and also radiate thermal energy to the surrounding air. The radiator is constructed with many thin fins which increase its surface area, meaning the radiator and its contents are in contact with a lot of air. As the car moves, cool air continually moves in through the radiator grille to surround the radiator and a fan is used to blow away hot air next to the grille.

○   The pump sends coolant up through the engine and is aided
        by the fact that the hot coolant expands, becomes less dense
        and rises as a result of the convection cycle within the radiator.
        The pump ensures that this is a continuous process.
        Car radiators are usually painted dull (matt) black to improve
        the emission of radiation.

How a coal or log fire transfers thermal energy

○   When coal or wood is burnt the chemical combustion releases
        infrared radiation. This is the main way by which we receive thermal
        energy directly from an open fire

○   In addition the air close to an open fire in a room heats and rises
        as a result of the change in density, pulling in cooler air and
        creating a convection cycle. Thus the warmer air spreads into the
        surroundings by convection (see page 115).

○   Thermal energy is also transferred by conduction to objects in
        contact with the burning fuel, e.g. the ground, fire basket, bricks,
        etc. These then become warmer and add to the radiation and
        convection processes.

Unit 3   Waves

Section 3.1   General properties of waves

❑   **Waves** transfer energy from one place to another. Consequently, waves can be used to carry signals from one place to another.

❑   Waves are produced by vibrations.

❑   Waves have repeating patterns.

❑   **Wave terms:**

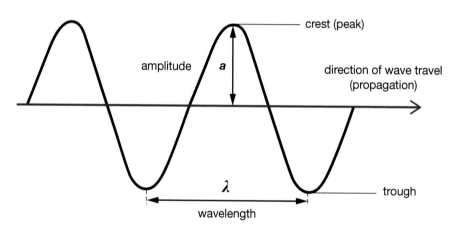

-   **amplitude *a*** – the maximum height of the wave from the **central equilibrium position**
-   **crest (peak)** – the highest point above the rest position
-   **trough** – the lowest point below the rest position
-   **wavelength *λ*** – the distance from any point on one wave to the same point on the next (adjacent) wave.

❑   Wave frequency is defined as the **number of wavelengths** produced or passing a specific point **per second**; it has the symbol ***f***, and its unit is the **hertz** (Hz).

Note

The larger the amplitude, the greater the energy a wave has.

○   The **period** of a wave is the time taken for one wavelength to pass a specific point; it has the symbol **T**, and its unit is the **second** (s).

$$T = \frac{1}{f} \quad \Rightarrow \quad f = \frac{1}{T}$$

❑   The speed of a wave **v** is the distance travelled by a particular point in a wave in one second.

❑   The wave equation is:

$$v = f\lambda$$

v = speed (m/s)
f = frequency (Hz)
λ = wavelength (m)

Types of waves

❑   There are two principal types of wave: longitudinal waves and transverse waves.

Longitudinal waves

❑   This type of wave can be shown by pushing and pulling a spring (slinky).

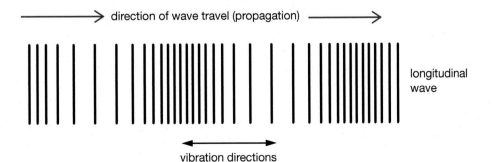

direction of wave travel (propagation)

longitudinal wave

vibration directions

- In a longitudinal wave the **oscillations** or **vibrations** are **parallel** to the direction the wave energy is travelling (propagation direction).

- Longitudinal waves need a medium to travel through, and as they pass through the medium the particles oscillate backwards and forwards.

- Examples of longitudinal waves are sound waves and seismic P-waves – the primary waves that follow an earthquake and that move the ground to and fro parallel to the direction of the wave.

Transverse waves

❑ This type of wave can be shown by moving a spring (slinky) or a rope from side to side, or by making ripples in water.

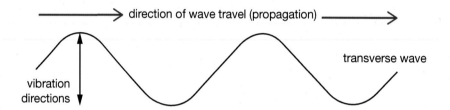

direction of wave travel (propagation)

vibration directions

transverse wave

- In a transverse wave the oscillations or vibrations are at **right angles (perpendicular)** to the direction the wave energy is travelling (propagation direction).

- Transverse waves do not need a medium to travel through.

- **Light**, radio, and other electromagnetic waves are transverse waves, as well as water waves, and seismic S-waves – the secondary waves that follow an earthquake and shake the ground up and down perpendicular to the direction of the wave.

Reflection and refraction

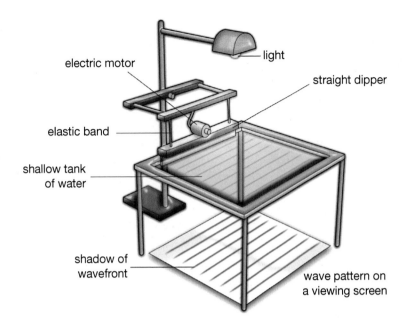

electric motor

light

straight dipper

elastic band

shallow tank
of water

shadow of
wavefront

wave pattern on
a viewing screen

❑   The ripple tank, as shown in the diagram above, is used to
produce waves. It can be used to study wave effects in different
situations. The **wavefronts** can generally be thought of as
continuous lines perpendicular to the direction of propagation.
This is rather like viewing sea waves from the top of a cliff.

Reflection off a plane surface

❑   A **straight dipper** can be used to create **plane** waves.

❑   If the waves strike a plane barrier they are reflected as
shown below.

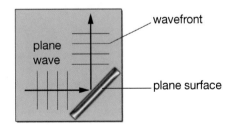

wavefront

plane
wave

plane surface

❑   The angle of incidence and the angle of reflection from a plane
surface are **equal**.

❑   With reflection, **speed**, **frequency** and **wavelength** remain the **same**. Only the direction changes.

Refraction due to a change in speed

❑   A straight dipper can also be used demonstrate **refraction**. By placing a sheet of clear glass in the ripple tank, the water above the glass is shallower compared to the rest of the ripple tank.

❑   Keeping the frequency of the waves constant, it can be shown that when a wave moves from one depth into another, it either **speeds up** or **slows down**. Water waves travel faster in deep water, and slower in shallow water. Notice (in the diagram below) that the wavefronts are closer together in the shallow region where they are slower.

❑   When a wave travels from deep water to shallow water:

-   wavelength decreases
-   speed decreases
-   frequency stays the same.

❑   When a wave moves from one depth to another at an **angle**, it **changes direction**. We say it is **refracted**.

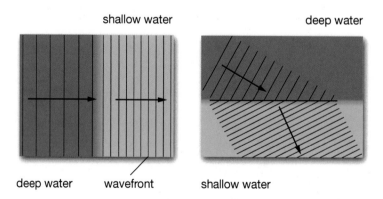

shallow water   deep water

deep water   wavefront   shallow water

Diffraction

❑   Diffraction occurs when a wave spreads out as it passes through a gap.

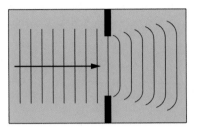
large gap

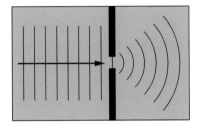
small gap

❑   Waves diffract when they pass an edge. The wavefront becomes bent.

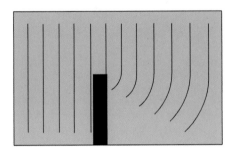

○   When waves are diffracted, the longer the wavelength, the more the wavefront is bent.

○   If a gap is about the same size as the wavelength, there is maximum diffraction and parallel wavefronts emerge as circular wavefronts (see 'small gap' diagram above).

○   **Sound waves** have long wavelengths and they diffract through large angles, hence we can hear sound around corners. **Light waves** have very short wavelengths and so **they diffract through negligibly small angles**, hence we cannot see or be seen around corners.

○   TV and FM radio reception is sometimes poor for people who live in hilly regions. The waves carrying the signal have a wavelength much smaller than the hill, and as they pass over the hill there is little diffraction. The people who live in the valley may not receive the signal. Long wavelength (low frequency) radio waves are diffracted more because the wavelength is comparable to the hill size, and they may be received as shown below.

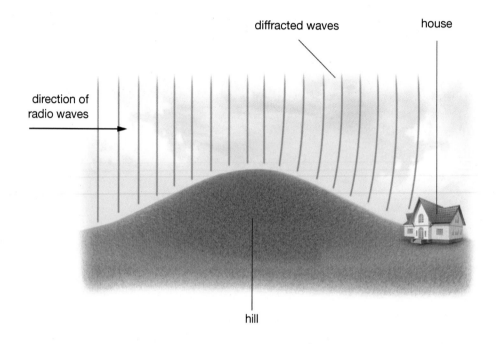

diffracted waves   house

direction of
radio waves

hill

Note

 During diffraction, **speed, frequency** and **wavelength** stay the same.

Top Tip

 When sketching diffraction diagrams, make sure the wavelength is the **same** either side of the gap. The emergent waves should be **curved** at the edges if the gap is **large** and **circular** if the gap is **small**, as shown on page 129.

Section 3.2   Light

Reflection of light

❑   Properties of light:

- it travels as **transverse** waves
- it transfers energy
- it can travel in a vacuum
- it travels at a speed of 3.0×10^8 m/s in a vacuum and is approximately the same in air.

❑   A light ray is a narrow beam of light that travels in a straight line. A light ray that reflects from a surface such as a **plane mirror** obeys the **law of reflection**.

❑   The angle of incidence is equal to the angle of reflection, where both angles are measured to the **normal**.

❑   The normal is a construction line at **90°** to the mirror, at the point where the light ray meets the mirror. It allows the angles shown in the diagram to be measured.

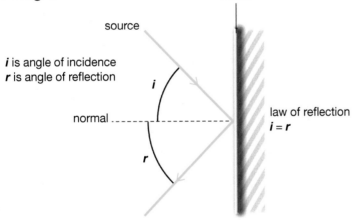

angle of incidence (i) = angle of reflection (r)

Note

    During reflection, **speed**, **frequency** and **wavelength** do not change; only **direction** changes.

❑   A plane mirror on a wall forms an **image** of an object, which has these properties:

- **upright** but **laterally inverted** i.e. the image is reversed left to right
- the **same size** as the object
- the **same distance** behind the mirror as the object is in front
- it is **virtual** (image cannot be formed on a screen).

❑   Plane mirrors are used in periscopes, security mirrors and dressing table mirrors.

○   **Finding the position of the image using a plane mirror**

1.   Draw any two incident rays from the object to the mirror.

2.   Draw in the reflected rays from these incident rays, making sure **angle of incidence** = **angle of reflection**.

3.   Continue these reflected rays back straight behind the mirror using a dotted line to the point where they appear to come from.

4.   The image is formed where the rays appear to come from behind the mirror. This is a **virtual image**. A virtual image cannot be formed on a screen. If you placed a screen at position 4 in the diagram below nothing would show.

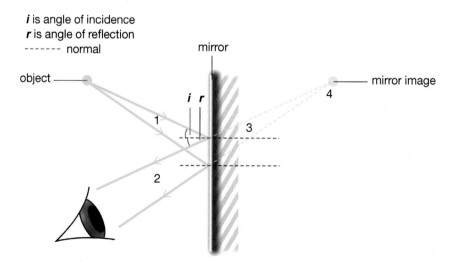

○   ***Example***

(a)   A lamp is placed in front of a mirror. Construct a ray diagram showing where the position of the image appears.

(b)   Describe two properties of the image.

Answer

(a) **Step 1**   Draw a ray A from the top of the object to the mirror. Mark in the normal and measure, using a protractor, the angle of incidence *i*.

        Step 2   Construct the reflected ray such that the angle of incidence *i* is equal to the angle of reflection *r*.

        Step 3   Draw a second ray B in the same way.

        Step 4   Use dotted lines to show where the reflected rays appear to come from. This is the top of the image.

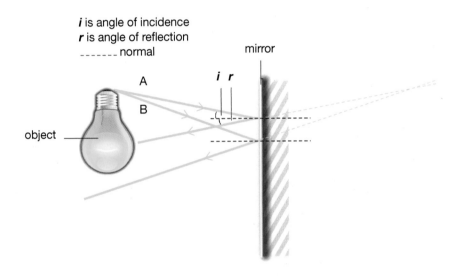

        Step 5   Repeat with two rays, C and D, from the bottom of the object.

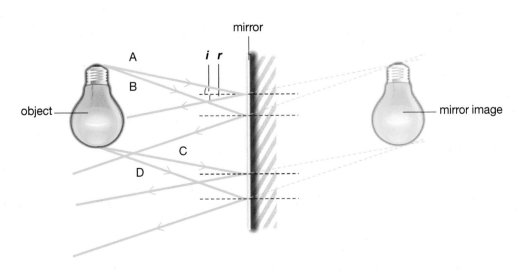

(b)   You could choose any two of the following:
- it is virtual
- the image is upright (the same way up as the object)
- it is the same size as the object
- it is the same distance behind the mirror as the object is in front.

Refraction of light

❑   Light rays can **change direction** when passing from one material into another because the rays move at **different speeds** in the two materials.

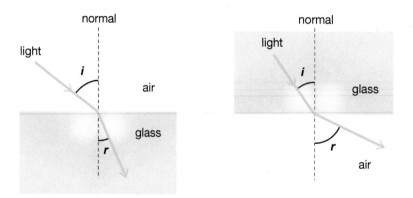

❑   Notice that the angle of incidence *i* and the angle of refraction *r* always lie between the light beam and the normal.

❑   A material in which light travels slowly is said to be **optically dense**.

❑   When travelling from an optically **less dense** material to a **more dense** material (such as air to glass), light **bends towards** the **normal** (diagram on the left above).

❑   When travelling from an optically **more dense** material to a **less dense** material (such as glass to air), light bends away from the **normal** (diagram on the right above).

❑   When light enters a different material:

- the frequency stays the same
- the wavelength changes
- the speed changes.

Refractive index

○ The **refractive index *n*** of a material indicates how strongly the material changes the direction of light. It is one of the few physical quantities that **does not have a unit**; it is just a number.

○ Refractive index, the speed of light in a vacuum (or air) and the speed of light in a medium (e.g. a material like glass, water or Perspex) are related by the equation:

$$n = \frac{\text{speed of light in air (or vacuum)}}{\text{speed of light in material}}$$

(Speed of light is given the symbol **c**.)

so $n = \dfrac{c_v}{c_m}$

○ Refractive index, the angle of incidence and the angle of refraction are related by the equation:

$$n = \frac{\sin i}{\sin r}$$

n = refractive index (no units)
i = angle of incidence (°)
r = angle of refraction (°)

This relationship is **Snell's Law**.

○   ### *Example 1*

Light travels from air into a glass block of refractive index 1.4. The angle of refraction in the glass is 35°. Calculate the angle of incidence in air.

Answer

Step 1   List all the information in symbol form and change into appropriate and consistent SI units if required.

$n = 1.4$

$r = 35°$

$i = ?$

Step 2   Use and rearrange the correct equation.

$$n = \frac{\sin i}{\sin r} \quad \Rightarrow \quad \sin i = n \times \sin r$$

$$i = \sin^{-1}(n \times \sin r)$$

(The term $\sin^{-1}(x)$ means the angle whose sine value is x.)

Step 3   Put the numbers into the equation and calculate the answer.

$$i = \sin^{-1}(1.4 \times \sin 35°) = 53.4$$
$$= 53° \text{ (to 2 sig. figs)}$$

ALWAYS REMEMBER TO STATE THE UNIT FOR CALCULATED QUANTITIES.

Top Tip

When a light ray travels from a **more optically dense** material (glass) to a **less optically dense** material (air) the **refractive index must be less than 1 ($n < 1$)**.

Make sure you know which way the light is travelling. If you are given $n > 1$ for light travelling from air to glass, but in the question the light is travelling from glass to air, you must first calculate the correct refractive index by finding the **reciprocal**.

If $n_{\text{air to glass}} = 1.43$ then $n_{\text{glass to air}} = 1/1.43 = 0.7$

Once you have the correct refractive index n, the equation in the example above can be used as normal.

○   *Example 2*

The speed of light in a vacuum is 3.0×10^8 m/s. Calculate the speed of light in glass of refractive index 1.6.

Answer

Step 1   List all the information in symbol form and change into appropriate and consistent SI units if required.

$n = 1.6$

c_v = speed in vacuum = 3.0×10^8 m/s

c_m = speed in material = ?

Step 2   Use and rearrange the correct equation.

$$n = \frac{\textbf{speed of light in vacuum}}{\textbf{speed of light in material}}$$

$$n = \frac{c_v}{c_m} \quad \Rightarrow \quad c_m = \frac{c_v}{n}$$

Step 3   Calculate the answer by putting the numbers into the equation.

$$c_m = \frac{3.0 \times 10^8}{1.6} = 1.875 \times 10^8 = 1.9 \times 10^8 \text{ m/s}$$
$$\text{(to 2 sig. figs)}$$

ALWAYS REMEMBER TO STATE THE UNIT FOR CALCULATED QUANTITIES.

Experiment to show refraction of light

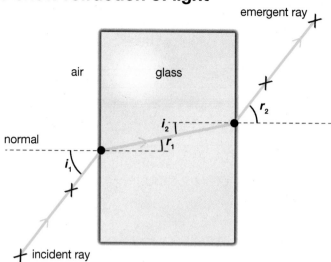

❑   The following experiment describes how to observe the refraction of a ray of light when it passes through a glass block.

1.   Place a transparent block in the middle of a plain sheet of paper; trace around the block in pencil.

2.   Position a raybox so that the light from it strikes the glass block at an angle.

Remember: If the light strikes the glass boundary at 90°, it passes straight through undeviated.

3.   Mark the positions where the light meets the glass boundary and where it leaves the glass boundary with dots (see the diagram).

4.   Mark two crosses (or place optical pins) on the paper along the incident ray and two crosses on the emergent ray approximately 5 cm apart.

5.   Remove the glass block and switch off the raybox.

6.   Using a ruler, complete the lines between the dots and the crosses.

7.   Draw in the normal at **90°** to where the light strikes the glass boundary.

8.   Draw the second normal where the light leaves the glass boundary, again at **90°**.

9.   Observe that the light bends towards the normal when it moves from air to glass, and away from the normal when it moves from glass to air.

○   **10.**   Using a protractor, measure the angles of incidence i_1 and refraction r_1 as shown on the diagram opposite.

○   **11.**   Divide $\sin i_1$ by $\sin r_1$ to find the refractive index of the glass.

Total internal reflection

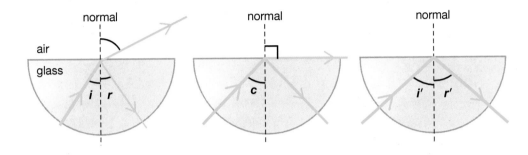

For small angles of incidence, the ray splits into a refracted ray and a weak internally reflected ray.	At the critical angle **c**, most of the light is refracted at 90° along the glass surface; the internally reflected ray has become a little stronger.	For angles of incidence greater than the critical angle, **total internal reflection** occurs. No light is refracted.

❑   **Total internal reflection** occurs when **light is travelling from a more optically dense to a less optically dense material** and the angle of incidence is greater than the **critical angle** of the material.

❑   The **critical angle** is defined as the angle in the optically denser material above which total internal reflection occurs.

❑   Each material has its own critical angle. For example, the critical angle of glass in air is 42° and for water in air it is 49°.

❑   Consequently, light incident at angles greater than 42° for glass and greater than 49° for water is completely reflected and none of it is refracted – total internal reflection (see page 140).

❑   The inside surface of diamond, water or glass can act like a mirror depending on the angle at which light strikes it.

○ The critical angle **c** is related to the refractive index **n** by the equation:

$$n = \frac{1}{\sin c}$$

n = refractive index (no units)
c = critical angle (°)

Uses of total internal reflection

○ Total internal reflection is used in fibre optic cables. A fibre optic cable is made up of a bundle of many very thin glass fibres. This means they are strong and flexible, allowing them to bend easily. The light travels along the fibre by being constantly totally internally reflected because the **angles of incidence** are always **greater** than the **critical angle** of the glass.

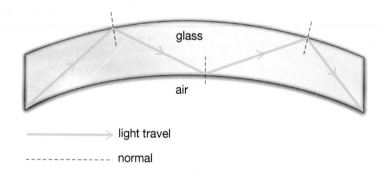

glass

air

→ light travel

------ normal

○ Fibre optic cables are used for TV transmission, telephone cables, internet communications (see page 150-1) and in medical devices such as endoscopes. An endoscope consists of a long, thin, flexible tube which has a light and a video camera. Images of the inside of the patient's body can be seen on a screen.

❏ The inside of a glass prism can be used as a mirror. Total internal reflection takes place on the **longest** face of the prism, as shown on the opposite page, and occurs because the angle of incidence (45°) is greater than the critical angle (42°). This arrangement is used in **periscopes**.

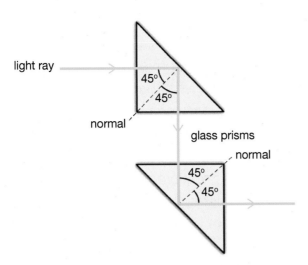

❑   Pairs of internally reflecting prisms are also used in **binoculars**.

Thin lenses

❑   Lenses bend light to form images. There are two main types of
      lens. The **converging** (convex) lens and the **diverging** (concave)
      lens as shown below:

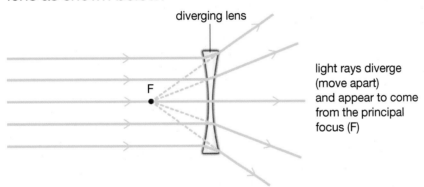

❑   A diverging lens diverges a light beam (**moves rays apart**) so they
      appear to come from the principal focus. A diverging lens
      produces a virtual image.

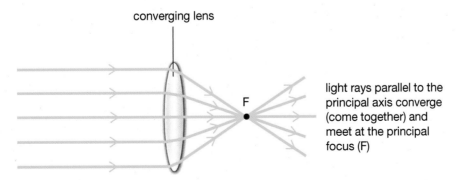

❑   A converging lens converges a light beam (**brings rays
      together**) to produce a focused image.

❑   The image formed by rays converging is a **real image** if the object is further from the lens than the focal length. A real image can be formed on a screen (see top diagram page 143).

Thin converging lens

❑   When a beam of light parallel to the principal axis passes through a converging lens, it is refracted so that it converges at a point known as the **focal point** or **principal focus**. There are two principal foci, one on each side of the lens.

❑   The **focal length f** of a lens is the distance between the **centre** of the lens and the **principal focus F**.

❑   The points **2F** are both a distance **2f** from the centre of the lens.

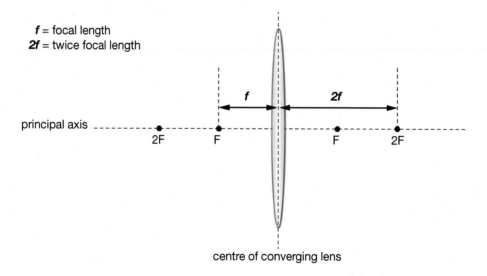

f = focal length
2f = twice focal length

principal axis

centre of converging lens

Drawing ray diagrams

❑   For a converging lens, to find the position of an image:

1.   draw a ray from the top of the object through the centre of the lens, which does not change direction

2.   draw a ray from the top of the object parallel to the principal axis until it reaches the central plane of the lens. The ray then passes straight through the principal focus on the other side of the lens. An image is formed where the rays meet.

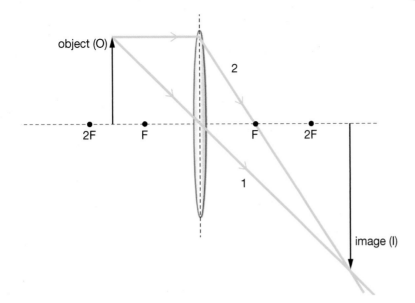

○   A converging lens can be used as a **magnifying glass** when an object is placed between **F** and the lens.

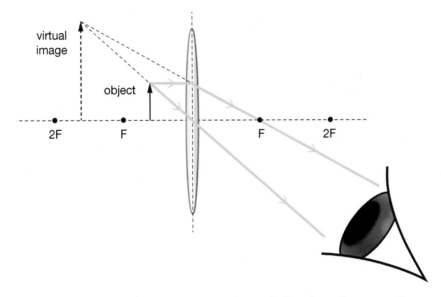

❏   In this case the rays do not meet when following the ray diagram rules explained at the bottom of page 142. When the lines are extended backwards (extrapolated), they appear to meet as shown by the dotted lines in the diagram above. This is known as a **virtual image**, which can be seen by positioning a human eye as shown.

Note

A **real image** forms where the light converges and it can be formed on a screen.

A **virtual image** is where all the light appears to come from and cannot be formed on a screen.

❑   Images can also be described as:

- upright (same way up) or inverted (upside down)

- magnified (larger) or diminished (smaller).

Top Tip

Sometimes you may be asked to draw a third ray when drawing a ray diagram. The rules are the same; the top ray goes parallel to the principal axis and then through F. The middle ray goes through the centre of the lens without changing direction. The bottom ray goes through F and then goes parallel to the principal axis as shown below.

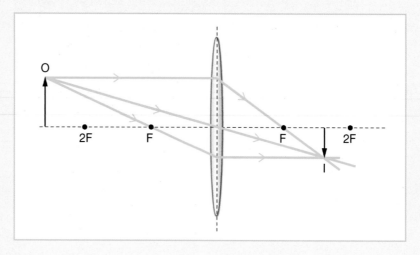

Formation of images by a converging lens

❑   **Object:** Further than **2f** from lens   **Image:**   **Uses:**

- between **f** and camera
  2f from lens
- inverted
- diminished
- real

❑   **Object:** Between **f** and **2f** from lens   **Image:**   **Uses:**

- more than **2f** projector
  from lens
- inverted
- magnified
- real

○   **Object:** Less than **f** from lens   **Image:**   **Uses:**

- rays do not magnifying
  converge glass
- virtual
- upright
- magnified

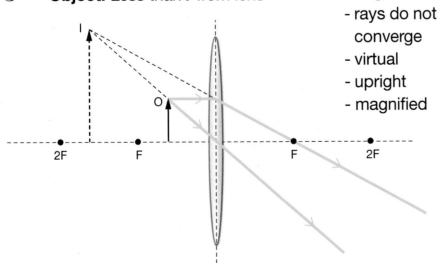

How do we see objects?

○ The normal human eye has a lens that converges light to form an image on the light-sensitive membrane at the back of the eyeball called the **retina**. The image is converted to an electrical signal, which is relayed to the brain via the optic nerve to translate the image into something meaningful. The focal length of the eye lens is very short – less than 20mm – the distance from the lens to the back of the eyeball.

○ If a person has **normal sight** the image is formed on the retina. If a person has **short-sight** (myopia) the image is formed in front of the retina, and if a person has **long-sight** (hypermetropia) the image is formed behind the retina. If the image is not formed on the retina the brain cannot translate the image into something meaningful and the person sees a blurred image.

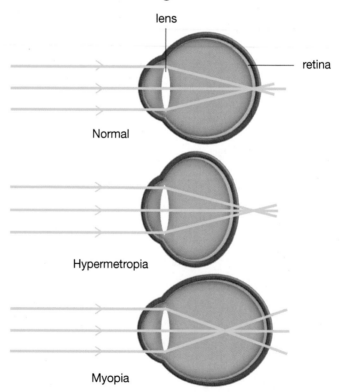

○ A person who is short-sighted (myopic), can see close objects, but objects far away are blurred. To correct short-sight, diverging lenses can be placed in front of the eyes (in a pair of glasses, or contact lenses). The lens diverges the parallel rays from a distant object before they hit the eye lens, so the image focuses on the retina. An example of a single eye is shown in the diagram opposite.

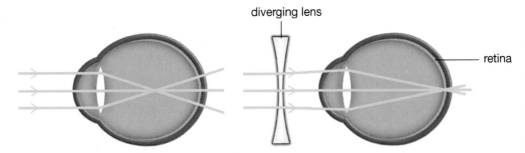

diverging lens

retina

○ A person who is long-sighted (hypermetropic) can see objects a long way away, but objects close by are blurred. To correct long-sight, converging lenses can be placed in front of the eyes. The lens converges the rays before they hit the eye lens so the image focuses on the retina as shown in the diagram below.

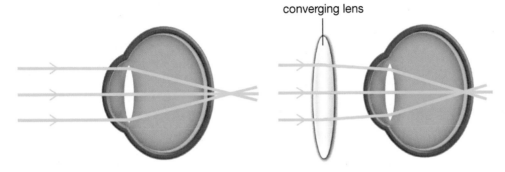

converging lens

Dispersion of light

❑ Visible light of different colours has different wavelengths.

❑ Red light has a longer wavelength and a lower frequency than green light, which has a longer wavelength and a lower frequency than blue light.

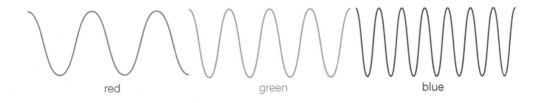

red   green   blue

Remember: If the velocity remains the same, as wavelength increases the frequency decreases, and vice versa.

○ Light of a single wavelength and therefore a single frequency, is known as **monochromatic** light. **Lasers** produce monochromatic light.

❑ **White** light is said to be made up of **seven** different colours. The colours travel at the same speed in space (vacuum) but slow down when they enter a denser medium like glass. The different wavelengths slow down by different amounts and so refract by different angles in a prism. This is known as dispersion and a **spectrum** is produced.

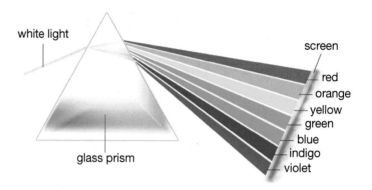

❑ The colours of the **visible light spectrum** can be memorised using the mnemonic: **ROYGBIV**: **R**ichard **O**f **Y**ork **G**ave **B**attle **I**n **V**ain.

Top Tip

Always describe white light **splitting up** into a **spectrum of light** and **not** 'colours of the rainbow'.

Section 3.3   Electromagnetic spectrum

❑ The electromagnetic (e.m.) spectrum is a family of **electromagnetic waves** that travel at the same high speed; they have different wavelengths and frequencies.

❑ Radio waves, microwaves, infrared, visible light, ultraviolet, X-rays and gamma (γ) radiation are all parts of the electromagnetic spectrum.

❑ The different wavelengths of the different types of wave are shown in the diagram opposite. Note, for example, that infrared radiation, responsible for the transfer of thermal energy by radiation, has a slightly longer wavelength than visible light.

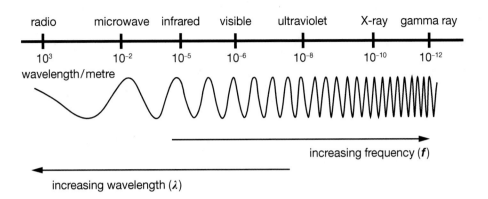

❑ Electromagnetic waves can travel through a vacuum and all electromagnetic waves travel at the same high speed.

❑ All electromagnetic waves are **transverse waves** and transfer energy but not matter.

◯ The **speed** of **all** electromagnetic waves in a vacuum (or approximately in air) is 3.0×10^8 m/s.

❑ Exposure to large doses of any type of electromagnetic radiation can be harmful. Microwaves, of the frequency used in microwave ovens, cause internal heating of body tissues and may cause burning, as may infrared radiation. Ultraviolet can damage the cells on the surface of the skin, leading to skin cancer, and the eyes, leading to eye defects such as cataracts.

Even small doses of short wavelength e.m. radiation can be harmful. Both X-rays and gamma rays can cause mutation or damage to living cells and can cause the death of living cells.

Summary of different electromagnetic waves

❑ *Gamma (γ-) rays*
   - very short wavelength
   - dangerous (γ-rays can kill living cells)
   - pass through skin and soft body tissue
   - come from radioactive substances such as uranium
   - used to kill cancer cells, sterilise food and hospital equipment

❏ **X-rays**
- short wavelength
- dangerous (X-rays can kill living cells)
- pass through skin and soft body tissue but not bone or metal
- used to photograph broken bones and scanning in security systems

❏ **Ultraviolet rays**
- wavelength a little shorter than visible light
- causes tanning and can damage the skin if over-exposed
- used to check for forged bank notes and sterilise water

❏ **Visible light**
- mid-range wavelength
- composed of a spectrum of colours
- comes from the Sun and other luminous objects
- used for vision, photography and illumination

❏ **Infrared rays**
- wavelength a little longer than visible light
- come from the Sun and any other hot objects
- used for cooking, in TV remote controls, optical fibres, thermal imaging and intruder alarms

❏ **Microwaves**
- long wavelength
- used in mobile (cell) phones, microwave ovens, satellite television and communication satellites

❏ **Radio waves**
- very long wavelength
- used for terrestrial television and radio broadcasts, astronomy, and RFID (radio frequency identification), an identification system used to tag objects and track them

Communications

❏ The longer wavelength electromagnetic waves, i.e. light, infrared, microwaves and radio waves, are used for communication.

❑   When you press a button on the remote control of a television you are communicating with the television from your comfortable seat. The remote control translates that button-press into a signal, usually infrared, which travels as an electromagnetic wave to the television, where it is translated into the action you asked for.

❑   Communication with **artificial satellites** usually uses microwaves because they can pass straight through the atmosphere. An artificial satellite is a human-made satellite that orbits the Earth. Some satellite phones and television broadcast systems use microwaves to communicate with low level artificial satellites.

❑   Most communications satellites occupy a **geostationary orbit**, i.e. they remain above the same point on Earth as they orbit. This means that a signal can be pointed at the artificial satellite and that a link can be established between that point on Earth and the satellite so that information can be passed between them.

○   Communications are an important part of the modern world, and many communication systems we use every day rely on electromagnetic radiation.

-   Cell phones and wireless internet connections (broadband) use microwaves, which can transmit both voice and data signals over large distances and are useful in remote locations. Microwaves have a shorter wavelength than radio waves and only require a short aerial for transmission and reception.

-   A Bluetooth device uses radio waves to connect with your cell phone, or computer so that when the device is close to the phone or computer it can connect or pair.

-   Optical fibres transmit visible light or infrared signals, which can carry high rates of data. They are used to transmit cable television signals, internet connection (high-speed broadband) and telephone signals. The light that enters the system is encoded with data and is transmitted along the cable due to total internal reflection (see page 140). At the receiving end, the light signal is decoded to reveal the data.

○ The word **signal** means a voltage, current or electromagnetic wave that varies with time and carries information.

○ There are two kinds of signal: an **analogue** signal, which varies continuously with time, and a **digital** signal, which is more like a series of on and off pulses.

○ On an oscilloscope these signals might look like:

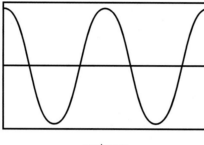
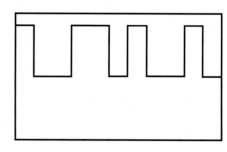

analogue   digital

○ Sound naturally occurs as an analogue signal, i.e. it has no breaks and is continuous. However, sound can be transmitted as a digital signal as a result of improvements in the way in which sound can be digitally recorded. The digital signal shows short bursts rather than one continuous sound, but if these bursts are close together, the ear distinguishes them as one sound.

○ Even though the process for digital signalling is more complex than for analogue signalling, there are many benefits:
  - digital signalling is more secure because the signal can be easily encrypted

  - digital signalling transmits information with less distortion and interference, i.e. the signal regeneration at the receiving end is more accurate

  - digital signalling gives a higher rate of transmission than analogue signalling

  - digital signalling can transmit data over very large distances because of the accuracy of the signal regeneration, i.e. the original signal is received and faithfully recreated.

Section 3.4 Sound

❏   Sound is caused by **vibrations**. It travels as a wave through a medium (which may be **solid**, **liquid** or **gas**) and transfers energy. Examples of how sound is produced include:

-   a hammer hitting a nail: the hammer and the nail vibrate, which in turn cause air particles to vibrate, creating a sound wave that travels to the ear

-   a door slamming: the door and its frame vibrate, causing air particles to vibrate, creating a sound wave that travels to the ear

-   a cricket bat hitting a ball: the bat and ball vibrate, causing air particles to vibrate, creating a sound wave that travels to the ear.

❏   Sound **cannot** travel through a **vacuum**. (There are no particles to vibrate.)

❏   The **speed of sound in air** is approximately **330–350 m/s**.

❏   Sound waves have a wide range of wavelengths and therefore frequencies. Our ears, however, do not respond to all frequencies. The normal **human hearing** frequency range is **20 Hz – 20 000 Hz**.

❏   Sound above 20 000 Hz is known as **ultrasound**. Humans cannot hear sounds with a frequency above 20 000 Hz, but some animals, including dogs, bats and mice can.

❏   Sound with a frequency lower than 20 Hz is called **infrasound**. Infrasound is used by some large animals for communication. For example, whales, giraffes and elephants can communicate over many miles using infrasound.

❏   Sound waves are **longitudinal waves**; their vibrations are **parallel** to the direction of propagation (see page 125).

○ **Sound waves** are a series of **compressions** and **rarefactions**.

- Areas where there is high pressure (where the molecules are squashed together) are known as **compressions**.

- Areas where there is low pressure (where the molecules are further apart) are known as **rarefactions**.

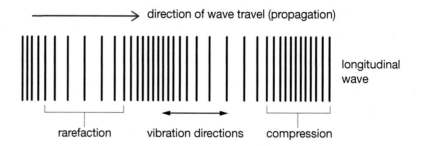

direction of wave travel (propagation)

longitudinal wave

rarefaction   vibration directions   compression

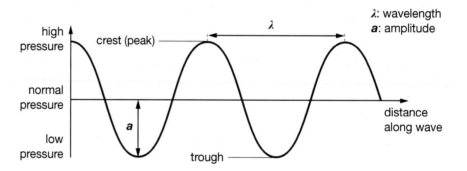

λ: wavelength
a: amplitude

high pressure

crest (peak)

normal pressure

distance along wave

low pressure

a

trough

Top Tip

Sometimes questions about sound can show what looks like a **transverse wave**; be careful as it is a **graphical** representation of **pressure** in a sound wave. Notice in the diagram above how the peaks of the graph correspond to the positions of compression and the troughs correspond to the positions of rarefaction in the longitudinal wave.

Speed of sound

❑   The following experiment describes how to determine the
       speed of sound in air.

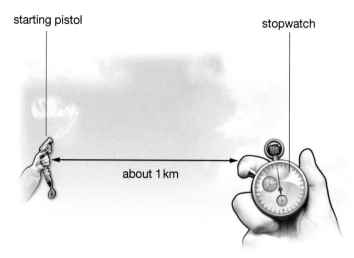

starting pistol   stopwatch

about 1 km

1.   A student with a stopwatch stands **a long distance** from
           a teacher with a starting pistol.

2.   The teacher fires the pistol in the air.

3.   The student starts the stopwatch when she sees the
           puff of smoke and stops it when she hears the bang.

Calculations to be made
Use the equation to calculate the speed of sound:

$$\text{speed} = \frac{\textbf{total distance travelled}}{\textbf{total time taken}} \qquad v = \frac{s}{t}$$

Improvements to the experiment
The experiment could be improved by:

1.   repeating it to find an average value, and using different
       students

2.   increasing the distance between the pistol and the
       stopwatch provided the smoke is visible, so that the
       timekeeper's reaction time has less effect on the time
       measured

3.   swapping the position of the pistol and the stopwatch to
       take account of any wind direction, because the direction
       of the wind affects the speed of sound.

> **Note**
>
> The speed of light (3.0 × 10⁸ m/s) is very much greater than the speed of sound (330 m/s). This is why we see lightning first and then hear thunder a little later.

Sound wave characteristics

○   The **speed of sound** varies from material to material. A sound wave compresses (pushes together) and rarefies (spreads apart) the particles of the material, and how easily this happens affects the speed of the wave.

○   Sound travels fastest in solids because the particles in a solid are very close together.

○   Sound travels second fastest in liquids because the particles in a liquid are only slightly further apart.

○   Sound travels slowest in gases because the particles in a gas are far apart.

○   **Remember**: Sound cannot travel through a vacuum because there are no particles.

○   Some examples of the speed of sound in different media are given below.

-    In dry air at 0 °C the speed is 330 m/s.
-    In dry air at 20 °C the speed is 340 m/s.
-    In water the speed is 1500 m/s.
-    In gold the speed is 3200 m/s.
-    In steel the speed is 5800 m/s.

❑   Frequency, pitch, wavelength and amplitude are terms associated with sound waves.

❑   **Frequency** is the number of wavelengths produced per second and its unit is the **hertz** (Hz).

❑   **Pitch** is how **high** or **low** a sound is and is dependent on frequency.

❑   **Wavelength** is the distance from any point on one wave to the same point on the adjacent wave. Its unit is the **metre** (m).

❑   **Amplitude** is the maximum disturbance of the wave particles from their equilibrium position. It determines how **loud** or **quiet** a sound is.

Oscilloscope wave traces

❑   The diagrams show graphical representations of sound waves as seen on an oscilloscope screen.

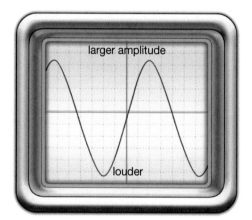
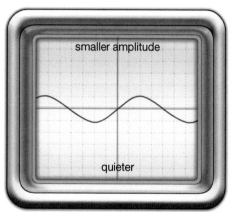

❑   Notice that the frequency for both the loud sound and the quiet sound is the same in the traces above. Only the amplitude is different.

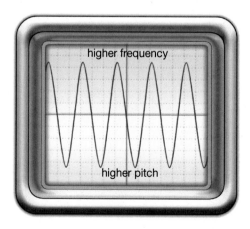
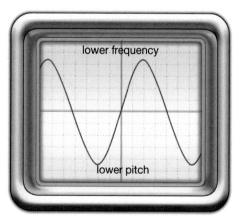

❑   Notice that the amplitude is the same for the high- and low-pitch sounds in the bottom two diagrams. Only the frequency differs.

Remember: Sound waves are longitudinal waves and not transverse waves. The diagrams on the previous page are graphical representations.

The speed of sound and echoes

❏   Sound is a longitudinal wave that can travel to a surface, be reflected and travel back again as an **echo**.

❏   If the distance between the source of sound and the reflective surface, and the time taken, are known then the speed the wave has travelled can be calculated using the equation:

$$v = \frac{s}{t}$$

❏   *Example*
Sara stands 200 m from a large wall and claps together two large blocks of wood. She hears an echo. She claps regularly and times her claps so that they coincide with hearing the echoes. A friend standing beside her with a stopwatch records the time taken for the sound of 10 claps to reach the wall and echo back again as 12.4 s. Calculate the speed of sound.

Answer

Step 1   List all the information in symbol form and change into appropriate and consistent SI units if required.
$s = 2 \times 200$ m (the distance to the wall and back)
The time taken for sound to travel there and back for 10 claps is 12.4 s, so

$t = 1.24$ s

Step 2   Use the correct equation.

$$v = \frac{s}{t}$$

Step 3   Calculate the answer by putting the numbers into the equation.

$$v = \frac{2 \times 200}{1.24} = 322.58 = 320 \text{ m/s (to 2 sig. figs)}$$

ALWAYS REMEMBER TO STATE UNITS OF CALCULATED QUANTITIES

❏   If the speed of sound in a medium and the time taken are known
       then the distance the wave has travelled can be calculated
       using $s = vt$.

○   Boats use a **SONAR** (**So**und **N**avigation **a**nd **R**anging) system to
       locate objects such as shipwrecks and shoals of fish beneath the
       surface of the sea, and to measure the depth of the ocean.
       An ultrasound pulse is sent from the boat to the object and the time
       taken for the pulse to reach the object and return to the ship,
       together with the speed of sound in seawater, enables the distance
       to be calculated.

○ ## *Example*

A fishing boat uses sonar (sound, navigation and ranging) to detect shoals of fish under the water. A ping of sound is sent from the surface, and is reflected back after it hits the shoal of fish. Sound travels at 1500m/s in water and the time between the ping and its echo is 0.40s. Calculate the depth of the water where the shoal is located.

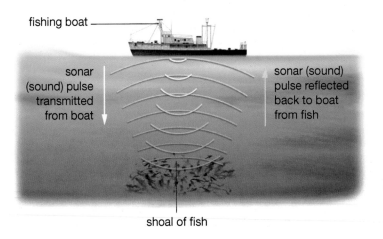

fishing boat

sonar (sound) pulse transmitted from boat

sonar (sound) pulse reflected back to boat from fish

shoal of fish

Answer

Step 1   List all the information in symbol form and change into appropriate and consistent SI units if required.

$v = 1500$m/s

The time taken for the sound to travel there and back is 0.40s, so

$t = 0.20$s

$s = ?$

Step 2   Use the correct equation.

$$v = \frac{s}{t} \quad \Rightarrow \quad s = vt$$

Step 3   Calculate the answer by putting the numbers into the equation.

$s = 1500 \times 0.20 = 300$m

ALWAYS REMEMBER TO STATE THE UNIT FOR CALCULATED QUANTITIES.

○   A similar technique is used in medical imaging to create an image of something that normally cannot be seen, for example, an unborn baby. An ultrasound scanner is run over the mother's body to direct an ultrasound pulse towards the unborn baby. The reflections that come from different parts of the baby's body are analysed by a computer to form an image of the unborn baby.

○   Ultrasound scanning can also be used to diagnose problems with various organs in the body, such as the heart, liver and kidneys. It is a non-invasive technique, i.e. doctors do not have to operate on patients to be able to 'see' what is inside them, and it does not have the same risks as X-rays.

○   Ultrasound scanning can also be used to search for defects in metals, pipes and other materials. If an ultrasonic pulse is aimed through a sheet of metal it would be expected to send an echo back from the far side, but if there is a crack within the metal an echo is sent back sooner than expected as shown below.

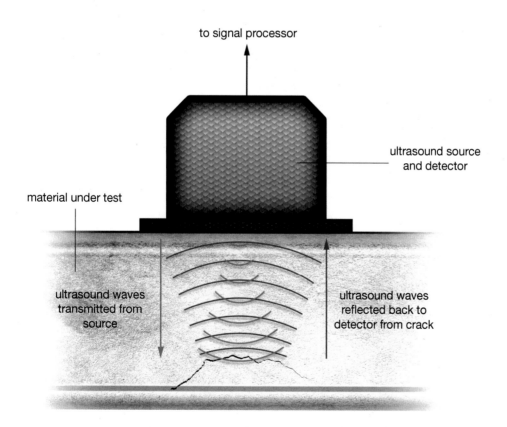

to signal processor

ultrasound source
and detector

material under test

ultrasound waves
transmitted from
source

ultrasound waves
reflected back to
detector from crack

Unit 4 Electricity and magnetism

Section 4.1 Simple phenomena of magnetism

❑   Properties of magnets:

-    they have north (N) and south (S) poles

-    like poles repel and unlike poles attract

-    magnets have a **magnetic field** around them – a region in space where their magnetism can affect magnetic materials

-    magnetic materials contain iron, nickel or cobalt
    Steel is a magnetic material; it is an alloy containing iron

-    magnetic fields can be described using magnetic field lines.

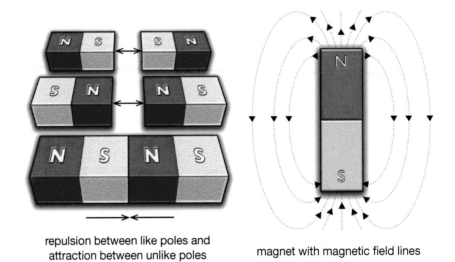

repulsion between like poles and
attraction between unlike poles

magnet with magnetic field lines

❑   If there is a N pole in the field, then the field at that point is in the direction of the force that acts on the N pole.

❑   The magnetic field lines point from the N pole of the magnet all the way back round to the S pole.

○   The magnetic field is strongest near the poles where the field lines are close together and is weaker away from the poles where the field lines are further apart.

○   If two magnets are placed close together their magnetic fields interact. This interaction produces a force that causes the magnets to move if they are free to do so.

❏   The diagram below shows the magnetic fields of two permanent magnets. The magnetic field patterns can be shown using iron filings or plotting compasses (see overleaf).

N.B. The same rules apply; the field lines travel from the N pole to the S pole and never cross or touch.

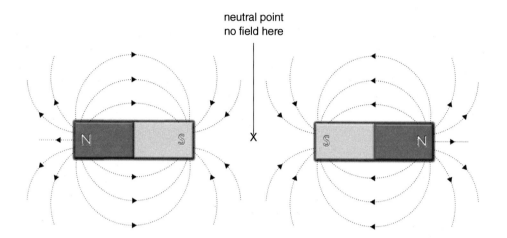

❏   In the diagram above the magnets are placed so that the poles repel. There is a point between the magnets where the magnetic fields cancel each other out; this is called the **neutral point**.

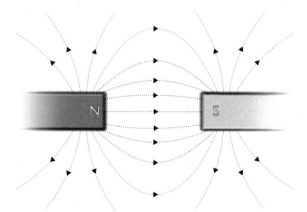

❏   In the diagram above the magnets are placed so that the poles are attracting. Between the magnets is a region where the field lines are straight and parallel. This means the field is uniform in that region.

Magnetic fields

❏   The pattern of magnetic field lines can be shown by sprinkling iron filings onto a sheet of clear plastic on top of a bar magnet. The iron filings arrange themselves in such a way as to show the magnetic field lines, as shown below.

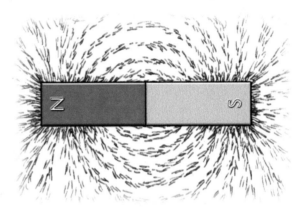

Determining the shape of a magnetic field

❏   Magnetic field lines can be plotted, and their direction determined, using a plotting compass. The field points from the N pole to the S pole. There are various types of plotting compasses; the front of the needle is red and the back of the needle is silver in the following example.

1.   Put the bar magnet on top of a piece of paper. Place a plotting compass near the North pole of the magnet as shown in the diagram opposite. The needle points in the direction of the magnetic field at that point. Mark a pencil dot at the front (B) and back of the compass needle (A) as shown on the diagram.

2.   Move the plotting compass so that the back of the needle is now pointing to the mark you made at the front (B), and mark another dot at the front (C).

3.   Continue until you reach either the magnet again or the edge of the paper. Join the dots and mark the line with an arrow indicating the direction of the magnetic field.

4.   Repeat with more lines. Your magnetic field pattern should look like the one on the opposite page.

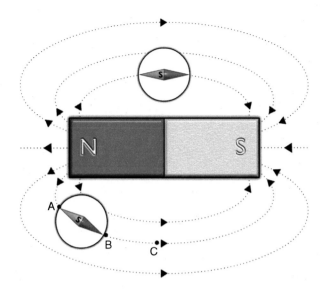

Note

The field lines are always drawn from the N pole to the
S pole and they never cross over each other or touch.

Ferromagnetism

❏ Many magnetic materials are described as **ferrous**. Alloys are
made by melting different metallic elements together. The resulting
material is ferrous if it contains **iron**. Steel is ferrous. Brass (an
alloy of copper and zinc) is an example of a non-ferrous alloy; it
does not contain any iron. Brass is non-magnetic.

Induced magnetism

❏ Magnets can **induce magnetism** in other magnetic materials,
i.e. make them into magnets.

The theory of magnetism

❏ Each iron atom in a magnetic material acts as a small magnet.
In an unmagnetised material, the atomic magnets do not line up;
they point in random directions. In a magnetised material, the
atomic magnets line up in groups called **domains**.

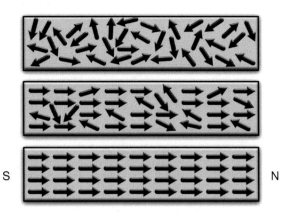

domains not lined up –
unmagnetised

some domains lined up –
weakly magnetised

S   N   all domains lined up –
fully magnetised

Note

Magnets always attract unmagnetised magnetic materials.
Just because they are magnetic materials does not mean
they are magnetised.

The **test** for magnetism is **repulsion**; only two magnets will
repel each other.

Hard and soft magnetic materials

❑   Steel is a **hard magnetic** material. It is difficult to magnetise but
once magnetised it is difficult to demagnetise. Steel is often used
to make **permanent magnets**.

❑   Iron is a **soft magnetic** material. It is easy to magnetise, but loses
its magnetism easily as well. Iron is often used to make
temporary magnets.

❑   The magnetic properties of steel make it a suitable choice to
produce permanent magnets such as **bar magnets**.

❑   Bar magnets have numerous applications, including use as
compass needles. They are always magnetised (permanent
magnets) and **cannot be switched off**.

❑   The magnetic properties of iron make it a suitable choice for
electromagnets. An electromagnet is a coil of wire with a soft
iron core. When a current is in the coil the iron becomes
magnetised.

❑   Electromagnets also have numerous applications, such as in door catches, alarm bells and magnetic inks and paints. They can also be used to lift cars in scrap-yards. They use the magnetic effect of current (see page 220) and can **be switched on or off** (temporary magnets).

Section 4.2   Electrical quantities

Electric charge

❑   All matter contains particles called **electrons**, which have a negative electric charge. When these electrons are taken from the surface of one material and transferred to the surface of another, and stay there, they produce a **static charge** (static means not moving). This branch of Physics is known as electrostatics.

❑   Everyday examples of static charges include:

-   rubbing a balloon on your hair and then sticking it to a wall

-   rubbing a comb on your jumper and then bringing it near to small pieces of paper; the paper jumps and sticks to the comb

-   rubbing polythene and bringing it close to a slow trickle of water; the water is attracted to the polythene.

❑   Some materials are easier than others to charge by rubbing (friction). **Electrical insulators** such as rubber, plastic and glass (non-metals) charge easily.

❑   When electrons are added to or removed from an insulator's surface by rubbing (friction), the charges stay on the surface because they are **not free to move** through the material.

❑   Silver, copper and gold are examples of **electrical conductors** (they are metals). Charge passes through them easily.

❑   Metals are good conductors because they contain **electrons** that are **free to move**. They are **difficult to charge** by friction because the electrons keep moving and the charge flows to earth.

The Earth is considered to be electrically neutral. It is so large it can gain or lose large numbers of electrons and still remain neutral. If a positively charged object is 'connected by a conductor' to Earth, electrons travel through the conductor from Earth until the object becomes electrically neutral. If a negatively charged object is connected to Earth, the excess electrons travel to Earth until the object becomes electrically neutral.

Determining whether a material is a conductor or an insulator

❑   Conductors allow charge to pass through them; insulators do not. Using the simple circuit shown in the diagram below, it is possible to determine whether a material is a conductor or an insulator.

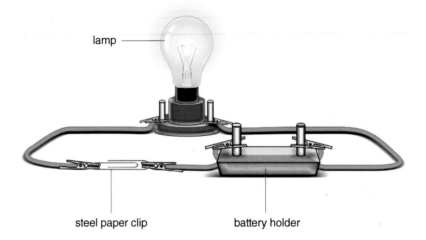

lamp

steel paper clip   battery holder

1.   Set up the circuit as shown to connect a dry cell to a lamp via a steel paper clip attached with crocodile clips.

2.   Observe that the lamp is lit, and conclude that the steel paper clip allows the flow of charge (electric current).

3.   Replace the steel paper clip with various other materials and observe the appearance of the lamp.

4.   List the materials that allow the charge to flow (and the lamp to light) as conductors and those that do not allow the lamp to light (i.e. no charge flows) as insulators.

❑   The table shows a list of some conductors and insulators.

Conductors	Insulators
copper	polythene
steel	wood
aluminium	air
gold	glass
earth	cotton
the human body	wool
sea water	rubber

❑   All atoms are made up of three kinds of particles, called **electrons**, **protons** and **neutrons**.

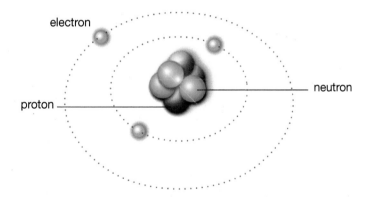

❑   **Protons** and **neutrons** are found in the densest part of the atom known as the **nucleus**, whereas **electrons** are found **orbiting** the nucleus.

❑   **Protons** are **positively** charged, **electrons** are **negatively** charged and **neutrons have no charge**.

❑   Atoms usually have **equal** numbers of electrons and protons, making the **resultant charge** of the atom **zero**.

❑   When two different insulators are rubbed together, electrons may be transferred from one insulator to the other. This leaves one insulator positively charged (having lost electrons) and the other one negatively charged (having gained electrons).

❑   **Protons do not** get transferred; it is **only electrons** that get transferred.

> **Note**
>
> Only **electrons** move when charges transfer by rubbing: the **protons do not**.
>
> If an object **gains electrons** it becomes **negatively charged** and if an object **loses electrons** it becomes **positively charged**.

Electric fields

❑   **Like charges** (+ + or − −) **repel** and **unlike charges** (− + or + −) **attract**.

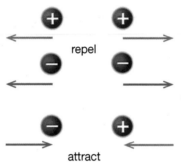

○   Around any charged object there is an **electric field**. A charged particle in this field feels a force towards or away from the charged object, depending on the type of charge on each.

○   An electric field is defined as a region in space in which an electric charge experiences a force.

○   The direction of an electric field at a point is the **direction of the force on a positive charge** at that point. If a positive charge was placed in the fields shown in the diagrams opposite it would begin to move in the direction of the field lines.

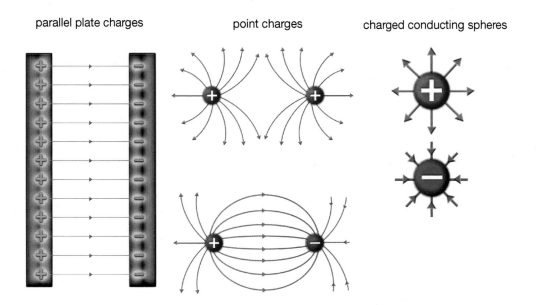

parallel plate charges   point charges   charged conducting spheres

○   The field lines for single point charges and for charged conducting spheres are radial. If the point charge (or sphere) is positive, field lines point away from it; if the charge is negative, field lines point towards it.

Note
Electric field lines are always drawn from positive charges to negative charges. They never cross or touch each other. The electric field is strongest where the electric field lines are closest.

Production of electrostatic charges

❑   Electrostatic charges can be produced in the following ways.

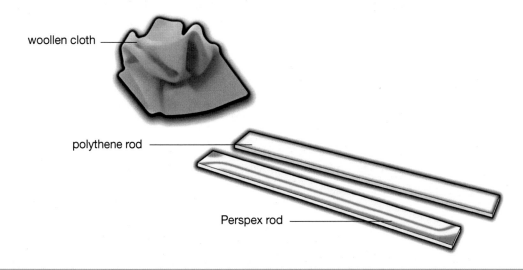

woollen cloth

polythene rod

Perspex rod

1.   Rub the polythene rod with a woollen cloth. This transfers electrons from the wool to the polythene, leaving the polythene **negatively charged** (it gains electrons) and the wool **positively charged** (it loses electrons).

2.   Rub the Perspex rod with a woollen cloth. This transfers electrons from the Perspex to the wool, leaving the wool **negatively charged** (it gains electrons) and the Perspex **positively charged** (it loses electrons).

Detection of electrostatic charges

❑   If one of the charged rods is suspended from a rod held in a clamp stand and a second charged rod is brought close, the suspended rod either moves towards or away from the second rod, depending on the charges.

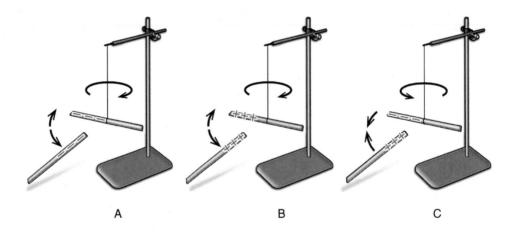

A   B   C

A   The two negatively charged rods repel each other.
B   The two positively charged rods repel each other.
C   The positively charged rod attracts the negatively charged rod.

Top Tip

The **true test** for charge is **repulsion**, just as with magnets. If you put a positively charged balloon close to an object such as a rod hanging from a thread, and it repels, the rod is definitely charged and has a positive charge.

❑ A **gold leaf electroscope** can be used to detect if an object is charged. The metal cap is connected to a metal rod and to a strip of very thin gold leaf, which is hinged so it can move.

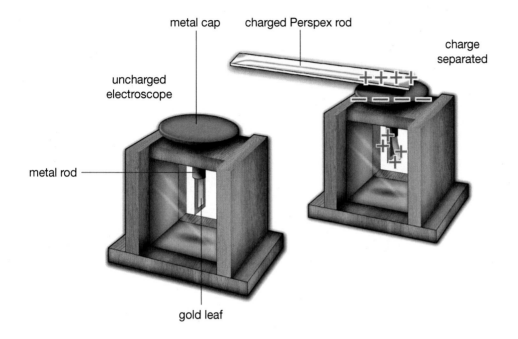

❑ If you put a positively charged Perspex rod near the cap of the electroscope (**but not touching it**), the gold leaf rises up, away from the metal rod.

◯ This happens because the electrons in the electroscope's metal rod and gold leaf are attracted to the Perspex rod. This leaves the cap with a negative charge, and a positive charge on the metal rod and gold leaf (as the free electrons move towards the cap). The positive charges on the metal rod and gold leaf repel each other and so the leaf rises.

Top Tip

Charged objects attract **uncharged objects**.
If you put a positively charged balloon close to some small pieces of paper it attracts them. The pieces of paper could be either neutral or negatively charged; you can't tell whether the paper is charged or not, so attraction is not a true test of whether an object is charged or not.

Circuit symbols

It is important to become familiar with the following electric circuit symbols for the rest of this topic. You have to be able to recognise and draw them.

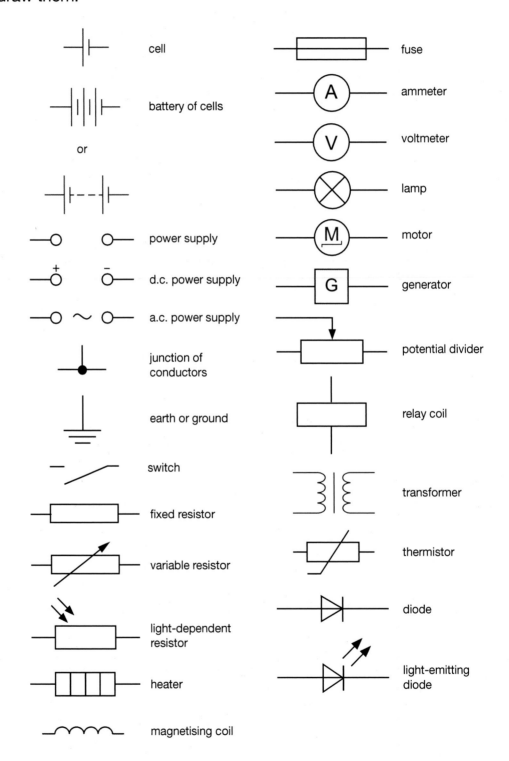

Electric current

- ❑ **Electric current** is the **rate of flow** of electric charge.

- ❑ **Direct current (d.c.)** is the flow of charge in one direction.

- ❑ **Alternating current (a.c.)** is the flow of charge backwards and forwards. It changes direction many times every second.

- ❑ The mains supply (electricity from wall sockets) is always a.c. A battery supply is always d.c.

- ❑ Electric current passes in a **conductor** because charges (electrons) are free to move. Current in metals is due to a flow of electrons.

- ❑ **Current** has the symbol **I**, and its unit is the **ampere** (A).

- ○ **Charge** has the symbol **Q**, and its unit is the **coulomb** (C).

- ○ There is a relationship between **charge**, **current** and **time**. They are related by the equation:

$$I = \frac{Q}{t}$$

I = current (A)
Q = charge (C)
t = time (s)

Note

The charge on an electron is **1.6×10^{-19}C**, which means **1.0 C** of charge has **6.25×10^{18} electrons**, a huge number.

○   **Example**

Calculate the current in a wire when 720 C of charge is transferred in 4.0 minutes.

Answer

Step 1   List all the information in symbol form and change into appropriate and consistent SI units if required.

$Q = 720\,C$

$t = 4.0$ minutes $= 4.0 \times 60 = 240\,s$

$I = ?$

Step 2   Use the correct equation.

$$I = \frac{Q}{t}$$

Step 3   Calculate the answer by putting the numbers into the equation.

$$I = \frac{Q}{t} = \frac{720}{240} = 3.0\,A$$

ALWAYS REMEMBER TO STATE THE UNIT FOR CALCULATED QUANTITIES.

Conventional current

○ In the early days, scientists assumed that current was a flow of charges from positive to negative. This was long before the discovery of the electron.

We now know that electric current is the flow of electrons away from the negative terminal towards the positive terminal. But to avoid confusion scientists decided to continue to define conventional current as the flow of charges from positive to negative.

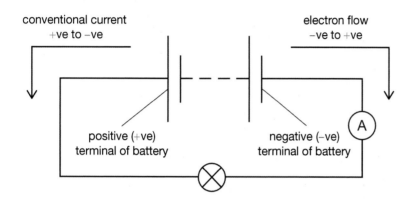

conventional current
+ve to −ve

electron flow
−ve to +ve

positive (+ve)
terminal of battery

negative (−ve)
terminal of battery

A

Note

Electrons flow from negative to positive. **Conventional current** is from positive to negative.

Remember: When we talk about current we mean conventional current.

❑ **Current** is measured using an **ammeter**.

❑ An ammeter has **very low resistance** to current and so does not affect the current in the circuit: it simply measures it. An analogue ammeter gives a reading with a needle moving across a scale; a digital ammeter has a numerical reading displayed.

❑   The analogue ammeter below shows a current of 0.50A.

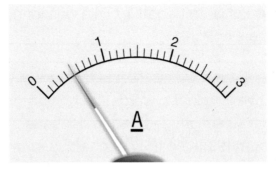

❑   The digital ammeter below shows a current of 1.26A.

❑   An ammeter is always placed in **series** with other components in a circuit.

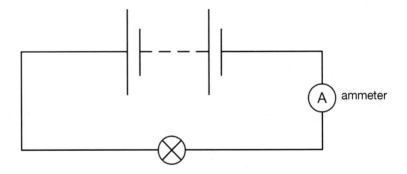

❑   When using an ammeter, choose one with a range that is appropriate for the current being measured. For example, if you are measuring a current of 0.8A and the ammeter you are using has a range of 10A, the deflection of the needle would be small. If the range was 1A, the deflection would be large and there would be less likelihood of error when taking the reading.

Electromotive force and potential difference

❑ **Electromotive force (e.m.f.)** is a measure of how much '**push**' or **energy** a battery or power source can provide to each unit charge in a circuit i.e. it is the electrical work done in moving unit charge all the way around the circuit. Its unit is the **volt** (V).

❑ The e.m.f. is defined as the amount of **energy** given to **one coulomb** of charge in a circuit (e.g. a **6.0V** battery gives **6.0J** to each coulomb of charge).

❑ **One volt** is defined as one joule per coulomb. **1V = 1J/C**

○ The equation for e.m.f. is

$$E = \frac{W}{Q}$$

E = e.m.f. (V)
W = work done (J)
Q = charge (C)

❑ Charges carry the energy round a circuit to the various components.

❑ When the charge enters a lamp, for example, the **electrical energy** carried by the charge is transferred as light and thermal energy.

❑ As charge flows through a circuit component it transfers energy, i.e. it has more energy as it starts to flow through the component than when it leaves.

❑ Voltage is a measure of the difference in electrical energy between two points of a circuit; the bigger the difference in energy, the bigger the voltage. This change in energy is known as the **potential difference (p.d.)** or sometimes the voltage drop or simply 'voltage'.

❑ The p.d. across a component has the unit **volt** (V).

❑ **Remember**: Work done is equal to energy transferred (see page 70) Thus p.d. can be defined as the work done by unit charge passing through a component.

Top Tip

E.m.f is a measure of the energy given to unit charge by a source to push it round the **whole circuit**.
P.d is the work done by unit charge passing through a **component**.

○   The equation for p.d. is:

$$V = \frac{W}{Q}$$

V = p.d. (V)
W = work done (J)
Q = charge (C)

❑   A **voltmeter** is used to measure the e.m.f. of a source or the p.d. across a component. It measures the **voltage (potential difference)** between two points.

Note

Voltage is defined as the energy given to each coulomb of charge.
1 volt = 1 joule/coulomb or **1V = 1J/C**

❑   A voltmeter can be either analogue or digital. An analogue voltmeter gives a reading with a needle moving across a scale; a digital voltmeter has a numerical reading displayed.

❑   The analogue voltmeter below shows a voltage reading of 2.4 V.

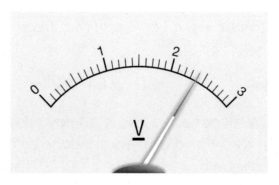

❑   The digital voltmeter below shows a voltage reading of 3.32V.

❑   Voltmeters are always connected in **parallel** with the component whose voltage is being measured, as shown in the diagram below. They do not affect the circuit. Voltmeters have very high resistance.

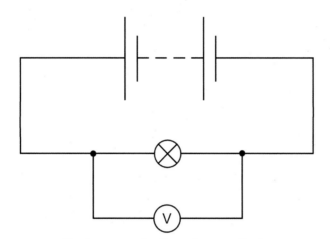

voltmeter measuring the p.d. across the lamp

❑   When using a voltmeter, choose one with a range that is appropriate for the voltage being measured. For example, if you are measuring a voltage of 1.0V and the voltmeter you are using has a range of 20V, the deflection of the needle would be small. If the range was 2V, the deflection would be larger and there would be less likelihood of error when taking the reading.

Resistance

❑ All components in an electrical circuit **oppose**, to a small or large degree, the current flowing in them.

❑ **Resistance** can be thought of as **electrical friction**.

❑ Resistance has the symbol **R**, and its unit is the **ohm** (Ω).

❑ When the total resistance in a circuit increases and the voltage of the source remains constant, the current in the circuit decreases.

❑ It can be difficult to visualise what is happening in an electric circuit because electric current is invisible. We can compare an electric circuit with a water circuit.

- Imagine a circuit consisting of water pipes and a pump moving the water round. The pump gives the water kinetic energy just as a battery gives the charges energy.

- A flowmeter would measure the rate of flow of the water just as an ammeter measures the rate of flow of charge.

- A constriction (narrowing) in the pipe reduces the flow rate (slows the water down) just as a **resistor** reduces the current (slows the charges). Note that the flow rate is reduced both before and after the constriction.

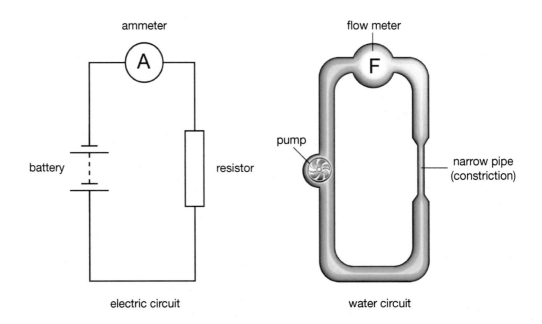

ammeter — battery — resistor — electric circuit

flow meter — pump — narrow pipe (constriction) — water circuit

Factors that affect resistance

❑ The resistance of a wire can be increased by increasing its **length**.

○ The resistance is proportional to the length.

$$R \propto l$$

Therefore, doubling the length of wire doubles the resistance. Imagine the effect on water flow of doubling the length of the constriction in a water pipe.

❑ The greater the **cross-sectional area A** of a wire, the **more electrons** there are available to carry the charge along a conductor's length and so the lower the resistance.

○ Doubling the cross-sectional area halves the resistance **R**. This is known as inverse proportion because the resistance is proportional to the inverse of the area (i.e. 1/**A**).

$$R \propto \frac{1}{A}$$

Note

Resistance is a measurement of a conductor's **opposition** to the **flow of electric current**. It is measured in ohms.

◯   ***Example 1***

A resistor is made of constantan wire that is 23 cm long and has a diameter of 0.38 mm. Its resistance is measured as 1.0 Ω.

Calculate:

(a)   the resistance if the length of the wire is increased to 46 cm but the diameter remains at 0.38 mm

(b)   the resistance if the length remains at 23 cm but the diameter is increased to 0.76 mm.

Answer

(a)   **Step 1**   List all the information in symbol form and change into appropriate and consistent SI units if required.

$$l_1 = 23 \text{ cm}$$
$$l_2 = 46 \text{ cm}$$
$$R_1 = 1.0 \, \Omega$$

Step 2   Recall that resistance is proportional to length.

$$R \propto l$$

Step 3   The length doubles, so the resistance doubles.

$$R = 2 \times 1.0 = 2.0 \, \Omega$$

(b)   **Step 1**   List all the information in symbol form and change into appropriate and consistent SI units if required.

$$d_1 = 0.38 \text{ mm}$$
$$d_2 = 0.76 \text{ mm}$$
$$R_1 = 1.0 \, \Omega$$

Step 2   The diameter doubles, so the cross-sectional area is four times as big and the resistance is a quarter of the original value.

$$R = \frac{1.0}{4} = 0.25 \, \Omega$$

ALWAYS REMEMBER TO STATE THE UNIT FOR CALCULATED QUANTITIES.

○ ***Example 2***

Hairdryer X contains a heating element made of resistance wire of length l and cross-sectional area A and has a resistance of R. A second hairdryer Y is made of resistance wire that is three times as long and has a quarter of the cross-sectional area of the wire used for X.

Calculate the ratio: $\dfrac{\text{resistance of element in X}}{\text{resistance of element in Y}}$

Answer

Step 1   List all the information in symbol form and change into appropriate and consistent SI units if required.

For X: length = l For Y: length = $3l$

area = A area = $A/4$

resistance = R resistance = ?

Remember: Because we are finding a ratio we do not need to include units for length and area.

Step 2   Recall how resistance depends on length and cross-sectional area:

$R \propto l$ and $R \propto \dfrac{1}{A}$

Step 3   If only the length was changed:

length of wire for Y would equal 3 × length of wire for X

$R_Y = 3 \times R_X$

If only the cross-sectional area was changed:

area of Y would equal one-quarter of area of X

$R_Y = 4 \times R_X$

considering both changes at the same time:
$R_Y = 3 \times 4 \times R_X$

$\dfrac{\text{resistance of element in X}}{\text{resistance of element in Y}} = \dfrac{1}{12}$

Ohm's Law

❑ **Potential difference**, **current** and **resistance** are related by the equation:

$$V = IR$$

V = potential difference (V)
I = current (A)
R = resistance (Ω)

By rearrangement:

$$\text{resistance} = \frac{\text{p.d.}}{\text{current}} \qquad R = \frac{V}{I}$$

❑ This equation **defines the resistance** of a component as V/I and it is constant for metallic conductors provided the temperature is constant.

❑ So if the **p.d.** across a resistor **doubles**, the **current** in it **doubles**.

○ If the resistance of a conductor **remains constant**, a graph of p.d. against current is a straight line. The **gradient** of the line is the resistance of the conductor.

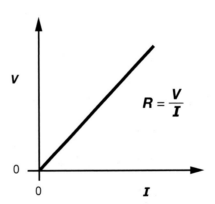

Note

For a given metallic conductor, V/I is constant provided that its **temperature** is **constant**. This is known as Ohm's Law.

❏   Such a conductor is known as an **ohmic resistor** because it obeys Ohm's Law. The voltage is proportional to the current ($V \propto I$).

❏   If a device has a fixed resistance of R, then you can calculate V or I if you know the other value from $V = IR$.

❏   ***Example***
Calculate the current in a resistor that has a 2.0 kΩ resistance and is connected across 240 V supply voltage.

Answer

Step 1   List all the information in symbol form and change into appropriate and consistent SI units if required.

$V = 240\text{V}$
$R = 2.0\text{k}\Omega = 2000\Omega$
$I = ?$

Step 2   Use and rearrange the correct equation.

$$V = IR \qquad \Rightarrow \qquad I = \frac{V}{R}$$

Step 3   Calculate the answer by putting the numbers into the equation.

$$I = \frac{V}{R} = \frac{240}{2000} = 0.12\,\text{A}$$

ALWAYS REMEMBER TO STATE THE UNIT FOR CALCULATED QUANTITIES.

Determining the resistance of an unknown resistor

❑ The following experiment describes how to determine the resistance of an unknown resistor.

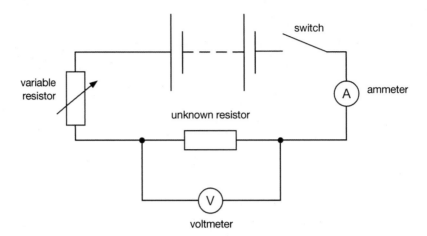

1. Set up the circuit as shown.

2. Vary the current by varying the resistance of the variable resistor.

3. Record the current and voltage.

4. Repeat for several different values of **I** and **V** and construct a table of results.

5. Calculate the value of **R** for each pair of current and voltage results, and determine the average value.

6. Alternatively plot a graph of **V** against **I** (see page 186).

Calculations to be made
Resistance of the unknown resistor.

$$V = IR \quad \Rightarrow \quad R = \frac{V}{I}$$

which is equal to the gradient of the **V–I** graph.

Improvements to the experiment
The experiment could be improved by:

1. **switching off** the circuit **between readings** to reduce the heating effect

2. carrying out the experiment at a **lower voltage** to reduce the heating effect.

Assumptions in the experiment

We assume that the changing temperature has **no effect** on the resistor's resistance. A straight-line graph through the origin confirms this.

The effect of temperature on resistance

❑   Current in a conducting wire produces a heating effect. This effect is used in toasters, kettles and filament lamps. This happens because the **moving free electrons** in the wire collide with the **particles** inside the wire. The electrons transfer energy to the particles, which vibrate faster. Therefore the internal energy of the wire increases and the wire becomes warmer.

Note

The resistance of a filament lamp increases as the voltage increases but the resistance of an ohmic resistor stays the same.

○   In the graph of current against voltage for the filament lamp shown below, the resistance increases as the voltage increases because the filament becomes hotter. This means that the current does not increase uniformly as it would in an ohmic resistor.

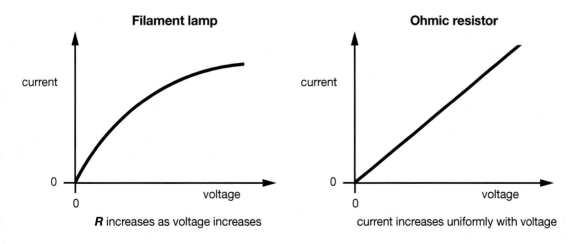

N.B. Notice that in these graphs the current is plotted on the **y**-axis, and the voltage on the **x**-axis.

Electrical energy and power

❑   Electric circuits transfer energy from the power source or the battery to the circuit components, where it is transferred into useful energy, e.g. a lamp provides light energy.

❑   **Energy** has the symbol E, and its unit is the **joule** (J).

❑   Other examples of electrical devices transferring energy include:

-   an electric motor – electrical energy transfers to kinetic energy which is useful, and thermal energy and sound which are dissipated to the surroundings

-   a television set – electrical energy transfers to light and sound which are useful, and thermal energy which is dissipated to the surroundings

-   an iPod – electrical energy transfers to sound energy which is useful, and thermal energy, which is dissipated to the surroundings

-   an immersion heater – electrical energy transfers to thermal energy in the water which is useful, but some thermal energy is dissipated to the surroundings.

❑   All electrical equipment has a **power rating**.

❑   **Power** is the **rate** at which energy is transferred from one form into another (e.g. 2000J of electrical energy being transferred to thermal energy per second by a 2000W electric kettle). Power has the symbol P, and its unit is the **watt** (W):

1W = 1J/s

❑   The power rating indicates how much energy is supplied to the device each second, e.g. a **100W** lamp receives energy at a rate of **100J/s**.

❑   Some of the energy is always dissipated to the surroundings, e.g. as well as giving out light, the lamp heats up and the thermal energy is 'wasted'.

○   The **power** of an item of electrical equipment depends on **voltage** and **current**.

| $P = IV$ | P = power (W)
I = current (A)
V = voltage (V) |

○   ***Example***
The current in a 240V electric cooker is 8.0A.
Calculate the power of the cooker.

Answer

Step 1   List all the information in symbol form and change into appropriate and consistent SI units if required.

$V = 240V$
$I = 8.0A$
$P = ?$

Step 2   Use the correct equation.

$P = IV$

Step 3   Calculate the answer by putting the numbers into the equation.

$P = IV = 8.0 \times 240 = 1920 = 1900W$ (to 2 sig. figs)

ALWAYS REMEMBER TO STATE THE UNIT FOR CALCULATED QUANTITIES.

○   The **energy** transferred by an appliance is related to **power** and **time**:

| $\Delta E = Pt$ | ΔE = energy transferred (J)
P = power (W)
t = time (s) |

❑   The kilowatt-hour (kWh) is a unit of electrical energy, and is defined as the energy transferred by a 1kW appliance when used for one hour.

1kWh = 3600 kJ

Energy suppliers often use this unit to calculate the cost of energy supplied to a home or business.

❏   *Example 1*

A 1 kW electric heater is left on for 12 hours. Each unit of electricity (each kWh) costs 11 cents. Calculate the cost of using the heater.

Answer

Step 1   List all the information in symbol form and change into appropriate and consistent SI units if required.

$$P = 1\,kW$$
$$t = 12\,h$$
$$cost/kWh = 11 \text{ cents}$$

Remember: We do not need to change these into SI units as we want our answer in kWh.

Step 2   Use the correct equations.

$$\Delta E = Pt$$
Cost = cost per unit x number of units

Step 3   Calculate the answer by putting the numbers into the equations.

$$\Delta E = Pt = 1 \times 12 = 12\,kWh$$
$$\text{Cost} = 11 \times 12 = 132 \text{ cents} = \$1.32$$

ALWAYS REMEMBER TO STATE THE UNIT FOR CALCULATED QUANTITIES.

❏   *Example 2*

Calculate how much energy is transferred by a 100 W lamp in 2.0 minutes.

Answer

Step 1   List all the information in symbol form and change into appropriate and consistent SI units if required.

$$P = 100\,W$$
$$t = 2.0 \text{ minutes} = 2 \times 60 = 120\,s$$
$$\Delta E = ?$$

Step 2   Choose the correct equation.

$$\Delta E = Pt$$

Step 3   Calculate the answer by putting the numbers into the equation.

$$\Delta E = Pt = 100 \times 120 = 12\,000\,\text{J}$$

ALWAYS REMEMBER TO STATE THE UNIT FOR CALCULATED QUANTITIES.

○   *Example 3*

A television set is connected to a 240V supply for 1.0 hour and the current is 0.33A. Calculate the energy transferred in this time.

Answer

Step 1   List all the information in symbol form and change into appropriate and consistent SI units if required.

$$I = 0.33\,\text{A}$$
$$V = 240\,\text{V}$$
$$t = 1.0\text{h} = 60 \times 60 = 3600\,\text{s}$$
$$\Delta E = ?$$

Step 2   Choose the correct equations.

$$P = IV \qquad \Delta E = Pt$$

Step 3   Calculate the answer by putting the numbers into the equations.

$$P = IV = 0.33 \times 240 = 79.2\,\text{W}$$
$$\Delta E = Pt = 79.2 \times 3600 = 285\,120$$
$$= 290\,000\,\text{J (to 2 sig. figs)}$$

ALWAYS REMEMBER TO STATE THE UNIT FOR CALCULATED QUANTITIES.

❑ Since power is related to voltage and current ($P = IV$) and energy is related to power and time, $\Delta E = Pt$ can be rewritten as:

$$\Delta E = IVt$$

ΔE = energy transferred (J)
I = current (A)
V = voltage (V)
t = time (s)

We simply substitute IV for P to get the equation above.

❑ **Example**

Calculate the energy transferred by a 240V hairdryer, running on a current of 6.0A, that is left on for 8.0 minutes.

Answer

Step 1   List all the information in symbol form and change into appropriate and consistent SI units if required.

$V = 240V$
$I = 6.0A$
$t = 8.0$ minutes $= 8.0 \times 60 = 480s$
$\Delta E = ?$

Step 2   Use the correct equation.

$\Delta E = IVt$

Step 3   Calculate the answer by putting the numbers into the equation.

$\Delta E = IVt = 6.0 \times 240 \times 480 = 691\,200$
$= 690\,000\,J$ (to 2 sig. figs)

ALWAYS REMEMBER TO STATE THE UNIT FOR CALCULATED QUANTITIES.

○   Another expression for electrical power is:

| $P = I^2R$ | P = power (W)
I = current (A)
R = resistance (Ω) |

○   The two expressions $P = I^2R$ and $P = IV$ can be shown to be related:

$$P = IV \text{ but } V = IR$$

Therefore, $P = I(IR)$

$$P = I^2R$$

We simply substitute IR for V to get the equation above.

○   This equation can be used to calculate the thermal energy dissipated in cables. When electrical energy is transmitted over large distances, the energy dissipated into the atmosphere can be quite large. A transformer can be used to reduce the current in the cables (see page 235).

○   **Example**
Calculate the power dissipated (given out) in a 40Ω pocket torch (flashlight) with a 100mA current in it.

Answer

Step 1   List all the information in symbol form and change into appropriate and consistent SI units if required.

I = 100mA = 0.100A

R = 40Ω

P = ?

Step 2   Use the correct equation.

$$P = I^2R$$

Step 3   Calculate the answer by putting the numbers into the equation.

$$P = I^2R = 0.100^2 \times 40 = 0.40\text{W}$$

**ALWAYS REMEMBER TO STATE THE UNIT FOR
CALCULATED QUANTITIES.**

Section 4.3 Electric circuits

Series and parallel circuits

❑ There is **only one path** for the current in a **series circuit**.

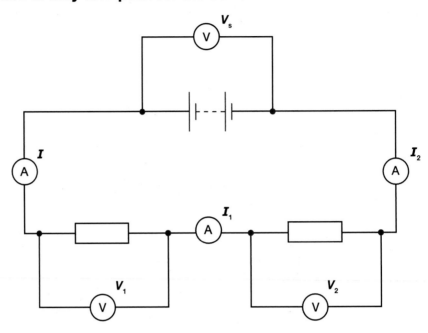

(The various meters are assumed not to be part of the circuit as they are simply there to measure values and have no effect on the circuit.)

❑ The **current** is the **same** at all points in a **series** circuit:

$$I = I_1 = I_2$$ I = supply current as measured by an ammeter wherever it is placed in the circuit

○ The **supply voltage V_s**, also known as the **electromotive force (e.m.f.)**, is equal to the sum of the voltages (potential differences) across each **individual component** in a series circuit:

$$V_s = V_1 + V_2$$ V_s = supply voltage (e.m.f.)

Note

Current is the same at all points in a series circuit.

The supply voltage (e.m.f.) is shared between components within the circuit.

❑   Sometimes the supply voltage (e.m.f.) is provided by several sources in series. In this case the total e.m.f. is the sum of the individual **e.m.f.s.** For example, if six 1.5V cells are connected in series, the total e.m.f. is 9.0V.

❑   There is **more than one path** for the current in a **parallel circuit.**

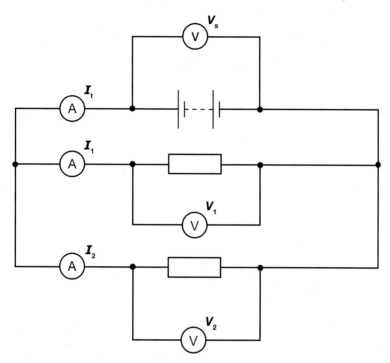

(The various meters are assumed not to be part of the circuit as they are simply there to measure values and have no effect on the circuit.)

○   The **voltage (p.d) across individual** components in a **parallel** circuit is **equal to the supply voltage:**

$$V_s = V_1 = V_2$$

V_s = supply voltage (e.m.f.)
V_1 and V_2 = **p.d.** across resistors

❑   The **current** in a parallel circuit is larger in the branch containing the battery than in the other branches.

○   The **sum of the currents** in the individual parallel branches is **equal to the current drawn from the supply I_t:**

$$I_t = I_1 + I_2$$

I_t = total supply current as measured by the ammeter in series with the battery

○   The sum of the currents entering any junction in a parallel circuit equals the sum of the currents leaving that junction.

❑   The combined total resistance R_t of **N** resistors connected in a **series** circuit can be found by using the following equation:

$$R_t = R_1 + R_2 + ...R_N$$

R_N = integer number of resistors

○   The combined total resistance R_t of two resistors connected in a **parallel** circuit can be found by using the following equation:

$$\frac{1}{R_t} = \frac{1}{R_1} + \frac{1}{R_2}$$

○   If two **identical** resistors (each of resistance R) are in parallel then R_t is equal to $R/2$. The total resistance is half of the resistance of one of the two identical resistors. For example, the combined total resistance of two $10\,\Omega$ resistors in parallel is $5.0\,\Omega$.

❑   If two resistors in parallel are not identical then R_t is less than the resistance of either of the two individual resistors (see example below and opposite).

Top Tip

The total resistance of any two resistors in parallel is less than the resistance of either of the individual resistors.

○   ***Example***
Calculate the total resistance R_t of the following circuit.

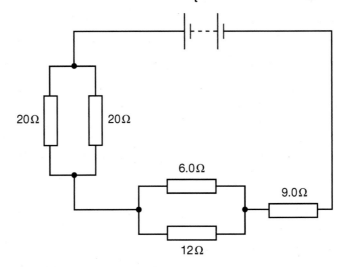

Answer

Step 1   Calculate the resistance of the pairs in parallel, effectively replacing each pair with a single **equivalent** resistor.

For the two 20Ω resistors in parallel:

$$R_t = \frac{R}{2} = \frac{20}{2} = 10\,\Omega$$

For the 6.0Ω and 12Ω resistors in parallel:

$$\frac{1}{R_t} = \frac{1}{R_1} + \frac{1}{R_2} = \frac{1}{6.0} + \frac{1}{12}$$

Both fractions need to be put over a common denominator:

$$\frac{1}{R_t} = \frac{2}{12} + \frac{1}{12} = \frac{2+1}{12} = \frac{3}{12}$$

Turn both sides upside down (**invert**):

$$\frac{R_t}{1} = \frac{12}{3} = 4.0\,\Omega$$

(In mathematics, this is called finding the **reciprocal**.)

Step 2   Now the circuit becomes:

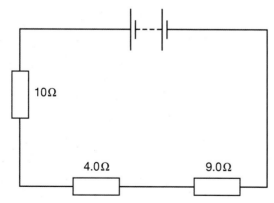

The total resistance of the circuit can be calculated by using the resistors in series equation:

$$R_t = R_1 + R_2 + R_3 = 10 + 4.0 + 9.0 = 23\,\Omega$$

ALWAYS REMEMBER TO STATE THE UNIT FOR CALCULATED QUANTITIES.

Series circuit with identical lamps

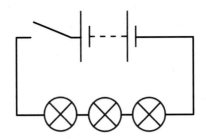

- ❏ In a **series** circuit, if one lamp blows the others **go out** (e.g. some festival tree lights).

- ❏ In a series circuit, the lamps **cannot** be switched on and off **independently**. When the switch is open there is no current in the circuit.

- ❏ In a series circuit all lamps **share** the supply voltage (**e.m.f.**) from the battery, so identical lamps are **equally lit** when the switch is closed.

- ❏ Current is the **same** at **all points** in a series circuit.

- ❏ If more lamps are added, the dimmer they all become.

- ❏ A practical example of a series circuit is a simple flashlight consisting of a battery, a switch and a lamp.

Note

The **brightness** of the lamps **depends** on **power** (*P* = *IV*). Lamps in series in a circuit are dimmer than they would be if they were in parallel because there is less voltage per lamp and less current in the lamp because of the higher resistance of the circuit. This in turn causes the power used per lamp to be less.

Parallel circuit with identical lamps

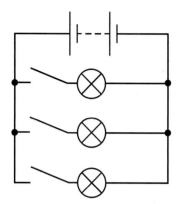

- ❑ In a **parallel** circuit, if one lamp blows the others remain **on**. (Consider the lighting in your house.)

- ❑ In a simple parallel circuit, the lamps **can** be switched on and off independently. If one switch is open it only affects the lamp in the same branch of the circuit.

- ❑ In a simple parallel circuit as shown above, all lamps have the **same voltage** as the **e.m.f.** of the **battery**.

- ❑ The total **current**, found by adding the current through each lamp, **adds** up to the **supply** current in a **parallel** circuit.

- ❑ If more lamps are added in parallel the brightness stays the same.

- ❑ A practical example of a parallel circuit is the domestic wiring in your home. You can switch the television off without switching off the computer.

Note

The advantages of parallel circuits are:
- when one component such as a lamp goes off the others stay on (because there is more than one path for the current)
- each component such as a lamp has the same voltage as the supply voltage
- each component can be switched on and off independently.

Action and use of circuit components

Potential dividers

○   **Resistors** in series **share** the supply **voltage (e.m.f.).**

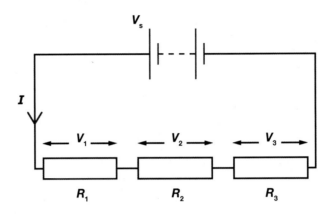

V_s = supply voltage (e.m.f.)

Total resistance: $R_t = R_1 + R_2 + R_3$

Voltage across R_1: $V_1 = I R_1$

but $I = \dfrac{V_s}{R_t}$ ⟹ $I = \dfrac{V_s}{R_1 + R_2 + R_3}$

and therefore $V_1 = \dfrac{V_s}{R_1 + R_2 + R_3} \times R_1$

this can be simplified $V_1 = \dfrac{R_1}{R_t} \times V_s$

often written as $\dfrac{R_1}{R_t} = \dfrac{V_1}{V_s}$

Similarly the voltage across V_2 and V_3 can be found as shown on the next page.

○ **Example**

Calculate the potential difference (p.d.) across each of the three resistors shown in the circuit diagram below.

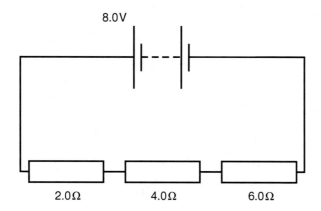

8.0V

2.0Ω   4.0Ω   6.0Ω

Total resistance $= 2.0 + 4.0 + 6.0 = 12\,\Omega$

p.d. across 2.0Ω: $V = \dfrac{2.0}{12} \times 8.0 = 1.3\,\text{V}$ (to 2 sig. figs)

p.d. across 4.0Ω: $V = \dfrac{4.0}{12} \times 8.0 = 2.7\,\text{V}$ (to 2 sig. figs)

p.d. across 6.0Ω: $V = \dfrac{6.0}{12} \times 8.0 = 4.0\,\text{V}$

Note: $1.3 + 2.7 + 4.0 = 8.0\,\text{V}$

This is **same** as the **e.m.f.** because p.d. in a series circuit adds up to the supply voltage (e.m.f.) (see page 196).

ALWAYS REMEMBER TO STATE THE UNIT FOR CALCULATED QUANTITIES.

○ The device shown below can be used as a variable resistor (or rheostat) when it is connected into a circuit using terminals X and Z. It can also be used as a **potentiometer** or **potential divider** when all three terminals are used as shown in the circuit diagram.

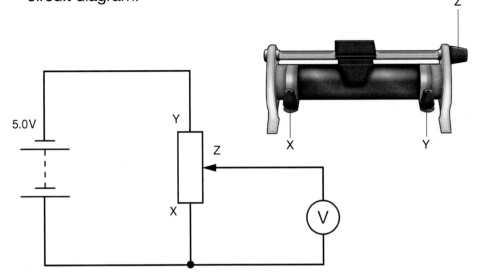

○ As the slider Z is moved from X to Y, the resistance between X and Z increases, so the voltage across XZ increases. This is the voltage measured by the voltmeter. Therefore the resistance between Z and Y decreases, so the voltage across ZY decreases.

Remember: The current between Y and X stays the same. The voltmeter is measuring the p.d. between X and Z, and as X moves closer to Y the resistance between X and Z increases, thus the p.d. increases.

○ If Z is in the middle of the potentiometer, then the voltage across XZ and the voltage across ZY are 2.5V each (for the example above).

Other circuit components

❑ Many real-life circuits are used for controlling something.

❑ Circuits with microchips and other **electronic** devices are called **electronic** circuits.

❑ Most electronic circuits operate on **very low current**, although they can control much more **powerful circuits**.

❑   All control systems have an input, a **processor** and an output.

❑   An input sensor sends a signal to a processor, which controls the flow of power to an output device.

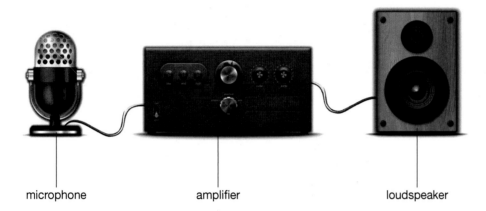

microphone   amplifier   loudspeaker

❑   **Sound energy** is transferred by the microphone into **electrical energy**, which is then amplified (increased) by the amplifier. The resulting output is a loud noise as **electrical energy** is transferred into **sound again** by the loudspeaker.

❑   Devices that **transfer** energy from one form to another or electrical signals into some other form of energy are called **transducers**. The components below are all transducers.

Input sensors	Output devices
light-dependent resistor (LDR)	light-emitting diode (LED)
microphone	lamp
thermistor	buzzer
variable resistor	loudspeaker
pressure switch (switch operated by pressing it)	electric motor

❑   A **relay** is an **electromagnetic switch**; it can be used to switch on high-powered circuits. See page 224 for an explanation of how a relay works. The symbol for a relay coil is:

❑   A **variable resistor** controls the current (and can, as a result control the potential difference/voltage across other circuit components). The symbol for a variable resistor is:

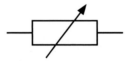

❑   A **thermistor** is a resistor with a resistance that depends on temperature. As the **temperature increases** the **resistance decreases**, and vice versa. The symbol for a thermistor is:

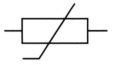

❑   The resistance of a **light-dependent resistor** (**LDR**), varies according to the amount of light falling on it; as the **light intensity increases** the **resistance decreases**, and vice versa. The symbol for a light-dependent resistor is:

○   A **diode** allows **current** to pass in **one direction** only. The symbol for a diode is:

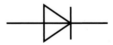

○   A **light-emitting diode** is a diode that glows when current passes through it. The symbol for a light-emitting diode is:

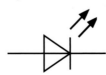

Diodes as rectifiers

○ The process of changing **a.c.** into **d.c.** is known as **rectification**.

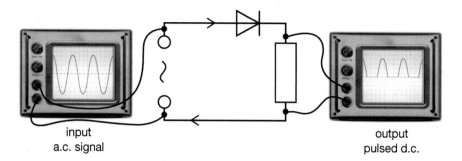

input
a.c. signal

output
pulsed d.c.

○ **Diodes** are used to change a.c. into d.c. in devices that are known as **rectifiers**.

○ Diodes are found in computers, television sets and battery chargers.

○ Diodes have to be **forward-biased** for current to pass. They often need approximately 0.7V to begin operating.

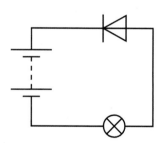

No current
The diode is reverse-biased.
The diode has an infinitely high
resistance.

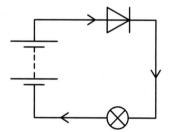

There is a current
The diode is forward-biased.
The diode has a low resistance.

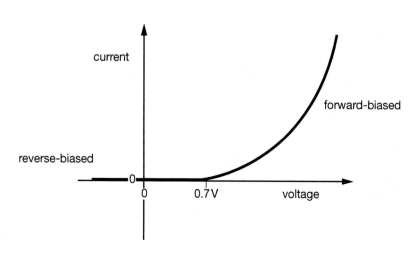

Light-sensitive switch

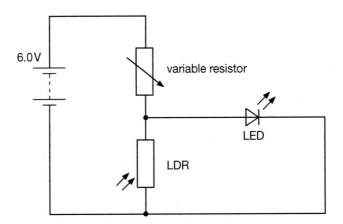

The circuit above switches on the LED when it gets dark. The light from the LED does not fall on the LDR.

How it works

- The light-dependent resistor (LDR) and variable resistor together behave as a potential divider. The **resistance** of the LDR changes depending on how much light is falling on it.

In daylight:

- As the intensity of light on the LDR is large, the resistance of the LDR is small.

- The **potential difference** (**voltage**) across the LDR is therefore small, so the current through the light-emitting diode (LED) is small and the LED is **off**.

As it becomes dark:

- As the light intensity incident on the LDR decreases, the resistance of the LDR increases.

- The potential difference across the LDR increases and consequently it switches the LED **on**.

- If the **variable resistor** and **LDR** were **swapped**, the lamp would be lit during daylight and be off at night.

Temperature-operated alarm

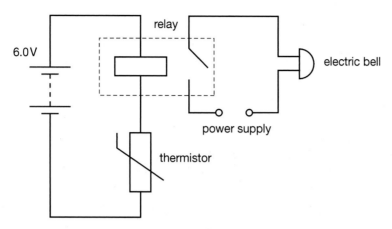

The circuit above causes the alarm to sound when it gets too hot.

How it works

○　The thermistor and relay together behave as a potential divider. The resistance of the thermistor changes depending on the surrounding temperature.

○　A relay is a magnetic switch. When there is a current in the coil of the relay it magnetises and causes the switch to close in the second circuit so the bell rings. See page 224 for further explanation of how a relay operates.

When cold:

○　When the temperature is low the resistance of the thermistor is high and therefore the **potential difference** across the thermistor is **high**.

○　The potential difference across the relay coil is **low** and so the current in it is low and its coil does not magnetise enough to close the switch. The bell does not ring.

When warm:

○　When the temperature is high the resistance of the thermistor is low and therefore the **potential difference** across the thermistor is **low**.

○　The potential difference across the relay coil is **high** and so the current in it is large. The coil magnetises and the switch closes and therefore the bell rings.

○ **Example**

The circuit below is designed to light up a warning LED when the temperature falls below a set value.

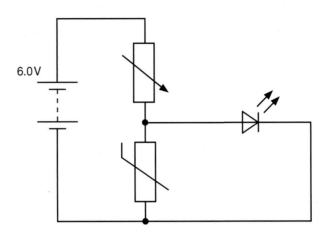

(a)   Describe the action of a thermistor.

(b)   Explain, with reference to the components in the circuit, why the LED switches on when the temperature falls below a set value.

(c)   Describe what happens when:

(i)   the resistance of the variable resistor is changed

(ii)   the variable resistor and the thermistor exchange positions.

Answer

(a)   The resistance of a thermistor is small when the temperature is high and is large when the temperature is low.

(b)   When the temperature decreases, the voltage across the thermistor increases. At a certain temperature, the potential difference across the input of the LED is high enough and so it switches on.

(c)   (i)   The temperature at which the LED switches on and off changes.

(ii)   The LED switches on when it is hot rather than when it is cold.

Section 4.4 Electrical safety

Potential hazards

❏ **Frayed cables** can lead to the **insulation** around the wires becoming **damaged**, which might lead to the live wire becoming exposed and dangerous. Accidentally touching this would cause an electric shock.

❏ In addition, exposed cables might touch each other, leading to a short circuit and a large current. **Overheated** cables could lead to a **fire**; this is particularly hazardous due to the fact that much of the wiring in any building is hidden in the walls and underneath floors.

❏ Having electrical appliances in **damp** conditions (**impure water conducts**) could lead to a person becoming directly connected to the live mains supply, which could lead to serious shock and possible death.

❏ Overloading a circuit, for example, by plugging too many plugs into one socket, usually leads to a trip switch (circuit breaker) switching off the supply (see page 212). If there was no trip switch the wires would overheat, and this could lead to a fire.

Safety measures

❏ A mains circuit consists of a live wire, a neutral wire and an earth wire. A switch is always connected to the live wire to make sure that, when the switch is off, the live wire is disconnected.

❏ A **fuse** is a deliberate weak link in a circuit for safety. It is also connected to the live wire.

❏ The **fuse** has the symbol: ──┤▭▭▭├──

❏ If there is **too much current**, the fuse wire **melts** and **disconnects the circuit**; it protects the flex (the flexible cable between the plug and appliance) and helps prevent electrical fires.

❑ The **fuse rating** is always **slightly higher** than the current the appliance usually draws. For example, a 10A appliance should use a 13A fuse. If it used a fuse smaller than 10A, the appliance would not even switch on. The fuse would melt immediately on switching on the appliance.

❑ A **circuit breaker** is an automatic safety switch, sometimes called a trip switch. It springs open (**trips**) if there is too much current. This switch can easily be reset once the fault is corrected.

Remember: Fuses and circuit breakers (trip switches) both stop current in a circuit if it is too high. Fuses need to be replaced and circuit breakers need to be reset.

❑ ***Example***
Determine the appropriate fuse rating for the following appliances. You can choose from a 3A, 5A or 13A fuse.

(a)   A 2.5kW electric kettle operating on a 240V supply

(b)   An 800W electric drill operating on a 240V supply

(c)   A 40W computer operating on a 16V supply

Answer

Step 1   List all the information in symbol form and change into appropriate and consistent SI units if required.

(a) $P = 2.5\text{kW} = 2500\text{W}$
$V = 240\text{V}$
$I = ?$

(b) $P = 800\text{W}$
$V = 240\text{V}$
$I = ?$

(c) $P = 40\text{W}$
$V = 16\text{V}$
$I = ?$

Step 2   Use and rearrange the correct equation:

$$P = IV \implies I = \frac{P}{V}$$

Step 3   Calculate the answer by putting the numbers into the equation.

(a) $I = \dfrac{2500}{240} = 10.4\,\text{A}$

You would need a 13A fuse.

(b) $I = \dfrac{800}{240} = 3.33\,\text{A}$

You would need a 5A fuse.

(c) $I = \dfrac{40}{16} = 2.5\,\text{A}$

You would need a 3A fuse.

ALWAYS REMEMBER TO STATE THE UNIT FOR CALCULATED QUANTITIES.

Other safety measures

The plug

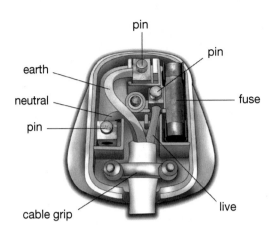

- [ ]   The **live** wire in a flex is normally brown and is connected to the right-hand pin of a three-pin plug. It is linked to the fuse.
  The **neutral** wire is normally blue and is connected to the left-hand pin.
  The green and yellow **earth** wire is connected to the top pin of the plug.
  Colour coding allows us to safely identify wires.
  Colours and plug designs may vary in different countries.

- [ ]   If the live wire were to become loose and make contact with the **external metal casing** of an appliance, the appliance would become dangerous. The **earth** wire provides the current with an **easy path** from the metal casing of the device to earth. A large current is produced and the **fuse blows**. The circuit is **disconnected**, removing the hazard.

- [ ]   Some appliances do not need an earth wire as they have a non-conducting (or insulating) casing such as **plastic**. The insulator can never become live. Appliances like this are said to be **double insulated**. Such appliances are marked with this symbol:

- [ ]   Two-pin plugs are sometimes used instead of three-pin plugs for devices that are double insulated. There is no earth wire, only live and neutral. The fuse protects the circuit and the cabling from an overload of current.

Electrical metal wires get hot when there is a current in them. **Thicker** wires can be used to **reduce** this heating effect as the greater cross-sectional area reduces resistance. Using thicker insulation only disguises the heating effect; the wires could still overheat.

Section 4.5   Electromagnetic effects

Electromagnetic induction

❑ Michael Faraday was the first person to generate electricity from a magnetic field using **electromagnetic induction**.

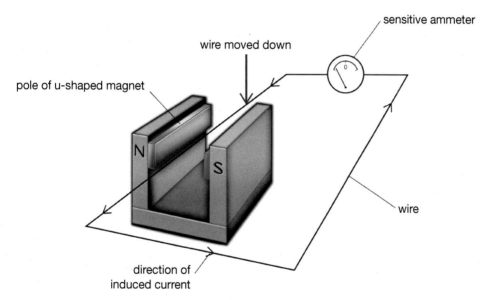

sensitive ammeter

wire moved down

pole of u-shaped magnet

N

S

wire

direction of induced current

❑ When a wire is moved through a magnetic field a small electromotive force (e.m.f.) is produced as the wire cuts the magnetic field lines. This is known as an **induced e.m.f.** If the wire is part of a complete circuit, a current is produced in the wire by the induced e.m.f.

❑ The diagram above shows a wire being moved down between the poles of a magnet and 'cutting' the magnetic field lines. The same effect could be achieved by moving a magnet near a conductor. The sensitive ammeter detects a current in the conductor if it is part of a complete circuit. The maximum current is observed when the wire cuts the magnetic field at right angles.

❑   The induced **e.m.f.** can be **increased** by:

-    moving the wire faster

-    using a stronger magnet to increase the magnetic field

-    increasing the length of wire cutting the magnetic field.
     (This is what happens when a bar magnet is pushed in and
     out of a coil of wire as each turn of the coil cuts the magnetic
     field, so the length of wire cutting the field is increased.)

○   When the induced e.m.f. produces a current its direction
     opposes the effect causing it (see page 217).

○   There is **no e.m.f.** and **no current** if the wire is **moved parallel** to
     the **magnetic field**. The wire must **cut** the magnetic field lines in
     order for an e.m.f. or current to be induced.

Note	
	- A conducting wire must cut the magnetic field lines in order for an e.m.f to be induced. - This e.m.f is a maximum when the field lines are cut at right angles.

○   **Fleming's right-hand rule – generators**
     This rule is used to indicate the direction of a current caused by
     an induced e.m.f.

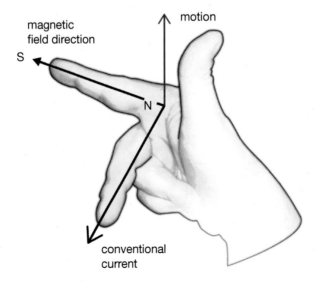

The directions of the current, magnetic field and motion are related to each other as shown.

All three fingers have to be at **right angles** to one another.

A tip to help you to remember what each finger represents is:

- *f*irst finger-*f*ield

- se*c*ond finger-*c*urrent

- thu*m*b-*m*otion

Induced current in a coil

❑   Electromagnetic induction can also occur in a coil. The wire may be stationary with the magnet moving.

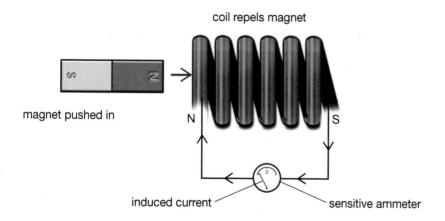

coil repels magnet

magnet pushed in

N   S

induced current   sensitive ammeter

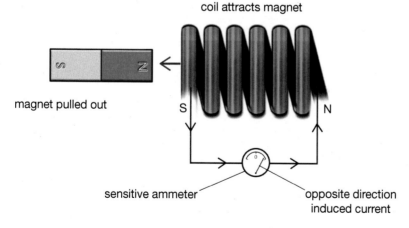

coil attracts magnet

magnet pulled out

S   N

sensitive ammeter   opposite direction
induced current

○   The direction of the current opposes the change causing it, whether the magnet is being pushed in or pulled out. This is Lenz's Law.

Remember: no movement = no current

N.B. If the magnet is flipped round in the examples above, the current will be reversed

❑   If the magnet is moved in and out several times, the needle on the sensitive ammeter indicates that the current changes direction (or alternates).

❑   The induced e.m.f. (and the current) can be **increased** by:

-    moving the magnet faster
-    using a stronger magnet to increase the strength of the magnetic field
-    increasing the number of turns in the coil.

The a.c. generator

❑   An **a.c.** generator produces **alternating** (backwards and forwards) e.m.f. and current.

Remember: The term a.c. stands for 'alternating current'.

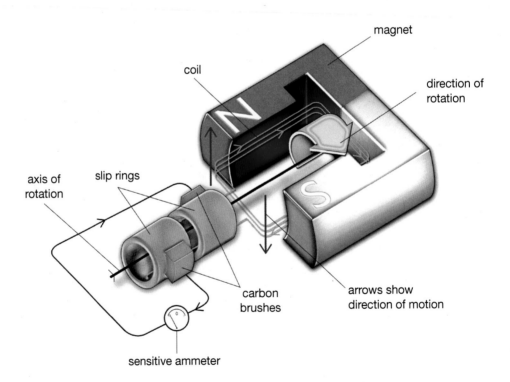

○   Generators often use a **rotating coil** between **fixed magnets**.

○   Each end of the coil is connected to a **slip ring** against which **carbon brushes** press. Carbon is a conductor.

○ The coil is made from copper wire as copper is a good electrical conductor.

○ The sensitive ammeter indicates the presence of a current.

❏ Again the electromotive force (e.m.f.) and current can be increased by:

- increasing the number of turns in the coil
- using a stronger magnet
- rotating the coil faster.

○ The diagram below shows a graph of voltage output against time, and how the output relates to the position of the coil in the magnetic field.

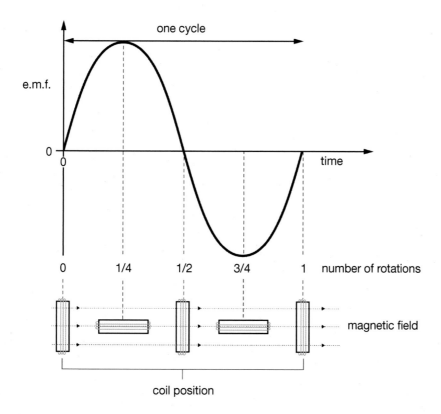

How it works

○ The coil is rotated in the magnetic field, **cutting** the magnetic field lines so that an alternating e.m.f. is induced.

○ This produces a.c. (alternating current) in an external circuit.

○   The direction of the current in each part of the coil can be found by applying Fleming's right-hand rule. The current in the two sides of the coil is in opposite directions.

○   Because one side of the coil is always connected to the same slip ring, as the coil rotates the current in the circuit changes direction every half-cycle.

○   The e.m.f. and the current are at a **maximum** when the coil is **horizontal** as it is cutting the field lines at the greatest rate.

○   The e.m.f. and the current are **zero** when the coil is **vertical** as no field lines are being cut.

Top Tip

How an a.c. generator works.
When the coil rotates it cuts the magnetic field of the permanent magnet and induces an alternating e.m.f.

The magnetic effect of a current

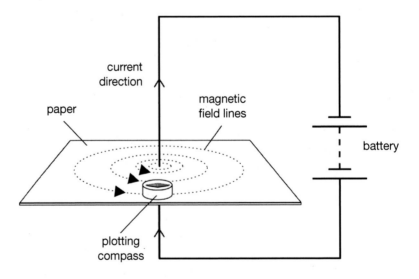

❑   A **magnetic field** is produced around a **current-carrying wire**. The field lines are **concentric circles** around the wire and can be shown using a plotting compass as in the diagram above. The magnetic field is strongest where the field lines are closest.

❑   The current produces a **weak** magnetic field if the current is small.

⭕   The magnetic field produced by a current-carrying wire has the following features.

-     Increasing the current increases the strength of the magnetic field.

-     The field is strongest closest to the wire and becomes weaker further away.

-     Reversing the direction of the current reverses the direction of the magnetic field.

❑   The magnetic field produced by a single wire carrying a current is not very strong. A stronger field can be produced by a coil of wire (see page 222).

❑   The direction of the magnetic field can be found by using the **right-hand grip rule**. Imagine gripping the wire in such a way that the thumb of your right-hand points in the same direction as the current, then your fingers curl around the wire in the direction of the magnetic field.

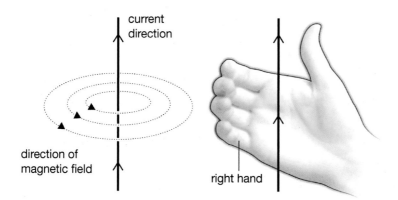

❑   In this example, the **magnetic field** is in an **anti-clockwise** direction when viewed from above.

❑   In practice, a coil of wire (a **solenoid**) is used to produce a magnetic field, instead of a single straight wire.

N.B. The magnetic field pattern around a solenoid is similar to a bar magnet.

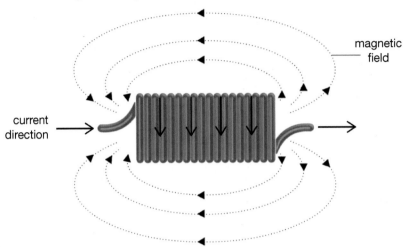

magnetic field

current direction

Determining the shape of the magnetic field due to a solenoid

❑   The following experiment describes how to determine the shape of a magnetic field around a solenoid.

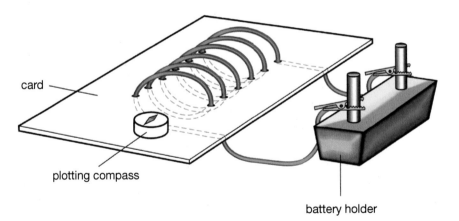

card

plotting compass

battery holder

1.   Make a simple solenoid by winding turns through a flat piece of card as shown in the diagram.

2.   Connect the ends of the solenoid to a cell of e.m.f. 1.5V using crocodile clips.

3.   Place a plotting compass on the card. The needle points in the direction of the magnetic field at that point.

4.   Using the method outlined on page 164-5 plot the magnetic field pattern. It should look like the one on the opposite page.

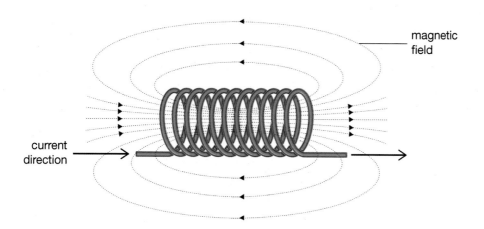

○   The magnetic field produced by a current-carrying coil or solenoid has the following features.

-   The field outside of the coil is similar to the field of a bar magnet and there are magnetic poles at each end of the coil.

-   The field lines inside the coil are almost parallel.

-   Increasing the current increases the strength of the magnetic field.

-   Increasing the number of turns in the coil increases the strength of the magnetic field.

-   Having an iron core (shown below) greatly increases the strength of the magnetic field.

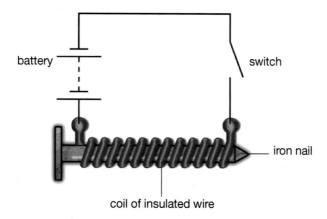

-   Reversing the direction of the current reverses the direction of the magnetic field.

- You can use the right-hand rule to predict the direction of the magnetic field. If you imagine holding the solenoid in your right hand with your fingers curled in the direction of the current then your thumb points in the direction of the North pole.

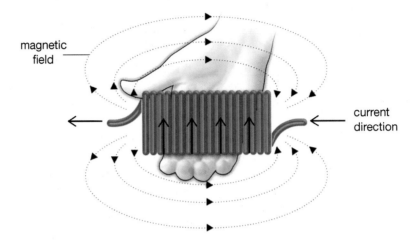

- The field is strong close to the coil and weaker further away.

Uses of magnetic effect of a current

The electric relay

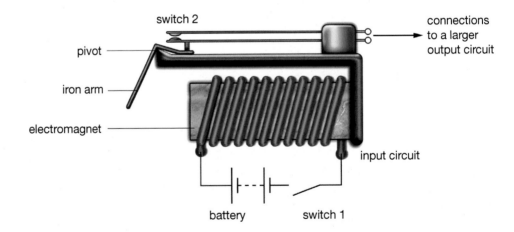

❑ When **switch 1** is **closed** in the diagram above, the input circuit is complete and there is a current in the circuit. The **electromagnet** becomes **magnetised** and it attracts the iron arm. The arm rotates about the pivot and pushes the two contacts of switch 2 together, switching on the output circuit. The output circuit is very often a more powerful circuit, such as the motor circuit for an elevator (lift). The rest of the output circuit is not shown in the diagram above.

❑   The advantage of using a relay is that a **small current** in the input circuit can switch on a **large current** in the **output circuit**.

The loudspeaker

❑   In a loudspeaker, energy is transferred electrically to kinetic energy, which is then transferred to the surroundings as sound.

❑   A loudspeaker contains an electromagnet and a permanent magnet connected to the speaker cone.

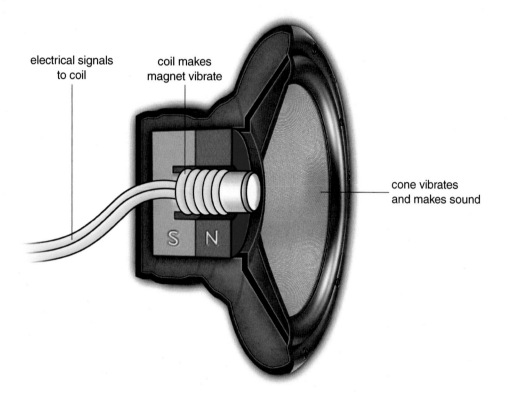

electrical signals
to coil

coil makes
magnet vibrate

cone vibrates
and makes sound

S   N

❑   The amplifier causes an alternating current in the coil of wire surrounding the electromagnet. Because the current is alternating, it produces a magnetic field in the electromagnet that is constantly changing direction.

❑   The changing magnetic field of the electromagnet interacts with the field of the permanent magnet, creating a force on the permanent magnet. This force is also constantly changing direction. As the magnet is attached to the speaker cone, the cone moves backwards and forwards, creating a sound wave as the air is alternately compressed and rarefied.

Force on a current-carrying conductor

❏   When a conductor carrying an electric **current** is placed in a **magnetic field** it experiences a **force**. That force causes the conductor to move if it is free to do so.

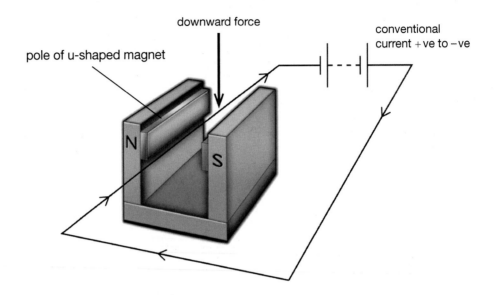

downward force

conventional current + ve to −ve

pole of u-shaped magnet

N

S

❏   The diagram shows a wire connected to a battery and placed between the poles of a magnet. When there is a current in the direction shown, the wire is seen to move downwards.

❏   This is because the current-carrying wire has its own magnetic field, which **interacts** with the field of the permanent magnet.

❏   If the current-carrying wire is placed in a magnetic field (whose lines of force are at right angles to the wire) then it experiences a force at right angles to both the current direction and the magnetic field lines.

❏   If either the direction of the current or the magnetic field is **reversed**, the direction of the **force** is **reversed**.

❏   If both the magnetic field and current are reversed, there is effectively no change.

❏   This effect is used in motors.

❑   The force can be **increased** by:

- increasing the current in the wire
- using a stronger magnet
- increasing the length of wire in the magnetic field.

Note

- If there is current in a wire in the presence of a magnetic field, a force is produced.
- This is because the current-carrying wire has its own magnetic field, which interacts with the field of a permanent magnet.

○   **Fleming's left-hand rule – motors**

Fleming's left-hand rule can be used to predict the direction of the force produced in d.c. motors.

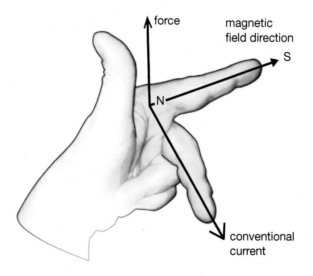

The directions of the current, magnetic field and force are related to each other as shown.

All three fingers have to be at **right angles** to one another.

A tip to help you remember what each finger represents is:

- *f*irst finger-*f*ield
- se*c*ond finger-*c*urrent
- *th*umb-*th*rust (force)

The d.c. motor

❑   A d.c. motor makes use of direct current (current in one direction).

❑   If there is a current in a coil placed between **fixed magnets**, forces act on the coil, producing a **turning effect**.

○   Each end of the coil is connected to one half of a **split-ring commutator** against which **carbon brushes** press. The coil is made of copper wire as it is a good electrical conductor.

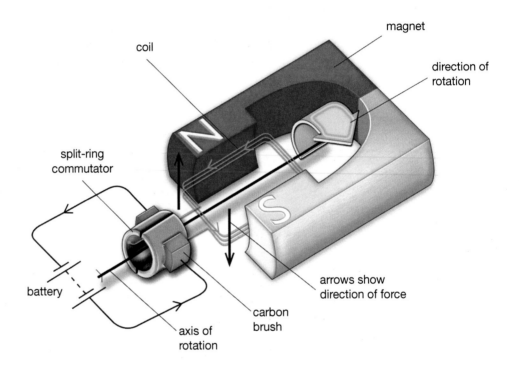

How it works

○   The battery supplies a current to the coil via the split-ring commutator.

○   Because the coil then has a current in it, it also has a magnetic field associated with it.

○   This magnetic field interacts with the magnetic field of the permanent magnet.

○   This causes an upward force on one side of the coil and a downward force on the other.

○   The direction of each force is given by Fleming's left-hand rule.

○   The **split-ring commutator** changes the direction of the current in the coil **every half-turn**, because as the coil rotates the commutator rotates.

○   Therefore, the turning force keeps acting in the same direction as the coil rotates, keeping the coil rotating.

❑   The turning effect, and therefore the speed of revolution of the motor, can be increased by:

-    increasing the number of turns in the coil

-    using a stronger magnet

-    increasing the current.

❑   In an electric drill, for example, the rotating coil causes a drill bit to rotate, which drills a hole in wood, plastic, metal or stone.

Top Tip

How a motor works in three easy steps

Step 1   When there is a current in a coil of wire, it produces a magnetic field around the coil.

Step 2   This magnetic field interacts with the field of the permanent magnet, which produces an upward force on one side of the coil and a downward force on the other side according to Fleming's left-hand rule.

Step 3   Therefore the coil rotates.

Forces on charged particles in a magnetic field

○ The diagram below shows an electron gun inside a vacuum tube. A beam of electrons is fired towards the fluorescent screen at the front. A spot of light appears where the beam hits the screen.

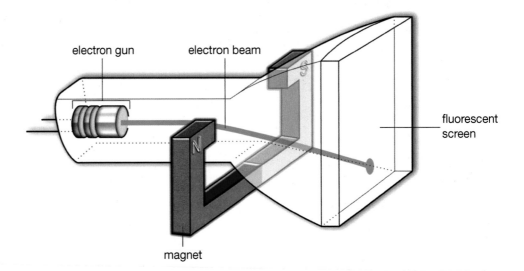

○ A magnet is placed against the outside of the tube and the spot on the screen moves downwards. This is because the direction of the magnetic field is from the N pole to the S pole and at right angles to the direction of movement of the electrons.
The electrons are negatively charged, so as they move they constitute an electric current in the opposite direction to their motion (see page 177).

○ Applying Fleming's left-hand rule shows that the electrons experience a force downwards. Hence, the spot on the screen moves downwards.

Transformers

❏ A transformer is used to **change** an **alternating voltage** from one size into another.

❏ It is made by winding two insulated coils around a soft iron core, as shown below. These coils are known as the **primary (input)** and the **secondary (output)** coils. (There are, of course, many more turns on the coils of a real transformer.)

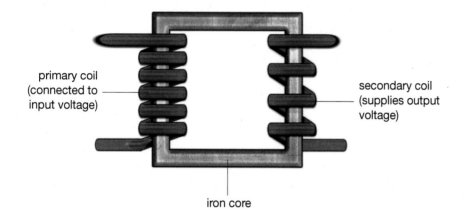

primary coil (connected to input voltage)

secondary coil (supplies output voltage)

iron core

❏ When there is an alternating current in the **primary** (input) coil, it sets up an **alternating magnetic field** in the primary coil and in the iron core.

○ This changing magnetic field is transferred through the core and into the **secondary** (output) coil.

○ This induces an **alternating e.m.f.** in the secondary (output) coil.

Top Tip

How transformers work in three easy steps

Step 1 An **alternating current** in the primary coil sets up an **alternating magnetic field** in the primary coil.

Step 2 This alternating magnetic field is **transferred** through the iron core.

Step 3 The **alternating magnetic field** cuts through the **secondary coil** and **induces** an e.m.f.

Step-up and step-down transformers

❑ There are more **secondary turns** than primary turns in a step-up transformer.
The **secondary voltage** is larger than the primary voltage, i.e. it is stepped up.

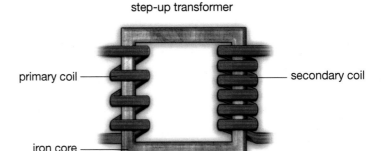

step-up transformer

primary coil —   — secondary coil

iron core —

❑ There are fewer **secondary turns** than primary turns in a step-down transformer. The **secondary voltage** is lower than the primary voltage, ie. it is stepped down.

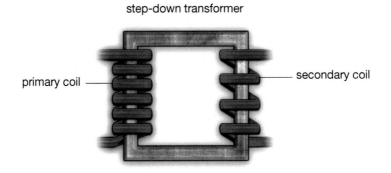

step-down transformer

primary coil —   — secondary coil

❑ The number of turns and voltage in the primary and secondary coil are related by the following expression:

$$\frac{V_p}{V_s} = \frac{N_p}{N_s}$$

V_p = primary voltage (V)
V_s = secondary voltage (V)
N_p = number of primary turns
N_s = number of secondary turns

❑ ***Example***

A transformer transforms 240V a.c. to 12V a.c. for a model car racing set. The secondary coil has 50 turns. Calculate the number of turns on the primary coil.

Answer

Step 1   List the information in symbol form and change into appropriate and consistent SI units if required.

$V_p = 240V$
$V_s = 12V$
$N_s = 50$
$N_p = ?$

Remember: There are no units for the number of turns.

Step 2   Use and rearrange the correct equation.

$$\frac{V_p}{V_s} = \frac{N_p}{N_s} \quad \Rightarrow \quad N_p = \frac{N_s \times V_p}{V_s}$$

Step 3   Calculate the answer by putting the numbers into the equation.

$$N_p = \frac{N_s \times V_p}{V_s} = \frac{50 \times 240}{12} = 1000$$

Efficiency of transformers

○ Transformers are **very efficient**; their power output is almost as high as their power input.

○ If a transformer could be made **100% efficient** then the power leaving the transformer would equal the power coming into the transformer.

$P_p = P_s$	P_p = primary power (W)
$I_p V_p = I_s V_s$	P_s = secondary power (W)
	I_p = primary current (A)
	V_p = primary voltage (V)
	I_s = secondary current (A)
	V_s = secondary voltage (V)

○ Note that if V_s is greater than V_p, as in a step-up transformer, then I_s must be less than I_p.

○ **No device is 100% efficient**, and the energy output is always less than the energy input. Even though transformers are not 100% efficient, we assume that they are in calculations.

○ One reason why transformers are not 100% efficient is because the **resistance** in both the primary and secondary coils causes heating.

○ Their efficiency might also be affected by the primary coil's magnetic field not linking the secondary coil with maximum effect.

○ *Example*

A transformer is 100% efficient. A 120V supply is connected across the primary coil and there is a current of 0.20A in the primary coil. A 12V lamp is connected to the secondary coil. Calculate the current in the lamp.

Answer

Step 1   List the information in symbol form and change into appropriate and consistent SI units if required.

$$V_p = 120V$$
$$V_s = 12V$$
$$I_s = 0.20A$$
$$I_p = ?$$

Step 2   Use and rearrange the correct equation.

$$I_p V_p = I_s V_s \quad \Rightarrow \quad I_s = \frac{I_p V_p}{V_s}$$

Step 3   Calculate the answer by putting the numbers into the equation.

$$I_s = \frac{I_p V_p}{V_s} = \frac{0.20 \times 120}{12} = 2.0A$$

ALWAYS REMEMBER TO STATE THE UNIT FOR CALCULATED QUANTITIES.

Transmission of electricity

❑ Power supplied to our home is generated in a power plant.

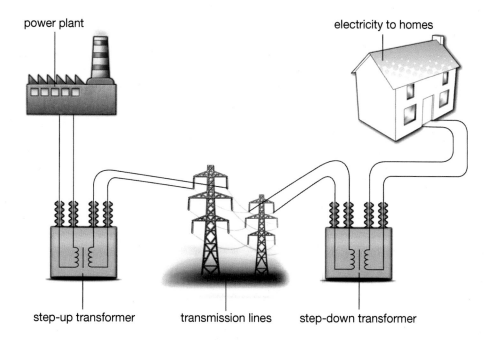

step-up transformer   transmission lines   step-down transformer

❑ **Step-up** transformers are used to **increase the voltage** and to **decrease the current** in cables used in transmission lines.

❑ The current is decreased **deliberately** in order to reduce the power 'loss' in the cables (when there is a current in the cables the cables heat up and energy is wasted).

○ The power 'loss' in the cables can be calculated using the following equation. Note that a smaller current gives a smaller power 'loss'.

$$P = IV = I\,(IR) = I^2R$$

P = power (W)
I = current (A)
R = resistance (Ω)

❑ So, by using step-up transformers to reduce the current, the **heating effect** is **minimised**. This is an advantage as it means cheaper and thinner cables can be used in transmission lines.

❑ **Step-down** transformers are used to **reduce the voltage** and increase the current before the electricity enters our homes.

❑ Transformers **only** work using **a.c.** and so that is why the current entering our homes is **a.c.** rather than **d.c.**

Note

Remember: Transformers only work if there is an **alternating magnetic field**. This alternating magnetic field is only present if there is an **alternating current**. Therefore transformers will only work using a.c. and not d.c.

Unit 5   Nuclear physics

Section 5.1   The nuclear model of the atom

The atom

Rutherford's scattering experiment

○   In 1910 Ernest Rutherford devised an experiment to investigate atomic structure.

○   Rutherford's experiment confirmed that the atom is made up of a **very dense nucleus** containing most of the mass and that the rest of the atom is mainly **empty space**.

○   This experiment was carried out by Hans Geiger and Ernest Marsden and involved firing alpha (α-) particles from a radioactive source at a piece of very thin gold foil in a vacuum.

○   A zinc sulfide screen was used as a detector. The α-particles were detected by the **scintillations**, or flashes of light, that they caused on the screen.

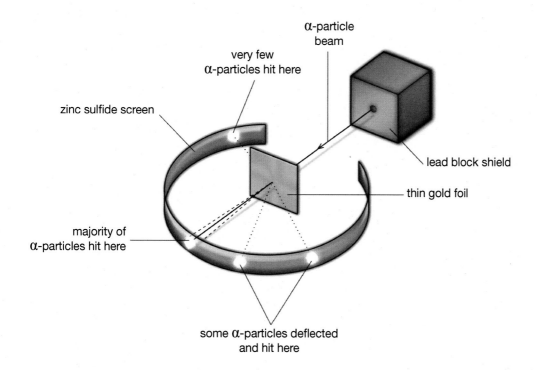

○   The results of this experiment were:

- the majority of the α-particles passed straight through the foil

- some particles were deviated through fairly large angles of up to 90°

- very few were deflected at angles greater than 90° (i.e. they bounced back).

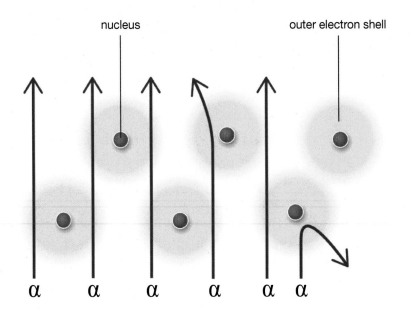

nucleus   outer electron shell

α   α   α   α   α   α

○   Rutherford concluded that:

- most of the atom must be made up of empty space because most of the α-radiation passed straight through unaffected

- the atom has a concentrated positive charge in the centre, because some of the positively charged α-particles were deflected by an appreciable angle or even bounced back

- since very few α-particles bounced straight back, this region of positive charge that repels the positive α-radiation must be very small in size and very dense.

He named this very dense and small centre the **nucleus**.

❑   We now know that the nucleus of an atom contains positive particles called **protons** and neutral (uncharged) particles called **neutrons**. The 'empty space' of the atom around the nucleus contains tiny negatively charged **electrons** in orbits or shells.

❑   An atom is electrically neutral, i.e. it has the same number of protons in the nucleus as the number of electrons in orbit.

❑   Atoms can gain or lose electrons to form ions. If an atom gains an electron it becomes a negative ion. If it loses an electron it becomes a positive ion.

The nucleus

❑   The number of **protons** in the nucleus is known as the **proton number Z** or **atomic number**. In a **neutral** (not ionised) atom the atomic number is also equal to the number of **electrons** orbiting the nucleus.

❑   The **nucleon number A** or **mass number** is the number of nucleons (protons and neutrons) in the nucleus.

❑   This is often written in the following format, known as nuclide notation:
$_Z^A X$ where **X** is the **chemical symbol** for the element.

❑   If the total number of protons and neutrons is A, and the number of protons is Z, it follows that:
the number of neutrons in the nucleus $= A - Z$

❑   Each **element** has a different **atomic number** (proton number) and the elements are arranged in order of **increasing** atomic number in the periodic table.

❑   The masses and charges of the subatomic particles are given in this table in terms of the mass and charge of the proton.

Particle	Relative mass	Relative charge	Symbol
proton	1	+1	$_1^1 p$
neutron	1	0	$_0^1 n$
electron	1/2000	−1	$_{-1}^0 e$

It follows that the proton number (atomic number) Z equals the relative charge on the nucleus, and the nucleon number (mass number) A equals the relative mass of the nucleus.

❑   This diagram is a simple representation of atomic structure.

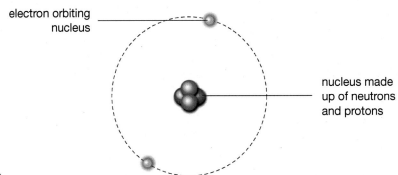

electron orbiting
nucleus

nucleus made
up of neutrons
and protons

Isotopes

❑   Nuclei with the same **atomic number** can have different
mass numbers.

For example:

$$^{12}_{6}C \qquad ^{14}_{6}C$$

These nuclei are called carbon-12 and carbon-14. They are
different **isotopes** of carbon.

❑   Isotopes of an element have the same number of **protons** but
a different number of **neutrons** (i.e. the same atomic number but
different mass number).

○   The isotope carbon-14 is radioactive and can be used in
carbon dating (see page 256).

Nuclear reactions

❑   The three types of nuclear reaction are nuclear fission, nuclear
fusion and radioactive decay. They all result in a release of energy.

Fission

○   Nuclear power reactors use a nuclear reaction called **nuclear
fission**. Fission means 'splitting'.

○   When an atom is split it releases energy.

○ Two isotopes commonly used as nuclear fuels are uranium-235 and plutonium-239. Both these isotopes have large nuclei and can be relatively easily split, especially when neutrons collide with them.

○ Naturally occurring uranium is mostly uranium-238 with a very small percentage of the isotope uranium-235. When a neutron strikes (collides with) a uranium-235 nucleus, the nucleus becomes unstable (uranium-236).

$$^{235}_{92}U + ^{1}_{0}n \rightarrow ^{236}_{92}U$$

○ The unstable uranium-236 splits into two smaller nuclei, **called daughter nuclei**.

○ Neutrons are released as well as energy. This energy appears as kinetic energy of the neutrons and γ-radiation. The energy transfers into thermal energy when it is absorbed by the surrounding materials in the reactor.

○ Neutrons produced from one fission strike other uranium-235 nuclei, causing further fissions and releasing even more neutrons, and a **chain reaction** can develop. The chain reaction could cause an atomic explosion because of the huge amount of energy that is released.

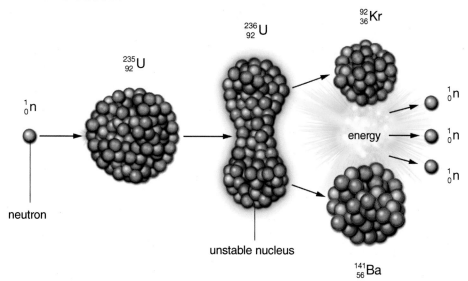

○ The equation for this reaction can be expressed as:

$$^{1}_{0}n + ^{235}_{92}U \rightarrow ^{141}_{56}Ba + ^{92}_{36}Kr + (3 \times ^{1}_{0}n) + \text{ENERGY}$$

Fusion

○   **Nuclear fusion** is the process that occurs in the Sun and other stars to create energy. In simple terms, hydrogen nuclei combine to form helium nuclei and release energy.

○   In one simple fusion reaction, deuterium ($^2_1$H) and tritium ($^3_1$H) (isotopes of hydrogen) nuclei combine to form helium nuclei and neutrons resulting in an overall loss of mass (the mass of the neutron and helium is less than the combined mass of the deuterium and tritium) and a release of energy.

$$^2_1H + \,^3_1H \;\rightarrow\; ^4_2He + \,^1_0n + ENERGY$$

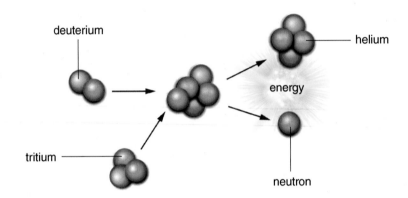

○   The nuclei have to get very close to collide, but the deuterium and tritium nuclei are both positively charged, as all nuclei have protons in them, and so there is electrostatic repulsion between them. As a result, fusion does not happen at low temperatures and pressures.

○   The nuclei must have enough kinetic energy to overcome this electrostatic repulsion and allow the positive nuclei to get close enough for fusion to occur. This requires extremely high temperature and high pressure, such as in the core of stars. The temperature at the core of the Sun can reach $1.5 \times 10^7 \,°C$.

Section 5.2 Radioactivity

Detection of radioactivity

❑   Many nuclei of elements in the periodic table are **stable** but some are **unstable**. Unstable nuclei undergo **radioactive decay**.

❑   When a radioactive nucleus decays it may emit one or more of the following: **alpha particles**, **beta particles** or **gamma rays**.

❑   The radiations alpha, beta and gamma have their own individual characteristics, as shown in the table below.

	Alpha particle	**Beta particle**	**Gamma ray**
Nature	2 protons and 2 neutrons (helium nucleus)	electron	electromagnetic radiation
Symbol	α or $^4_2$He	β or $^{\,0}_{-1}$e	γ
Charge	positive	negative	uncharged
Affected by magnetic and electric fields	yes	yes	no
Penetrating power	weak – stopped by thin paper	moderate – stopped by a few mm of aluminium	strong – only stopped by many cm of lead or many m of concrete
Relative ionising effect	strongest	medium	weakest
Dangerous	yes	yes	yes

❑   There is always radiation present all around us. This is known as **background radiation**. Background radiation comes from **cosmic rays**, **rocks and buildings**, and **atmospheric gases such as radon**. A small amount (about 3%) of background radiation comes from human-made sources such as **medical equipment**, **nuclear power stations** and **nuclear weapons testing**, and a very small amount comes from **food and drink** which can contain traces of radioactive isotopes.

❑   **Ionising radiation** is powerful enough to knock electrons from atoms, leaving them positively charged. These positively charged particles are called positive **ions**. (α) Alpha, (β) beta and (γ) gamma radiation all have an ionising effect, to some degree (see the table on the previous page).

○   Alpha particles have the strongest ionising effect. They have a double positive charge, and they tend to knock electrons from the atoms they collide with. They have the greatest mass of the three radiations, and they are relatively slow-moving, which means they can do a great deal of damage within a short distance. They also lose their kinetic energy quickly because of the number of collisions, so their penetrating power is weak.

○   Beta particles are high-energy electrons, so they have very little mass compared with an alpha particle, but they move very quickly (close to the speed of light) and tend to pass through air without very many collisions.

○   Gamma radiation consists of very short wavelength electromagnetic radiation; i.e. gamma rays have no mass and no charge. They are only weakly ionising but have a strong penetrating power.

❑   By ionising atoms, radiation may cause chemical reactions to occur.

❑   This is particularly dangerous if these reactions occur within the living cells of humans. Radiation can cause **sterility**, **anaemia**, **hair loss** and **cancer**, amongst other things.

❑   All radiation produced by radioactivity can be detected using **photographic film**, a **cloud chamber,** or more commonly a **Geiger–Müller tube** connected to a counter or ratemeter as shown opposite.

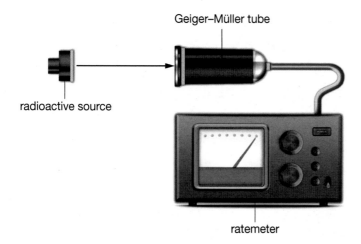

radioactive source

Geiger–Müller tube

ratemeter

❑ α-particles are stopped by paper, β-particles are stopped by 3 mm of aluminium, and γ-rays are greatly reduced in intensity by lead.

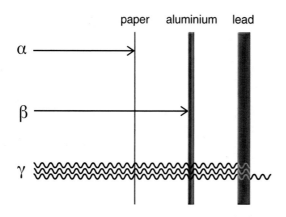

❑ By using a Geiger–Müller tube and sheets of paper and aluminium, it is possible to deduce what type of radiation a radioactive source is emitting.

❑   ***Example***

A teacher demonstrates an experiment to investigate what type of radiation a radioisotope emits, as shown below. The ratemeter measures the count rate in counts/minute.

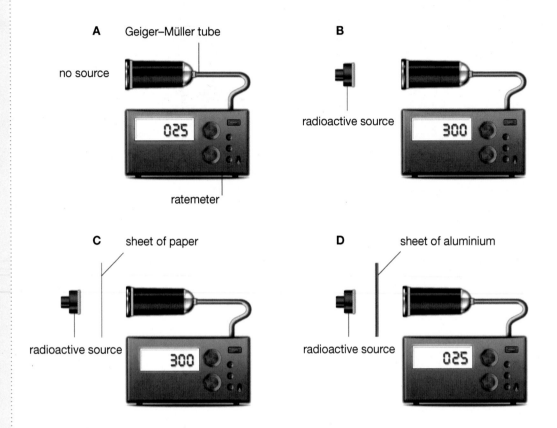

The following measurements were taken:

A   Detector and no source, giving a background reading of 25 counts/minute.

B   Detector and radioactive source, giving a reading of 300 counts/minute.

C   Detector, source and paper, giving a reading of 300 counts/minute.

D   Detector, source and aluminium, giving a reading of 25 counts/minute.

A student concludes that only β-particles are emitted by the radioisotope. Explain how the results obtained show that only β-particles are emitted.

Answer

When paper was placed between the source and the detector in diagram **C** the reading did not change, so there can be no α-radiation emitted, as this would have been stopped by the paper.

When the aluminium was placed between the source and the detector in diagram **D**, the reading dropped to the background value, showing that the radiation was stopped by the aluminium. Therefore the radiation must be β-particles.

There can be no γ-rays present. If there were, they would not be stopped by the aluminium, so the reading would not drop in diagram **D** to the background value.

○   Note that in the above experiment a reading of background count was taken first. To find the reading due to the source alone you would subtract the background radiation. In the example above, the reading for the source alone would be 300 – 25 = 275 counts per minute.

Characteristics of the three kinds of emission

❑   Radioactive emission is a completely **random** and **spontaneous** process. It is impossible to predict when, and in which direction, a particular nucleus will decay.

❑   α-particles are the most ionising (refer back to the table on page 243), so α-radiation is potentially the most **harmful** if ingested into our bodies. However, α-particles are not very penetrating and so cannot get past our skin when produced outside the body. Consequently, α-radiation is more dangerous within our bodies than on the outside of our bodies.

❑   β-particles and γ-rays are **weaker** at ionising if ingested into our bodies but can penetrate our skin more easily when travelling through air. This is what makes them dangerous from outside the body.

○ α-particles are **positively** charged and β-particles are **negatively** charged. Because they are charged, both α-particles and β-particles are affected by electric and magnetic fields.

○ γ-rays have no charge and therefore **are not** influenced by an electric or magnetic field.

○ The diagram shows how the three kinds of radiation behave in an **electric field**.

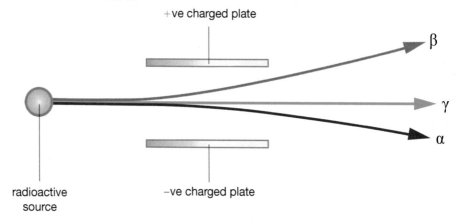

○ α-particles are **deflected less** than β-particles because they have a much **greater mass** and therefore need a much **bigger force** to deflect them.

○ The diagram below shows how the three kinds of radiation behave in a **magnetic field**.

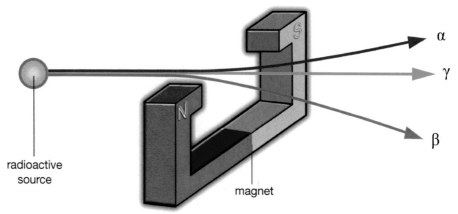

○ The deflection of α- and β-particles in a magnetic field can be found by using **Fleming's left-hand rule** (see page 227).

○ **Remember:** Fleming's left-hand rule is based on conventional current (positive to negative).

Radioactive decay

❑ Unstable elements undergo the random and spontaneous process of radioactive decay. The nucleus of an unstable atom breaks up to form a different nucleus (i.e. a different element) and releases energy.

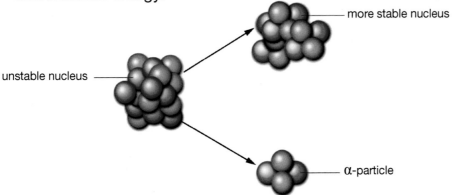

more stable nucleus

unstable nucleus

α-particle

❑ An α-particle is identical to a helium nucleus, so it has an **atomic number of two** and a **mass number of four**.

○ In α-decay a nucleus loses **two protons** and **two neutrons**, so the mass number is reduced by four and the atomic number by two. For example, using nuclide notation:

$$^{226}_{88}\text{Ra} \quad \rightarrow \quad ^{222}_{86}\text{Rn} + ^{4}_{2}\alpha$$

The mass numbers and proton numbers balance on both sides of the equation:

$$226 = 222 + 4$$
$$88 = 86 + 2$$

○ In β-decay a **neutron changes** into a **proton** and an **electron**. The **atomic number** of the nucleus therefore increases by **one** and the **mass number** stays the **same**. The new proton stays in the nucleus but the electron is expelled as a β-particle. For example, using nuclide notation:

$$^{131}_{53}\text{I} \quad \rightarrow \quad ^{131}_{54}\text{Xe} + ^{0}_{-1}\beta$$

Again the mass numbers and proton numbers balance on both sides of the equation.

❏　　A β-particle is a high-energy (high-speed) **electron** emitted from the nucleus.

❏　　γ-rays are emitted when a nucleus decays but is still in a slightly unstable state after emission of particles. γ-emission causes **no change** in atomic or mass number.

❏　　γ-radiation often occurs along with alpha or beta emission. For simplification purposes, this is often omitted from nuclide equations, but the full equations on the previous page would be written as:

$$^{226}_{88}Ra \rightarrow ^{222}_{86}Rn + ^{4}_{2}\alpha + ^{0}_{0}\gamma$$

$$^{131}_{53}I \rightarrow ^{131}_{54}Xe + ^{0}_{-1}\beta + ^{0}_{0}\gamma$$

○　　Unstable nuclei are found in elements where the nucleus has a great number of nucleons and is too heavy. For example, uranium-234 emits an alpha particle to become thorium-230, which is also unstable and decays to radium-226, which decays to radon-222 and so on until the stable nucleus of lead-206 is reached.

○　　The isotopes of an element can also be radioactive if there are too many neutrons in the nucleus. For example, carbon-12 has six protons and six neutrons, and carbon-13 has six protons and seven neutrons. Both these isotopes are stable. Carbon-14 has six protons and eight neutrons and is unstable (radioactive). A carbon-14 nucleus decays by emitting a beta particle from the nucleus, turning one of the neutrons into a proton, and becoming nitrogen.

Half-life

❑ The **count rate** due to any radioactive source is measured in counts per second (counts/s) or counts per minute (counts/minute).

❑ The rate of decay of radioactive sources **decreases with time**.

❑ Some radioactive sources are **more unstable** than others and decay at a **faster rate**.

❑ **Remember:** 'Decay' does not mean that radioactive material disappears. The unstable nuclei of the material change to stable nuclei of a different element.

❑ The bigger the mass of a given source, the greater the rate of decay.

❑ Radioactive decay is **not affected** by temperature or pressure; it is spontaneous (without any obvious cause).

❑ Radioactive decay is a **random** process. There is no way to predict which nucleus in a radioactive substance will be the next to decay.

❑ However, the average time taken for **half** of the unstable nuclei in a sample of a particular radioactive isotope to decay is **always the same**. This time is known as the **half-life**.

❑ The half-life is the time taken for the **rate of decay** of a radioactive isotope to **drop by half** of its original value.

○ When calculating the half-life, the **count rate** must be corrected to account for **background radiation**. You must subtract the background count rate from the measured count rate before you start.

❑ The graph overleaf shows a typical example of a radioactive isotope decaying over a period of time.

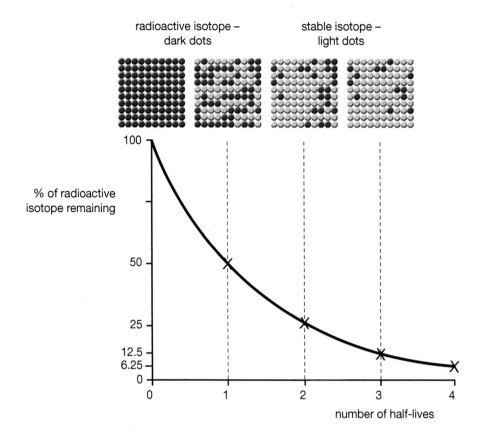

radioactive isotope –
dark dots

stable isotope –
light dots

% of radioactive
isotope remaining

number of half-lives

❑   Since the decay of an isotope is random, the curve is actually a
curve of **best fit**.

❑   ***Example***
The graph shows the decay curve for a sample of a radioactive
isotope, with count rate plotted against time. This graph has been
corrected for background radiation.

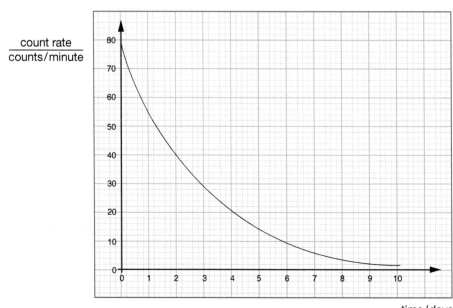

count rate
counts/minute

time/days

Use the graph to estimate the half-life of the isotope.

Answer

Step 1   The initial count rate is 80 counts/minute.
          The half-life is the time taken to reduce the count rate
          to half, i.e. 40 counts/minute.

Step 2   Draw a horizontal line from the count rate axis at
          40 counts/minute to reach the curve, and then a
          vertical line from the curve to reach the time axis.

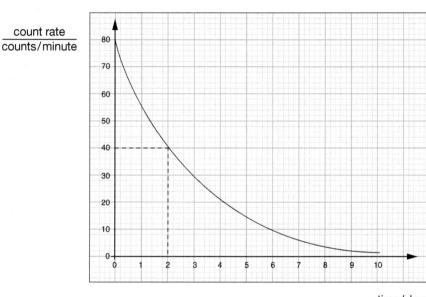

time/days

Step 3   Read the time axis to find the time at which the
          count rate is 40 counts/minute.
          Half-life = 2.0 days

ALWAYS REMEMBER TO STATE THE UNIT FOR
CALCULATED QUANTITIES.

Top Tip

To determine a more reliable value for the half-life, you could
use the graph to find the time taken for the count rate to
decrease to 25% i.e. when the count rate is 20 counts/minute.
This time is equivalent to two half-lives so the value of the
half-life can be determined.

❍ To calculate the **half-life** of an isotope without a graph, the count rates before and after a certain amount of time and the total time elapsed are needed.

❍ **Remember:** Count rate can be measured in counts/s, or counts/minute. It is acceptable to work in either unit, but never use both together in the same calculation.

❑ *Example*

In an experiment the count rate due to a sample of a radioactive isotope decreases from 200 counts/s to 25 counts/s in 75 minutes. Calculate its half-life.

Answer

200 counts/s ➡ 100 counts/s ➡ 50 counts/s ➡ 25 counts/s

The count rate has halved three times; therefore three half-lives have elapsed.

half-life = 75 minutes ÷ 3
half-life = 25 minutes

❑ To calculate the **count rate** due to an isotope after a period of time, the half-life, the starting count rate, and the time elapsed are needed.

❍ *Example*

The count rate on a detector near a radioactive isotope of half-life 3.0 days, is 2050 counts/minute. The background radiation count rate is is known to be 50 counts/minute. Calculate the count rate measured by the detector after 9.0 days.

Answer

The actual initial count rate is 2000 counts/minute, because the count rate due to background radiation is 50 counts/minute.
The half-life is 3.0 days; therefore after 9.0 days three half-lives have elapsed.

| 2000 counts/minute | ➡ | 1000 counts/minute | ➡ | 500 counts/minute | ➡ | 250 counts/minute |

Therefore, the count rate is 250 counts/minute 9.0 days later, but the count rate due to background radiation of 50 counts/minute is constant, so the actual count rate is 300 counts/minute.

Uses of radioactive isotopes

○ γ-rays can be used to **sterilise medical equipment** because they kill bacteria.

○ Some **smoke detectors** contain a radioactive isotope called americium-241, which emits alpha particles. These alpha particles ionise the air in the detector, making it a better conductor. There is a p.d. across the chamber of the smoke detector and this causes a current. If smoke enters the detector it reduces the flow of charge and the alarm is triggered. The alpha particles are unable to penetrate the casing of the detector and so do not present a risk to people.

○ Food can be irradiated with gamma rays to **kill bacteria** and to increase shelf-life. The radiation does not change the appearance, taste, or texture of the food.

○ Radioactive isotopes can help to **detect leaks** in underground water pipes. When there is a leak, water seeps into the ground. A detector indicates a greater count rate in the region of the leak and indicate where to dig to repair the leak.

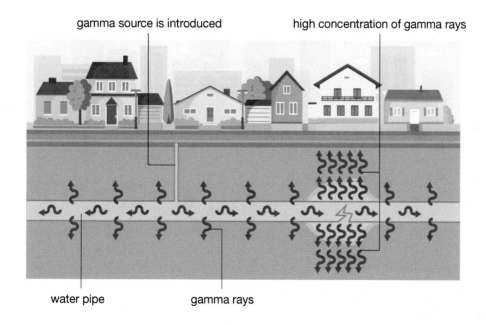

gamma source is introduced   high concentration of gamma rays

water pipe   gamma rays

○ β-particles can be used to monitor the **thickness of paper** during manufacture. In this thickness-monitoring process the number of β-particles that pass through the paper is inversely related to the thickness of the material. If the paper produced is too thick, fewer β-particles are detected. If the paper produced is too thin, more β-particles are detected.

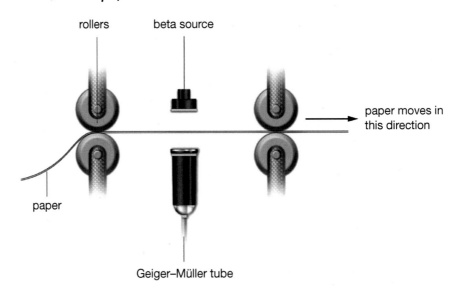

○ α-particles would not pass through at all and γ-radiation would pass through unimpeded. So neither α-particles nor γ-rays would be useful in this process.

○ **Medical tracers** are used to detect blockages in vital organs. A small amount of radioactive isotope is injected into a patient's bloodstream. Such isotopes usually emit γ-radiation, which passes through the body to an external imager. The imager can follow the path the isotope takes. The isotopes have very short half-lives (see page 250), so they are quickly eliminated from the body.

○ γ-rays can be used in **radiotherapy**; beams of γ-radiation are fired directly at **cancer cells** to kill them.

○ An isotope of carbon is used in **radioactive carbon dating**. All living organisms contain a small amount of carbon-14, which has a half-life of 5700 years. When the organism dies, the remaining carbon-14 decays slowly. The ratio of carbon-14 to the non-radioactive carbon-12 can be used to calculate when the organism was last living. Carbon dating is therefore very useful in archaeology.

Safety precautions

❑   **Radioactive radiation** can **damage** living cells. It can kill cells, and/or cause mutations, including cancer.

❑   α-particles, due to their strong ability to **ionise** other particles, are particularly dangerous to human tissue when inside the human body.

❑   γ-radiation outside the body is highly dangerous because of its high **penetrating** power.

❑   **Safety precautions** for storing and handling include, but are not limited to:

- using forceps or robotic manipulators to hold radioactive sources
- storing radioactive materials in thick lead containers
- reducing the amount of time a person is exposed to radiation
- wearing lead-lined clothing and gloves
- working behind a lead-glass shield
- wearing a film badge that alerts the wearer to the possibility of dangerous levels of radiation.

⭘   In general terms, the aim is to limit the effect of any exposure on living human tissue. This can be achieved by reducing the time of exposure, increasing the distance from the source and/or using shielding to absorb the radiation.

Unit 6   Space physics

Section 6.1 Earth and the Solar System

The Earth

❑   The Earth is a planet, and it orbits the Sun.

❑   The Earth takes just over 365 days to complete one orbit.

❑   The Earth also spins on its axis and it takes about 24 hours to rotate once.

❑   The Earth's axis (an imaginary line through the Earth from the North pole to the South pole) is tilted at an angle of about 23.5 degrees, so parts of the Earth receive more light than others and this is what causes our seasons (see page 260).

❑   The Earth is about 150 million kilometres (1.50×10^8 km) from the Sun, and the Moon is about 384 thousand kilometres (3.84×10^5 km) from the Earth.

❑   ***Example***
The Earth is 150 million kilometres (to 2 sig. figs) from the Sun and the speed of light in space (vacuum) is 3.0×10^8 m/s. Calculate the time taken for light to reach the Earth from the Sun in minutes.

   Answer
   Step 1   List all the information in symbol form and change into appropriate and consistent SI units if required.

   s = 150 million kilometres = 150 000 000 000 m
   $= 1.50 \times 10^{11}$ m

   $v = 3.0 \times 10^8$ m/s
   $t = ?$

   Step 2   Use and rearrange the correct equation.

   $$v = \frac{s}{t} \quad \Rightarrow \quad t = \frac{s}{v}$$

Step 3   Calculate the answer by putting the numbers into the equation.

$$t = \frac{s}{v} = \frac{1.50 \times 10^{11}}{3.0 \times 10^{8}} = 497\,s = 8.3\,min \text{ (to 2 sig. figs)}$$

ALWAYS REMEMBER TO STATE THE UNIT FOR CALCULATED QUANTITIES.

Day and night

❑   Because the Earth spins on its axis, sometimes you are facing the Sun and sometimes you are facing away from the Sun. The Sun only shines on the half of the Earth that is facing it. When you are facing the Sun, you are experiencing day-time. When you face away from the Sun, you are experiencing night-time.

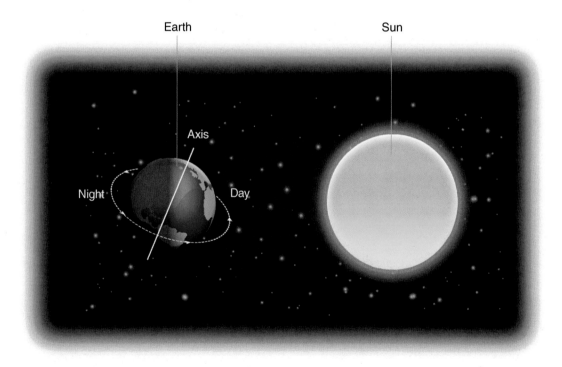

❑   The Earth spins towards the East. That is why the Sun appears to rise in the East and set in the West. At midday in the Northern Hemisphere it appears to be in the South.

Remember: It is the Earth that is rotating, not the Sun that is moving.

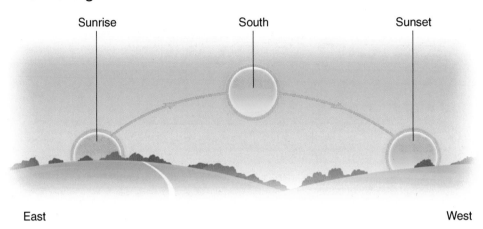

East   West

The seasons

❑   The Earth moves round the Sun once in approximately 365 days. The fact that it is tilted on its axis affects how much sunlight is received at different times of the year, and this varies depending on where you live on the Earth.

❑   We experience different seasons due to the amount of direct sunlight we receive. The diagram below shows the Earth orbiting the Sun.

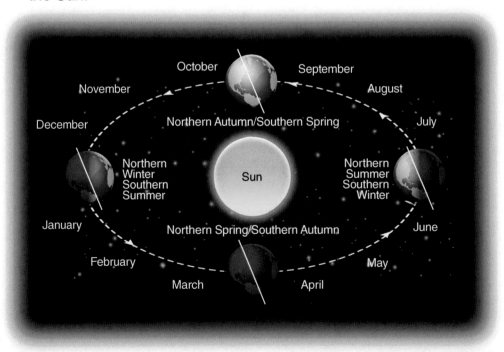

❑   The diagram below shows that in December the Northern Hemisphere is tilted away from the Sun and in June it is tilted towards the Sun. In June the Northern Hemisphere receives more direct sunlight and so it is summer. At the same time, the Southern Hemisphere is tilted away from the Sun and it is winter.

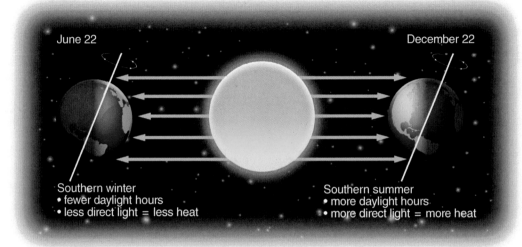

June 22

December 22

Southern winter
• fewer daylight hours
• less direct light = less heat

Southern summer
• more daylight hours
• more direct light = more heat

❑   At the equator the seasons do not vary as much because there is direct sunlight all year round.

❑   At the poles during winter there are days when the Sun never rises, and days during summer when the Sun never sets.

❑   The maximum height of the Sun in the sky varies according to the seasons. In summer it is high and casts short shadows. In winter it is low and casts long shadows. The variation is more pronounced nearer the poles. The diagram below shows how shadows vary in the Northern Hemisphere.

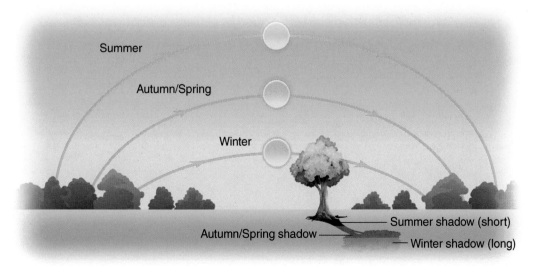

Summer

Autumn/Spring

Winter

Summer shadow (short)

Autumn/Spring shadow

Winter shadow (long)

Sunrise

Sunset

Phases of the Moon

❑   It takes about a month for the Moon to orbit the Earth. It orbits with the same side of the Moon facing the Earth all the time.

❑   We can only see the Moon because it is illuminated by (reflects light from) the Sun, which shines on it. It does not produce its own light.

❑   The diagram below shows how the Moon reflects sunlight as it orbits the Earth.

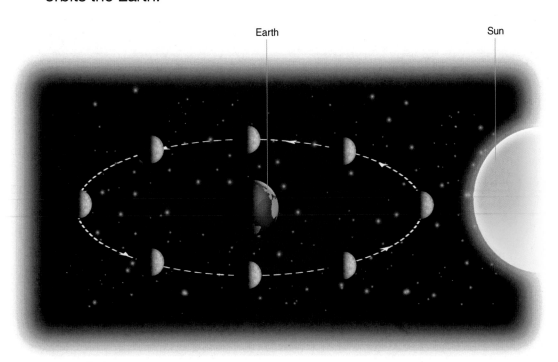

N.B. The diagram is not to scale.

❑   As the Moon orbits the Earth it reflects different amounts of light towards Earth. When the Moon is between the Sun and the Earth it does not reflect any light towards the Earth. We call this a New Moon. As it continues to orbit we see more and more of the Moon, and we say it is **waxing**, towards a Full Moon, and then it **wanes** again as shown opposite.

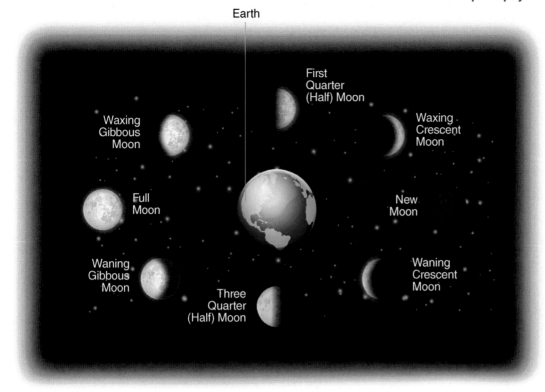

Earth

First
Quarter
(Half) Moon

Waxing
Gibbous
Moon

Waxing
Crescent
Moon

Full
Moon

New
Moon

Waning
Gibbous
Moon

Waning
Crescent
Moon

Three
Quarter
(Half) Moon

N.B. The diagrams of the Moon are what would be seen from the surface of the Earth.

Orbital speed

○   The speed at which a planet orbits the Sun is known as its **orbital speed**.

❏   The further the object is from the body that it orbits:
- the longer it takes to complete an orbit
- the slower it moves.

❏   For example, the closest planet to the Sun, Mercury, takes 88 Earth days to complete an orbit. But Neptune, the furthest planet from the Sun, takes 60 190 Earth days (approximately 165 Earth years) to complete an orbit.

○   The orbital speed, the radius of a planet's orbit (orbital radius) and the time it takes for the planet to orbit the Sun once (orbital period) are related by the following equation:

$$\text{orbital speed} = \frac{2 \times \pi \times \text{orbital radius}}{\text{orbital period}}$$

$$v = \frac{2\pi r}{T}$$

v = orbital speed (m/s)
r = orbital radius (m)
T = orbital period (s)

○   **Example 1**
The Earth is 150 million kilometres (to 2 sig. figs) from the Sun and takes one year to complete its orbit. Calculate the orbital speed of the Earth in m/s.

Answer

Step 1   List all the information in symbol form and change into appropriate and consistent SI units if required.

r = 150 million kilometres = 150 000 000 000 m
$$= 1.50 \times 10^{11} \text{m}$$
T = 1 year = 365 × 24 × 60 × 60 = 31 536 000 s
v = ?

Step 2   Use the correct equation.

$$v = \frac{2 \pi r}{T}$$

Step 3   Calculate the answer by putting the numbers into the equation.

$$v = \frac{2 \pi r}{T} = \frac{2 \times \pi \times 1.50 \times 10^{11}}{31\,536\,000} = 29\,885.77$$
$$= 29\,900 \text{m/s}$$
$$\text{(to 3 sig. figs)}$$

ALWAYS REMEMBER TO STATE THE UNIT FOR CALCULATED QUANTITIES.

○   **Example 2**
The Moon takes 27.3 days to orbit the Earth and its orbital speed is 1022 m/s. Calculate the radius of its orbit.

Answer

Step 1   List all the information in symbol form and change into appropriate and consistent SI units if required.

v = 1022 m/s
T = 27.3 days = 27.3 × 24 × 60 × 60 = 2 358 720 s
r = ?

Step 2   Use and rearrange the correct equation.

$$v = \frac{2 \pi r}{T} \quad \Rightarrow \quad r = \frac{vT}{2\pi}$$

Step 3   Calculate the answer by putting the numbers into
the equation.

$$r = \frac{vT}{2\pi} = \frac{1022 \times 2358720}{2 \times \pi} = 383660790.2 = 3.84 \times 10^8\,m$$
(to 3 sig. figs)

ALWAYS REMEMBER TO STATE THE UNIT FOR CALCULATED QUANTITIES.

❑   The diagram below shows our Milky Way galaxy and where our Sun
and Solar System are located in relation to the rest of the galaxy.

Sun

950 000 000 000 000 000 km (9.5 × 10²⁰ m)

The Solar System

❑   Our Sun is in a spiral galaxy with 'arms' of stars, called the **Milky Way**. The Sun is about half way out from the centre of the galaxy, on one of the arms, as shown above.

❑   Our Solar System is only a very small part of the Milky Way galaxy. If our Sun was the size of a grain of sand, the Milky Way would stretch across the continent of North America.

❑   The Sun is a star at the centre of our Solar System. It appears much bigger than other stars in the sky because it is much closer to the Earth. In terms of stars, it is rather average; there are much bigger stars than our Sun in the Universe. For example, Antares A (Alpha Scorpii) is 700 times the size of our Sun. The closest star to the Earth outside our Solar System is Proxima Centauri, which is about 4.24 light-years from Earth.

❑ Our Solar System is made up of planets, dwarf planets, asteroids and comets, which all **orbit** the Sun. The Earth is one of eight planets in our Solar System. Smaller dwarf planets include Eris, Ceres and Pluto.

❑ Planets are not hot enough to emit their own light. We only see them because they are illuminated by (reflect light from) the Sun.

❑ The diagram below shows all the planets and their relative sizes. It does not show their relative distances from the Sun. To show their relative sizes and distances on the same diagram is impossible, because the distances are so large.

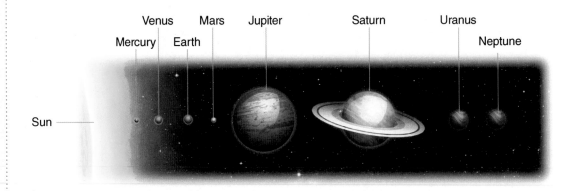

❑ The four planets closest to the Sun, sometimes called the **inner planets**, are rocky and small. The four planets furthest from the Sun, the **outer planets**, are large and gaseous and are sometimes called the **gas giants**.

❑ The planets that make up our Solar System in order from closest to the Sun are given below.

- Mercury is the closest planet to the Sun. It has no atmosphere and has a cratered surface very much like our own Moon.

- Venus is almost the same size as the Earth. The planet is covered with clouds of sulfuric acid and its atmosphere is almost entirely made up of carbon dioxide. This causes a severe greenhouse effect, where temperatures on the surface can reach 500°C.

- Earth is the only planet in the Solar System known to support life. It contains free oxygen and oceans of liquid water.

- Mars, known as the red planet, has a thin atmosphere made mainly of carbon dioxide. It has a dusty surface and polar ice caps.

- Jupiter is bigger than all the other planets put together. It has no solid surface but may have a rocky core deep below; it is a planet made mainly from gas. It is mostly composed of hydrogen and a feature of this planet is the great red spot. This spot represents a storm that has been going on for hundreds of years.

- Saturn is also mainly a gas planet. It is surrounded by rings made up of pieces of rock and ice ranging in size from grains to boulders.

- Uranus is another gassy planet. It also has rings but they are much fainter than those of Saturn.

- Neptune is very similar in size to Uranus and it is mostly made up of ice and gas.

❑   To remember the planets in order, you can use this mnemonic (a mnemonic is a phrase using the first letters of the planets in order): **M**y **V**ery **E**ducated **M**other **J**ust **S**erved **U**s **N**oodles.

❑   Our Solar System first formed about 4.6 **billion** years ago from a cloud of dust and hydrogen gas called a **nebula**. Gravity caused the cloud to collapse in on itself and most of the mass gathered in the centre. The temperature and pressure increased, and the mass began swirling, driving the matter inwards and increasing its density.

  N.B. a billion years is a thousand million years, or 10^9 years.

❑   This was the beginning of the protostar that became our Sun. The temperature and pressure continued to increase until nuclear fusion occurred, converting the hydrogen gas into helium (see page 242).

❑   As the swirling cloud of gas and dust collapsed it began to rotate faster and faster. Eventually the cloud became a flat, rapidly rotating accretion disc.

  N.B. Accretion is the name given to the process of collapsing and the joining together of dust and gas under gravity.

❑   In the remaining cloud, other solids gathered together to form large objects, which eventually became planets, and smaller objects, which became dwarf planets, moons, asteroids and comets.

Planets

○   The planets are kept in orbit by the gravitational pull of the Sun. They mostly **orbit** around the Sun **in an elliptical**, **near circular path**, much like electrons orbiting the nucleus of an atom.

○   An ellipse is a squashed circle with two foci (plural of focus). The Sun sits at one focus. This means that the Sun is not at the centre of the orbit, unless the orbit is spherical.

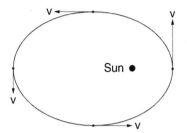

Sun ●

○   Different planets take different amounts of time to go around the Sun. A single orbit is called the planet's year, and the further out a planet is the longer its year is, because the orbital circumference is larger, and the planet is also travelling slower.

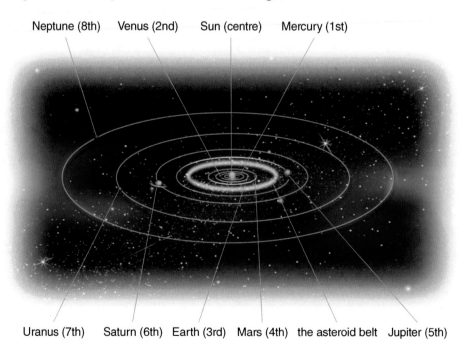

Neptune (8th)   Venus (2nd)   Sun (centre)   Mercury (1st)

Uranus (7th)   Saturn (6th)   Earth (3rd)   Mars (4th)   the asteroid belt   Jupiter (5th)

Remember: That the planets orbit the Sun in elliptical (almost circular) paths.

Gravitational field strength

❑ A galaxy containing billions of stars is held together by the **force due to gravity**.

❑ The force due to gravity is the force of **attraction** between any two objects with mass. For example, we are attracted to the Earth and we have seen in Unit 1 (page 18) that the force due to gravity acting on a mass on Earth is called **weight**.

$W = m \times g$ where g is the **gravitational field strength**.

❑ The size of the gravitational field strength depends on:
- the mass of the object causing the gravitational field; the greater the mass of the object, the greater the gravitational force of attraction
- the distance between the objects; doubling the distance between the objects reduces the gravitational force by one quarter.

❑ The gravitational field strength near to a celestial body (positioned in space) varies depending on the mass and size of the celestial body. For example, g on Earth is 9.8N/kg but on the Moon it is only 1.6N/kg. Close to the Sun the gravitational field strength is 270N/kg. This means that a man with a mass of 70kg weighs 686N on Earth, 112N on the Moon and 18900N close to the Sun (if he didn't vaporise first). Other examples are given in the table below.

Planet	g in N/kg
Venus	8.8
Mars	3.8
Saturn	10
Jupiter	25

Orbits

❑ An attractive force is required to keep a planet in orbit around the Sun, and a moon around a planet. This force is the gravitational force that exists between all masses. A planet, moon, asteroid, comet or any other object would travel in a straight line if no force were acting on it (see pages 31-2).

❑ In our Solar System, the Sun's gravitational field keeps the planets, dwarf planets, comets and asteroids in orbit around the Sun. This is because the Sun is the largest object in our Solar System and therefore has the greatest gravitational field strength. In fact, the Sun contains most of the mass of the whole Solar System.

○ As the distance from the Sun increases, the time to complete an orbit for a planet increases because:

- the orbital distance increases

- the speed of a planet in its orbit decreases as gravitational field strength decreases.

○ An object orbiting the Sun has kinetic energy E_k because it is moving and gravitational potential energy E_p because of its distance from the Sun.

○ In an elliptical orbit, the distance from the Sun changes and so the gravitational potential energy changes. However, because of the principle of Conservation of Energy, the total energy of the planet must remain the same.

total energy $= E_k + E_p$

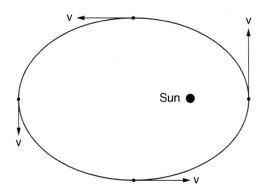

○ When the planet is closer to the Sun its E_p is smaller, and so its E_k is greater and it moves faster. When the planet is further from the Sun its E_p is greater, and so its E_k is smaller and it moves slower.

Example

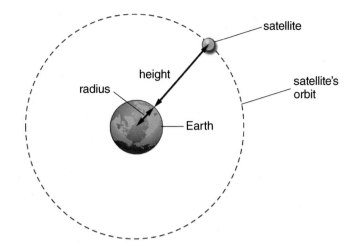

A geostationary satellite stays at exactly the same point above the equator, taking 24 hours to complete one orbit, just as the Earth takes 24 hours to rotate on its axis. The height of its orbit above sea level is 35800km, and the radius of the Earth is 6370km.

(i)   Calculate the radius of the orbit.
(ii)   Calculate the orbital speed of the geostationary satellite.

Answer

(i)   orbital radius = radius of Earth + height of satellite

                = 6370 + 35800 = 42170 = 42200km (to 3 sig. figs)

(ii)   **Step 1**   List all the information in symbol form and change into appropriate and consistent SI units if required.

                r = 42200km = 4.22 × 10^{7}m
                T = 24 hours = 24 × 60 × 60 = 86400s
                v = ?

        Step 2   Use the correct equation.

                $$v = \frac{2\pi r}{T}$$

        Step 3   Calculate the answer by putting the numbers into the equation.

                $$v = \frac{2\pi r}{T} = \frac{2 \times \pi \times 4.22 \times 10^7}{86400} = 3068.87 = 3100\,\text{m/s}$$
                                                    (to 2 sig. figs)

**ALWAYS REMEMBER TO STATE THE UNIT FOR
CALCULATED QUANTITIES.**

○   The table below shows some data for the eight planets of the Solar System.

	Mercury	Venus	Earth	Mars	Jupiter	Saturn	Uranus	Neptune
Mass (10^{24} kg)	0.330	4.87	5.97	0.642	1900	568	86.8	102
Diameter (km)	4880	12100	12756	6790	143000	121000	51100	49500
Density (kg/m³)	5430	5240	5515	3930	1330	687	1270	1640
Gravitational field strength (N/kg)	3.70	8.8	9.8	3.7	24.7	10.5	9.0	11.7
Distance from Sun (10^6 km)	57.9	108	150	228	779	1430	2870	4500
Orbital period (days)	88.0	225	365	687	4330	10700	30600	59800
Mean temperature (°C)	170	464	15	−65	−110	−140	−195	−200

○   It can be seen that:
- as the distance from the Sun increases, the orbital period increases
- the diameters of the inner rocky planets are less than the diameters of the outer gaseous planets
- the densities of the gaseous planets are less than the densities of the rocky planets
- generally (apart from Venus) the mean temperature falls as the distance from the Sun increases.

Section 6.2 Stars and the Universe

Stars

❑　Stellar evolution is the process by which a star changes during its lifetime. On human timescales, most stars don't change much at all. Stars are born, age and die over millions and billions of years. The lifetime of a star depends upon its **mass**.

❑　When we first look at stars they all appear to be white, but if we look more closely we notice a range of **colours**. Stars can be classified according to their colour. Their colour has a direct correlation with their surface temperature; so, for instance, a red star is cooler than a white star and a white star is cooler than a blue star. By looking at the colour of a star, astronomers can have an understanding of its temperature.

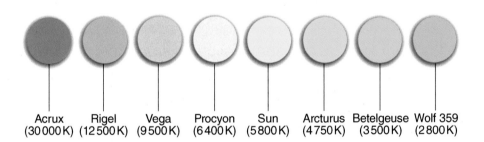

Acrux
(30 000 K)　Rigel
(12 500 K)　Vega
(9 500 K)　Procyon
(6 400 K)　Sun
(5 800 K)　Arcturus
(4 750 K)　Betelgeuse
(3 500 K)　Wolf 359
(2 800 K)

○　Our Sun is a yellowish-white star and its surface temperature is about 6000 K. It releases an enormous amount of energy, mostly in the form of ultraviolet, visible light and infrared radiation.

○　Our Sun is made mostly of hydrogen and helium, and it produces its energy by nuclear fusion of hydrogen into helium. This energy is emitted in the form of electromagnetic radiation, including visible light, infrared radiation and ultraviolet radiation (see pages 148-9).

The life cycle of a star

Nebula

○   Stars begin in a cloud of dust and gas (mostly hydrogen) known as a **nebula**, most of which was left when previous stars blew apart in **supernovae**. The denser clumps of the cloud contract very slowly under the **force due to gravity**.

○   As the cloud collapses, it fragments into smaller, denser regions, which themselves contract further to form stellar cores. These stellar cores, known as **protostars,** continue to contract, and heat up as they do so. The very smallest stars have masses about half that of our Sun and the very largest have masses about 25 times that of our Sun

Main sequence stars

○   Main sequence describes the longest period of a star's life.

○   The temperature of the core of the contracting protostar increases to the point where a nuclear reaction begins (a few million kelvins). At this point, **hydrogen** (H) nuclei fuse together to form **helium** (He) nuclei in the core of the star (see page 242).

○   This process releases extremely large amounts of energy and creates enough pressure to stop the collapse of the star due to its **gravitational field**. The outward force due to the gas pressure from the nuclear fusion of hydrogen in the core balances the gravitational force trying to compress the star. This stage is called '**hydrogen core burning**', and the star emits huge amounts of radiation from its surface – it shines. It is now in the stable part of its life, called the **main sequence**.

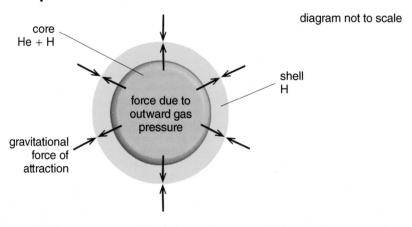

○   For about 90 % of its life, the star continues to convert hydrogen into helium and will remain a main sequence star. An average mass star – with a mass similar to the mass of our Sun – remains in the main sequence stage for about 10 billion years.

○   Our Sun is in its **main sequence** stage and is stable because the forces in it are balanced.

Red giant

○   Eventually the hydrogen in the core runs out, nuclear fusion stops and the core begins to contract again as the outward force due to gas pressure stops but the gravitational force of attraction remains. The inert helium core continues to contract and heat up under the gravitational field of the star.

○   The temperature of the helium core eventually becomes high enough to cause the hydrogen which surrounds the core to fuse. This is known as '**hydrogen shell burning**'.

○   This causes a release of energy that pushes the outer layers of the star even further out and causes the star to expand rapidly and become much larger and brighter. The outer layer is cooler than the inner core giving it a reddish colour. The star is now a **red giant**, a star which might have a mass similar to the Sun's, but it is much larger in size.

○   The core continues to contract and heat up until it is hot enough for the helium to fuse into carbon and oxygen. This is known as '**helium core burning**'. This stage lasts a much shorter time and the star does not reach stability; the outward force never balances the inward force. The fusion of helium releases enormous amounts of energy. Further stages of fusion are possible all the way up to the production of iron; the number of stages depends on the mass of the star.

White dwarf - stars with low mass

○   When the helium in the core runs out, nuclear fusion in the core stops. The core made of carbon and oxygen begins to contract again as the outward pressure stops but the gravitational force of attraction remains. The inert carbon – oxygen core will continue to contract and heat up under the gravitational field of the star.

○ The temperature of the core eventually becomes big enough to cause the helium that surrounds the core to fuse. This is known as '**helium shell burning**'.

○ The core continues to contract and get hotter. This time the temperature may not be not sufficient to cause any further fusion in the core.

○ The core continues to contract under its own weight but it does not have enough weight to collapse completely. The situation becomes unstable, as there are now two outer burning shells, one made of helium and one made of hydrogen.

○ This instability causes the star to eject its outer layer, and lose mass The ejected gas forms a planetary nebula.

○ The core of the star is now a very dense hot solid known as a **white dwarf**, a star with a mass similar to the Sun's, but much smaller in size. This will eventually cool to a 'black dwarf'.

○ In about 5 billion years from now the Sun will start to run out of fuel and will end up as a white dwarf.

Red supergiant - stars with high mass

○ Stars with higher mass evolve in a similar way up to the main sequence stage. A massive star only remains in this stage for millions, rather than billions of years.

○ When the hydrogen in the core runs out, the star swells and becomes a **red supergiant**, a star with a mass higher than the Sun's, and very much larger in size.

○ Unlike lower mass stars, the contracting carbon – oxygen core of high-mass stars can heat up enough to cause fusion, this time forming neon.

○ This process of core fusion followed by core contraction and shell fusion is repeated in a series of nuclear reactions. These produce successively heavier elements, until iron is formed in the core.

○ Iron cannot be fused into heavier elements. The star has therefore run out of fuel and collapses under its own gravity.

○   What happens next depends on the mass of the star. If it's about three to ten times the size of our Sun, it explodes in a **supernova** and leaves behind a **neutron star**.

N.B. A supernova is the name given to an exploding star.

○   As the star explodes it casts its outer layers into space forming a nebula made up of gas and dust. This material may form new stars with their own orbiting planets.

○   If the mass of the star is even bigger, such as in very large giants or super giants, a **black hole** is formed. A black hole is a point in space with an extremely large gravitational field.

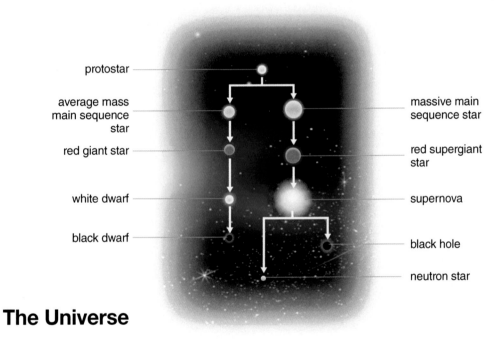

protostar

average mass main sequence star

red giant star

white dwarf

black dwarf

massive main sequence star

red supergiant star

supernova

black hole

neutron star

The Universe

Galaxies

❏   We have already seen that our Sun is in a galaxy called the Milky Way.

❏   The **universe** is a vast space which is continually expanding. There are regions within this space known as **galaxies** where billions of stars are grouped together.
(One billion = one thousand million, $1\,000\,000\,000$ or 10^9.)

❏   Each brightly coloured region in the diagram overleaf represents a galaxy containing billions of stars. The diagram shows the galaxies much closer together than they actually are.

diagram not to scale

❑ There are billions of galaxies distributed throughout the universe.

❑ Distances in space are commonly described in units called a **light-year (ly)**. This is because the distances are very, very large. **One light-year (1 ly) is the distance light travels in one year**.

○ In one year there are approximately 365 days; each day is 24 hours long, each hour has 60 minutes and each minute has 60 seconds. Therefore one year is:

$365 \times 24 \times 60 \times 60 = 31\,536\,000\,s$

Light travels at 3×10^8 m/s (300 000 000 metres in one second)

$s = v \times t = 300\,000\,000 \times 31\,536\,000$
$= 9\,460\,800\,000\,000\,000\,m = 9.5 \times 10^{15}\,m$

One light-year is approximately 9.5 million million kilometres.

❑ Each galaxy spans thousands of light-years. The distance **between** galaxies is even bigger. For example, the Milky Way spans about 100 000 light-years, but the nearest galaxy to us, known as Andromeda, is 2.5 million light-years away.

❑ A car travelling at 20 m/s would take approximately 65 million years to reach our nearest star, Proxima Centauri, which is 4.24 light-years away.

❑ If one light-year in space was represented by one kilometre, you would travel around the Earth approximately 60 times to travel the equivalent distance from the Milky Way to the Andromeda galaxy.

Big Bang Theory

❑   We do not know exactly how the Universe was formed, nor how big it actually is. We do know that gravitational forces have had a significant impact on what has happened. Gravitational forces will continue to influence the future of the Universe.

❑   The **Big Bang Theory** is the most popular theory on how the universe was formed. According to this theory the Universe was formed 13.7 billion years ago. All matter and energy in the Universe came from an extremely hot and dense single point known as a 'singularity'. Nothing existed before this singularity – everything that we know today came after this event.

❑   The Universe started from this extremely hot, extremely dense and extremely small singularity and consequently began expanding and cooling.

❑   It went from this extremely hot, dense and small singularity to the size and temperature of the Universe today, filled with billions of stars, countless planets, moons, asteroids, gas clouds, and vast amounts of empty space. The Universe continues to cool.

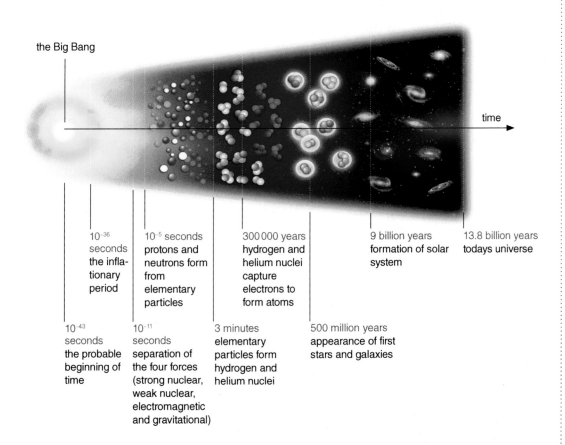

the Big Bang

time

| 10^{-36} seconds the inflationary period | 10^{-5} seconds protons and neutrons form from elementary particles | 300 000 years hydrogen and helium nuclei capture electrons to form atoms | 9 billion years formation of solar system | 13.8 billion years todays universe |

| 10^{-43} seconds the probable beginning of time | 10^{-11} seconds separation of the four forces (strong nuclear, weak nuclear, electromagnetic and gravitational) | 3 minutes elementary particles form hydrogen and helium nuclei | 500 million years appearance of first stars and galaxies |

Evidence that supports the Big Bang Theory

❑   The observation of **redshift** in the spectra of distant galaxies
        (see pages 285-6) shows that almost all galaxies are moving away
        from us at speeds proportional to their distance, suggesting
        that the Universe was once compact and started from a single point.

○   The discovery of **cosmic microwave background radiation**
        (**CMBR**), which is uniform across the sky and does not come from
        any one star or galaxy, also supports the Big Bang Theory. This
        suggests that it is the left-over radiation from an extremely hot original
   ,   source that has cooled over time. The source currently has a
        temperature of around 3 K, just as predicted by the Big Bang Theory.

○   In the middle of the 20th century, the Big Bang Theory was
        becoming popular. It suggested that if there had been a Big Bang,
        there would be left-over radiation in the Universe today. CMBR was
        first discovered, by chance, in the 1960s.

○   CMBR is a remnant of the Big Bang. This radiation is now spread
        thinly throughout the whole Universe. When the energy was first
        released billions of years ago it was a bright light but as the
        Universe has expanded, so has the wavelength of the radiation
        and it is now in the microwave range of the electromagnetic
        spectrum.

Note

A common misconception is that the Big Bang was a huge
explosion with a fireball and a sound much like a bomb.
It wasn't; it was more like a tiny balloon being blown up that
expanded in all directions.

Redshift

❑   When a source of waves, such as sound waves, moves
     towards or away from an observer, there is a change in its
     observed frequency. If you hear a police car or an ambulance
     with its siren sounding, it is noticeable that when the source of
     sound is coming towards you it has a higher frequency (pitch)
     than when it is going away from you. This effect is called the
     Doppler effect, and the change in frequency is called the
     Doppler shift.

❑   The diagram above shows a motor cycle travelling from left to
     right. The lines show the wavefronts as the sound of the motor
     cycle travels through the air. For the boy the wavefronts are
     pushed together more because the motor cycle is travelling
     towards him and the sound he hears has a shorter wavelength,
     or a higher frequency, than the sound heard by the girl.

❑   All waves demonstrate the Doppler effect when the source is
     moving relative to (towards or away from) the observer, but the
     effect is less obvious when the speed of the source is very
     small compared with the speed of the wave.

❑   Light travels at approximately 300 000 000 m/s (3.0×10^8 m/s) in air, so we rarely notice the Doppler effect in light, but it is seen when viewing stars and distant galaxies. As already mentioned, the light from galaxies that are moving away from Earth undergoes a **redshift**.

We saw earlier in Unit 3 (pages 147-8) that white light is composed of a spectrum of colours with varying wavelengths. A shift to the red end of the spectrum in the light from a galaxy means the **wavelength has increased** (and the frequency has decreased), so it must be moving away from us.

Remember: The Doppler effect is the apparent change in frequency of a wave caused by the relative motion between the source of the wave and the observer.

❑   If a distant star and the Earth were stationary objects, the frequency of light observed on the Earth from the star would appear the same as the frequency from a similar source on Earth.

❑   Visible light is dispersed to form a spectrum of colours (see page 148). When astronomers view the light from a star or a galaxy, they see black lines in the spectrum. These black lines are caused by various elements absorbing particular wavelengths of light; for example, our Sun contains helium and hydrogen and the (simplified) spectrum from the Sun is shown below. This is known as an **absorption spectrum**.

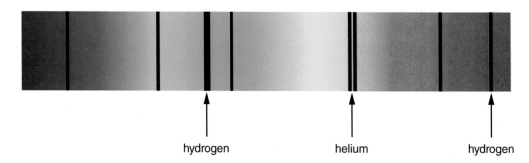

hydrogen   helium   hydrogen

❑   If a star or galaxy containing hydrogen and helium were moving **away** from the Earth, the frequency of these black lines would appear **lower** (longer wavelength). This is known as **redshift**. The visible light observed is shifting towards the red end of the spectrum.

❑ In the spectrum of the very few galaxies that are moving towards the Earth, the frequency of these black lines would appear **higher** (shorter wavelength). This is known as **blueshift**.The visible light observed is shifting towards the blue end of the spectrum.

❑ The diagram below gives an example of an absorption spectrum and shows how the black lines shift to the red end of the spectrum if the star is moving away from an observer, or to the blue end if it is moving towards the observer.

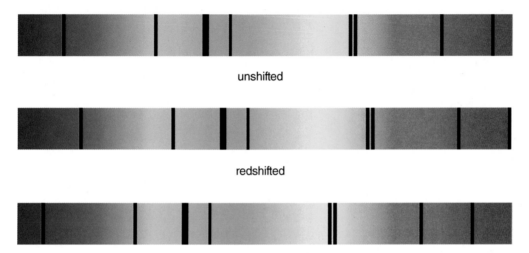

unshifted

redshifted

blueshifted

❑ When we view stars in a nearby rotating spiral galaxy, some stars will be moving towards us and others will be moving away from us as the galaxy rotates. We observe both blueshift and redshift.

star in rotating galaxy

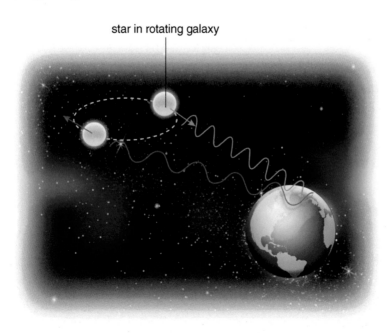

○   This shift in frequency (and wavelength) relates to the speed of the star moving towards or away from the Earth. For example, the bigger the redshift, the faster the star is moving away from us.

○   When observing very distant galaxies, the light from individual stars cannot be distinguished; the light from the whole galaxy is analysed. The Doppler shift tells us how fast the galaxy is moving away from us.

Note

Remember: Redshift means that the object, such as a star emitting light waves, is moving further away from the observer, such as an astronomer on Earth. The bigger the change in frequency towards the red end of the visible spectrum, the faster the star is moving.

The Hubble constant

○   Edwin Hubble was one of the first to observe redshift in the spectra from Earth and distant galaxies; he also showed that this shift was bigger for galaxies further away from Earth. **No distant** galaxies observed showed blueshift.

○   Hubble's Law states that a galaxy's recessional velocity (its velocity away from us) is directly proportional to the galaxy's distance from Earth.

○   A graph of recessional velocity against distance from Earth is a straight line passing through the origin.

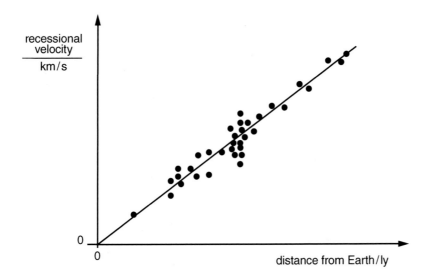

○ This graph shows that galaxies that are further away from Earth are moving away even faster than those closer to Earth.

○ The distance **d** of a far away galaxy can be determined using the brightness of a supernova in that galaxy. If you were to stand in a large dark field with two people holding identical lamps, the light from the person closer to you would be brighter than that from the person who was further away. Astronomers know precisely how much light a supernova produces, and they can use this knowledge to calculate the distance to a far away galaxy by measuring how much light a supernova in that galaxy produces.

○ The Hubble constant is defined as the ratio of the speed at which the galaxy is moving away from the Earth (recessional velocity) to its distance from the Earth.

$$H_0 = \frac{v}{d}$$

H_0 = Hubble constant (/s or s^{-1})
v = speed of galaxy (m/s)
d = distance of Earth from galaxy (m)

N.B. The Hubble constant is equal to the gradient of the graph at the top of the page.

○ Currently H_0 is estimated to be 2.2×10^{-18} per second.

N.B. Although we call this the Hubble constant it will vary over time as the Universe expands.

○   The time it has taken for the galaxies to reach their current separations is given by:

$$t = \frac{d}{v} = \frac{1}{H_0}$$

○   So, you can take $\frac{1}{H_0}$ as an estimate for the age of the Universe.

This is further evidence that all matter in the Universe came from an extremely hot and dense point known as a 'singularity'.

○   ***Example***

Calculate the estimated age of the Universe in years given that the value of the Hubble constant is estimated to be 2.2×10^{-18} s^{-1}.

Answer

Step 1   List all the information in symbol form and change into appropriate and consistent SI units if required.

$H_0 = 2.2 \times 10^{-18}$ s^{-1}

Step 2   Use the correct equation.

$$t = \frac{1}{H_0}$$

Step 3   Calculate the answer by putting the numbers into the correct equation

$$t = \frac{1}{H_0} = \frac{1}{2.2 \times 10^{-18}} = 4.5 \times 10^{17} \text{ s (to 2 sig. figs)}$$

N.B. Because the Hubble constant is only given to 2 sig. figs, we can only express our answer to 2 sig. figs. to convert to years

$$4.5 \times 10^{17} \text{ s} = \frac{4.5 \times 10^{17}}{365 \times 24 \times 60 \times 60} = 1.4 \times 10^{10} \text{ years}$$

$$= \text{approximately 14 billion years}$$

ALWAYS REMEMBER TO STATE THE UNIT FOR CALCULATED QUANTITIES.

Additional support material

Physical quantities and units
Supplement level in grey tint

Quantity	Symbol	Unit (usual unit bold)
Motion, forces and energy		
■ period	*T*	**s**
■ length	*l, h, s, d, x*	**m**, mm, cm, km
■ area	*A*	**m²**, cm²
■ volume	*V*	**m³**, cm³, dm³
■ distance	*s, d*	**m**, cm, km
■ time	*t*	**s**, min, h, ms, µs
■ speed	*u, v*	**m/s**, km/h, cm/s
■ acceleration	*a*	**m/s²**
■ mass	*m*	**kg**, g, mg
■ weight	*W*	**N**
■ acceleration of free fall	*g*	**m/s²**
■ gravitational field strength	*g*	**N/kg**
■ momentum	*p*	**kgm/s**
■ impulse		**Ns**
■ density	*ρ*	**kg/m³**, g/cm³
■ force	*F*	**N**
■ spring constant	*k*	**N/m**, N/cm
■ moment of a force	*M*	**Nm**
■ energy	*E*	**J**, kJ, MJ, kWh
■ work done	*W, E*	**J**, kJ, MJ
■ power	*P*	**W**, kW, MW
■ pressure	*p*	**N/m²**, **Pa**
Thermal physics		
■ pressure	*p*	**N/m²**, **Pa**
■ volume	*V*	**m³**, cm³, dm³
■ energy	*E*	**J**, kJ, MJ, kWh

■ power	*P*	**W**, kW, MW
■ time	*t*	**s**, min, h, ms, µs
■ current	*I*	**A**, mA
■ voltage	*V*	**V**, mV
■ temperature	*θ, T*	**°C, K**
■ thermal capacity	*C*	**J/°C**
■ specific heat capacity	*c*	**J/(kg°C)**, J/(g°C)

Waves

■ frequency	*f*	**Hz**, kHz
■ wavelength	*λ*	**m**, cm, nm
■ focal length	*f*	**cm**
■ angle of incidence	*i*	**degree** (°)
■ angle of reflection	*r*	**degree** (°)
■ angle of refraction	*r*	**degree** (°)
■ critical angle	*c*	**degree** (°)
■ refractive index	*n*	no units
■ distance	*s, d*	**m**, cm, km
■ time	*t*	**s**, min, h, ms, µs
■ speed	*v*	**m/s**, km/h, cm/s

Electricity and magnetism

■ time	*t*	**s**, min, h, ms, µs
■ charge	*Q*	**C**
■ current	*I*	**A**, mA
■ voltage/potential difference	*V*	**V**, mV, kV
■ resistance	*R*	Ω
■ e.m.f.	*E*	**V**
■ energy	*E*	**J**, kJ, MJ, kWh
■ power	*P*	**W**, kW, MW

Nuclear physics

■ count rate	counts/minute, counts/second
■ half-life	**s**, min, h, days, weeks, years

Space physics

■ Hubble constant	H_0	s^{-1}, /s

How to use equations effectively

❏   **Learn all the equations** presented on the following pages. You must know them all for the supplementary level and the ones marked with a square for the core level.

❏   Read each examination question carefully and follow the steps below.

Step 1   List the values given in the examination question using **symbol**, **value** and **units** that represent each quantity, including the symbol for the answer you are being asked to find.

   For example $v = 10\,cm/s$
                         $s = 5.0\,m$
                         $t = ?$

Step 2   Change all units to appropriate and consistent SI units if required.

   For example $v = 0.1\,m/s$

Step 3   Write down the correct equation.

   For example $v = \dfrac{s}{t}$

Step 4   Rearrange the equation so that the subject of the equation you are trying to find is on its own on the left-hand side.

   For example $t = \dfrac{s}{v}$

Step 5   Write down the figures in the equation and calculate the answer, **remembering to include units for calculated quantities**. (You may get marks for your working on the paper; remember this is the only way you can communicate with an examiner.)

   For example $t = \dfrac{5.0}{0.1} = 50\,s$

Equations

Motion, forces and energy

The triangles provide a learning aid. They are not an alternative way of writing the equation.

❏   period of pendulum = $\dfrac{\text{total time}}{\text{number of swings}}$

$$T = \dfrac{t}{\text{number}}$$

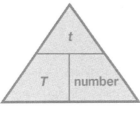

❏   speed = $\dfrac{\text{distance}}{\text{time}}$

$$v = \dfrac{s}{t}$$

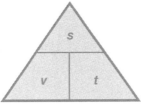

◯   acceleration = $\dfrac{\text{change in velocity}}{\text{time taken}}$

$$a = \dfrac{\Delta v}{\Delta t}$$

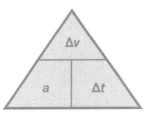

❏   gravitational field strength = $\dfrac{\text{weight}}{\text{mass}}$

$$g = \dfrac{W}{m}$$

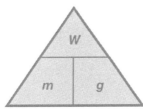

❏   density = $\dfrac{\text{mass}}{\text{volume}}$

$$\rho = \dfrac{m}{V}$$

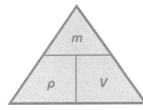

◯   force = mass × acceleration

$$F = ma$$

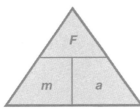

◯   spring constant = $\dfrac{\text{force}}{\text{extension}}$

$$k = \dfrac{F}{x}$$

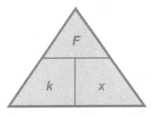

❑   moment = force × perpendicular distance

$M = Fd$

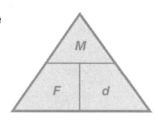

❑   sum of anti-clockwise moments = sum of clockwise moments

$F_1 d_1 = F_2 d_2$

○   momentum = mass × velocity

$p = mv$

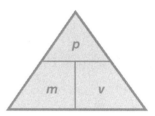

○   impulse = change in momentum

$F \Delta t = \Delta (mv)$

○   resultant force = change in momentum per unit time

$F = \dfrac{\Delta p}{\Delta t}$

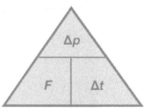

○   kinetic energy = $\dfrac{1}{2}$ × mass × velocity^2

$E_k = \dfrac{1}{2} mv^2$

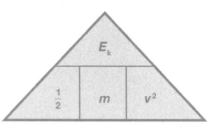

○   change in gravitational potential energy = mass × gravitational field strength × change in height

$\Delta E_p = mg \Delta h$

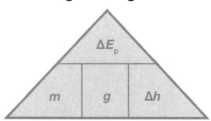

○   efficiency = $\dfrac{\text{useful energy output}}{\text{total energy input}} \times 100\%$

efficiency $= \dfrac{E_{out}}{E_{in}} \times \mathbf{100\%}$

○   work done = force × distance = energy transferred

$W = Fd = \Delta E$

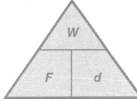

○   power = work done per unit time = energy transferred per unit time

$p = \dfrac{W}{t} = \dfrac{\Delta E}{t}$

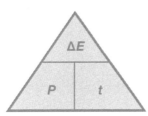

❑   pressure = $\dfrac{\text{force}}{\text{area}}$

$p = \dfrac{F}{A}$

○   change in fluid pressure =
        density × gravitational field strength × height/depth

$\Delta p = \rho g \Delta h$

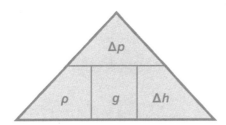

Thermal physics

○ Boyle's Law:
pressure × volume = constant
pV = constant
$p_1V_1 = p_2V_2$

○ specific heat capacity = $\dfrac{\text{thermal energy transferred}}{\text{mass × change in temperature}}$

$$c = \frac{\Delta E}{m\Delta\theta}$$

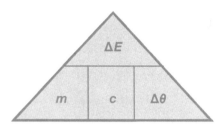

○ energy transferred = power × time

$$\Delta E = Pt$$

○ power = current × voltage

$$P = IV$$

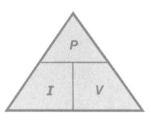

○ energy transferred = current × voltage × time

$$\Delta E = IVt$$

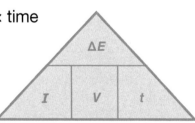

Waves

○   velocity = frequency × wavelength

$$v = f\lambda$$

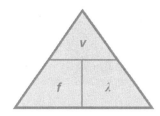

❑   frequency = $\dfrac{1}{\text{period}}$

$$f = \dfrac{1}{T}$$

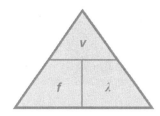

○   refractive index = $\dfrac{\text{sine of angle of incidence}}{\text{sine of angle of refraction}}$

$$n = \dfrac{\sin i}{\sin r}$$

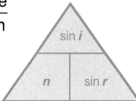

○   refractive index = $\dfrac{\text{speed of light in vacuum}}{\text{speed of light in material}}$

$$n = \dfrac{c_v}{c_m}$$

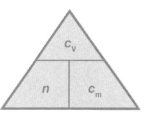

○   refractive index = $\dfrac{1}{\text{sine of critical angle}}$

$$n = \dfrac{1}{\sin c}$$

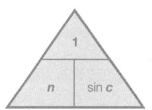

❑   distance = speed × time

$$s = vt$$

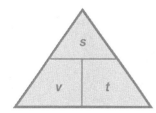

Electricity and magnetism

○ current $= \dfrac{\text{charge}}{\text{time}}$

$$I = \dfrac{Q}{t}$$

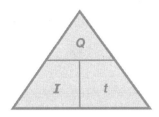

❑ resistance $= \dfrac{\text{voltage}}{\text{current}}$

$$R = \dfrac{V}{I}$$

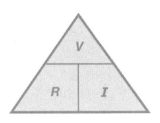

❑ total resistance in series: $\quad R_t = R_1 + R_2$

○ total resistance in parallel: $\quad \dfrac{1}{R_t} = \dfrac{1}{R_1} + \dfrac{1}{R_2}$

○ e.m.f. = work done in moving unit charge round a circuit

$$E = \dfrac{W}{Q}$$

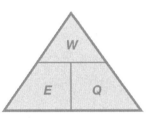

○ potential difference = work done by unit charge passing through a component

$$V = \dfrac{W}{Q}$$

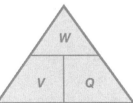

○ For a potential divider:

$$\dfrac{R_1}{R_2} = \dfrac{V_1}{V_2}$$

- power = current × voltage

  $P = IV$

  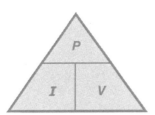

- energy transferred = power × time

  $\Delta E = Pt$

  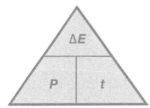

- power = current² × resistance

  $P = I^2R$

  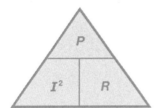

- energy transferred = current × voltage × time

  $\Delta E = IVt$

  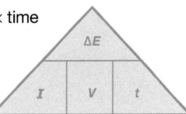

- For a transformer:

  $$\frac{\text{voltage in primary coil}}{\text{voltage in secondary coil}} = \frac{\text{number of turns in primary}}{\text{number of turns in secondary}}$$

  $$\frac{V_p}{V_s} = \frac{N_p}{N_s}$$

- For a 100% efficient transformer:

  voltage in primary × current in primary

       = voltage in secondary × current in secondary

  $V_p I_p = V_s I_s$

Space physics

○ For orbital speed:

$$v = \frac{2\pi r}{T}$$

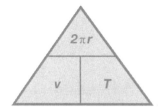

○ The Hubble constant is defined as the ratio of the speed at which a galaxy is moving from the Earth to its distance from the Earth.

$$H_0 = \frac{v}{d}$$

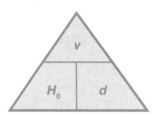

○ The age of the Universe is represented by:

$$\frac{d}{v} = \frac{1}{H_0}$$

Working with numbers

Understanding significant figures

❑ Numbers can be expressed in many different ways. Let us say the calculated value for a particular quantity was 2. One student may write it as 2 and another as 2.0. They may appear the same but they mean different things. 2 has one significant figure. Writing 2 means the value is 1.5 or above but below 2.5. 2.0 has two significant figures. Writing 2.0 means the value is 1.95 or above but below 2.05.

❑ In physics calculations, many numbers may appear on the calculator, e.g. 5.046754327. Expressing your answer like this is **wrong** because it claims you know the answer far more precisely than any instrument you have used or any information you have been given. For example, let us say you are calculating the average time for an oscillation. If you use the answer above, you are claiming incorrectly that you can measure time with a stopwatch to this high degree of precision.

❑ As a general rule, giving answers to **two or three significant figures** is normally acceptable for the majority of Cambridge IGCSE Physics questions. It is usually possible to express values from a graph to **three significant figures**.

Rounding to three significant figures

❑ Rounding means reducing the digits in a number while trying to keep its value similar.

❑ In the number 6.0469812 the fourth figure is above 5, so you would increase the third figure by one unit, e.g. 6.05. This is **rounding up**.
In the number 6.0429812 the fourth figure is below 5, so you would leave the third figure as it is, e.g. 6.04. This is **rounding down**.

❑ **Remember:** Round up if the figure to the right is 5 or above and round down if it is below 5.

Standard form

❑   Many very large or very small numbers in physics are expressed in standard form, also commonly known as **scientific notation**.

❑   Standard form consists of two parts, a number between 1 and 10 followed by × 10 to the power of a number, known as the **index**.

e.g. 3.0×10^8 m/s is the speed of light

❑   The following numbers written out in full give:

$$1.0 \times 10^5 = 100\,000$$
$$3.0 \times 10^8 = 300\,000\,000$$
$$3.56 \times 10^7 = 35\,600\,000$$

The value of the index depends on how many places the decimal point has been moved. For example $35\,600\,000$ becomes 3.56 by moving the decimal point 7 places to the left. The index is 7.

❑   To represent very small numbers, a negative index is used. The following numbers written out in full give:

$$2.1 \times 10^{-5} = 0.000\,021$$
$$9.3 \times 10^{-8} = 0.000\,000\,093$$
$$3.56 \times 10^{-4} = 0.000\,356$$

This time the decimal point moves to the right and the index is a negative number. For example $0.000\,356$ becomes 3.56 by moving the decimal point 4 places to the right. The index is −4.

❑   Values can be entered in standard form on a calculator by using the EXP button or $\times\,10^x$. For example:

$7.6 \times 10^4 =$ [7][.][6][EXP][4]

$3.2 \times 10^{-3} =$ [3][.][2][EXP][(−)][3]

Do not include the 10. You would only use the 10 when using the [xʸ] button, for example: [3] [.] [2] [×] [1] [0] [xʸ] [(–)] [3] and so on.

❑ Sometimes, **prefixes** are used with SI units to simplify large or small values.

$$\text{kilo (k)} = 10^3 \qquad \text{milli (m)} = 10^{-3}$$
$$\text{mega (M)} = 10^6 \qquad \text{micro (μ)} = 10^{-6}$$
$$\text{giga (G)} = 10^9 \qquad \text{nano (n)} = 10^{-9}$$
$$\text{tera (T)} = 10^{12} \qquad \text{pico (p)} = 10^{-12}$$

For example, you can write 2000m as 2km and 0.003m as 3mm.

Always change prefixed units to base units but notice that the kilogram is the base SI unit for mass.

Graphs

Plotting graphs

You may be advised which set of numbers is to be plotted on the **x**-axis and the **y**-axis.

❑ **Choosing the appropriate scale for the x- or y-axis**
   - Find the maximum and minimum value needed for each axis. **Remember:** You do not have to start the axis from zero if the numbers given are all greater than zero unless you are trying to show that the two variables are directly proportional, in which case you must show that the line passes through the origin.
   - Make the scale easy to interpret. Choose a scale where each square on the graph paper equals 1, 2, 5, 10, 50 or 100. For smaller values use 0.01, 0.02, 0.05, 0.1 or 0.5.

❑ **The axes**
   - The **x**-axis will usually represent the **independent variable** and will rise in regular intervals, e.g. 2, 4, 6, etc. not 2, 4, 9 etc. The independent variable is the one you control. For example if you take a measurement every 10s, time is your independent variable.

- The **y**-axis will usually represent the experimental results – the **dependent variable**. This will usually give rise to a straight line or a curve.

- Label the axes clearly with both variable and units.

❑ **Drawing the graph**

- The graph you draw (i.e. the points you plot) should cover as much of the graph paper as possible – three-quarters of the page is a good guide.

- Plot plus signs (+), crosses (x) or encircled dots (⊙) rather than dots (·) on your graph. Re-check any points that do not appear to fit the pattern.

- Draw a smooth continuous line that will not necessarily pass through all the points, known as a **line of best fit**. If the graph looks like a straight line, then use a ruler.

○ **Finding the gradient of a line**

- Use $m = \dfrac{\Delta y}{\Delta x}$ to find the gradient of a line. Make sure you pick two points that are **on the line**. It is helpful to show the values you choose by drawing dotted lines from the axes (see below). Choose values as **far apart** as possible to give a more accurate gradient.

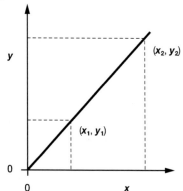

Example

Let (x_1, y_1) be (5.0, 50) and (x_2, y_2) be (10, 100).

$$m = \frac{y_2 - y_1}{x_2 - x_1} = \frac{100 - 50}{10 - 5.0} = 10$$

In many cases the gradient will have units. For example, if **y** is distance measured in metres and **x** is time measured in seconds, the gradient calculated above will be 10 m/s.

Understanding the graph you have plotted

❑ **Proportionality and linearity**

Many quantities in Physics are **directly proportional** to each other. Many equations are derived from **straight-line** (**linear**) relationships.

The equation of a straight line on a graph is made up of a **y** term, an **x** term, and sometimes a number, and is written in the form of $y = mx + c$.

Graph 1

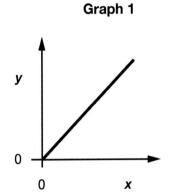

Graph 2

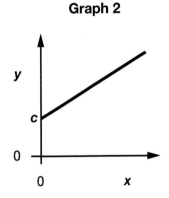

❑ *Graph 1 – directly proportional*

As **x** increases, **y** increases. The graph is a straight line and passes through the origin. Importantly the ratio of **x:y** is always the same. The graph equation is $y = mx$, where **m** is the steepness of the line, also known as the gradient:

$$m = \frac{y_2 - y_1}{x_2 - x_1}$$

❑ *Graph 2 – straight line with y-intercept*

As **x** increases, so does **y** as before. The difference is when $x = 0$, as this time **y** is not zero. The graph equation is $y = mx + c$, where **m** is the gradient. The **y**-intercept (the value of **y** when $x = 0$) is **c**.

Glossary

absolute magnitude the brightness of a celestial body if it were at a distance of 32.6 ly from an observer on the Earth

absolute zero the theoretical temperature at which all molecular motion ceases; equal to $-273.15°C$

a.c. generator a device used to produce alternating current

acceleration how much an object's speed is increased per second – the rate of change of velocity of an object

acceleration due to gravity the acceleration of an object falling freely under gravity

accretion the increase in mass of a celestial object as it gathers surrounding gas and objects by gravity

accurate how close a measured value is to a known value

activity the rate of decay of nuclei in a radioactive sample

air resistance the frictional force on an object moving through air

alpha (α) particle a type of nuclear radiation consisting of a helium nucleus ejected from an unstable nucleus

alternating current (a.c.) electric current that changes its direction repeatedly in a circuit; the charges flow one way and then the other way

ammeter an instrument for measuring electric current in amperes (A)

ampere (A) the base unit of current; it is the electric charge that flows past a point in one second

amplified increased in size

amplitude the maximum height or disturbance of a wave from its central equilibrium (rest) position

analogue a quantity that can be represented by a continuously varying signal

angle of incidence the angle measured between the normal and a ray of light arriving at a surface

angle of reflection the angle measured between the normal and a ray of light reflecting at a surface

angle of refraction the angle measured between a refracted ray and the normal to a surface

anode a positive electrode; another name for the positive terminal of a battery

anomalous odd results not in keeping with the rest of your results; not fitting the pattern

atomic number see proton number

average speed the speed calculated by dividing total distance by total time taken

background radiation the radiation in the surrounding environment that we are exposed to all the time

balanced equal in size but opposite in sign or direction and therefore adding to zero

beta (β) particle a type of nuclear radiation consisting of a high-speed electron emitted from an unstable nucleus

Big Bang Theory a scientific theory describing the origin of the Universe

black hole a massive object with a gravitational field so strong that nothing can escape, not even light

blueshift the apparent change in wavelength of light, due to the Doppler effect, when stars in rotating galaxies move towards us

boiling point the temperature at which a liquid changes to a gas at normal pressure

Boyle's Law for a given mass of a gas at constant temperature, the volume of the gas is inversely proportional to the pressure

Brownian motion the motion of small particles in a fluid (liquid or gas), caused by collisions with other particles in fluid

calibrate to mark an instrument with a standard scale of readings such as the Celsius scale on a thermometer

cargo goods carried by a large vehicle such as a ship or a plane

cathode a negative electrode; another name for the negative terminal of a battery

cathode ray a beam of electrons travelling from a cathode (–ve) to an anode (+ve) in a vacuum tube

celestial of or relating to the sky or the Universe

centre of gravity the point in an object where all the weight appears to act

centripetal force the radial force required to keep an object moving in a circular path; the force always acts towards the centre of the circle

charge a property of certain materials, which can be positive or negative; a charged particle will experience a force if placed in an electric field

circuit breaker a safety device that switches off automatically when the current in it becomes too high; it can easily be reset

comet a small icy body that orbits the Sun

cloud chamber a device used to detect ionising radiation using alcohol vapour in an enclosed environment

collision where two or more objects strike each other and each object exerts a force on the other(s)

component part of a mechanical or electrical system

compression a region of a sound wave in which the particles are pushed close together

conduction the process by which thermal energy or electrical energy is transferred

conductor a material that transfers thermal energy or allows charges to pass through it easily

conserved maintained at a constant overall; does not change; for example, energy into and out of a system

constriction the act of narrowing, such as the narrowing of a tube

conventional current the imagined flow of electric charge, from the positive terminal in a battery round the circuit to the negative terminal

coolant a fluid (liquid or gas) used to cool down a system

cosmic microwave background radiation (CMBR) left over from the Big Bang

cosmology the study of the origin and evolution of the universe

count rate the number of decaying radioactive nuclei detected per second or minute

critical angle the angle above which total internal reflection occurs

current the rate of flow of electric charge in a circuit

decay see radioactive decay

deceleration (also known as negative acceleration) how much an object's speed is decreased per second; the rate of change of velocity of an object

density the mass per unit volume of a substance

depleted used up to the point of it running out, such as an empty fuel tank in a car

depth the distance from the top to the bottom, such as in a swimming pool

determine find a quantity as a result of calculation or from a graph; often used when the quantity cannot be measured directly

deviated moved away from the original intended course

diffraction the spreading out of a wave when it passes through a gap or past an edge

digital signal a signal that has only two possible values and is represented by a 1 for on and a 0 for off

diminished smaller; for example, a diminished image is smaller than the object

diode a circuit component that allows current in one direction only

direct current (d.c.) electric current that is always in the same direction

directly proportional two quantities are directly proportional if their ratio is constant; as one increases, the other increases by the same percentage; if a graph of one quantity (y) is plotted against the other (x), the graph is a straight line that passes through the origin (0,0)

dispersion the splitting of white light into its component wavelengths (colours) due to refraction; for example, when white light falls onto a triangular prism

dissipate to disperse or scatter, to give out

domains can be thought of as small atomic magnets that need to line up for a magnetic material to become magnetised

Doppler effect the apparent change in frequency of a wave for an observer moving relative to the source of the wave

drag a type of friction (sometimes called air resistance) that opposes the motion of an object

earthing when a charged object is connected to earth (or ground) and the charges flow to earth; for example, the casing of an electrical appliance is connected to the earth wire for safety

echo the reflection of sound from a surface heard some time after the original sound

efficiency a fractional measure (usually expressed as a percentage) of how effectively energy or power is transferred into a useful form in comparison to the total energy or power

elastic collision a collision in which the total kinetic energy is the same before and after the collision

electric current see current

electric field a region in space in which an electric charge will experience a force

electromagnet a coil of wire with an iron core that becomes magnetic only when there is an electric current in the coil

electromagnetic induction a method of producing an e.m.f. by moving a magnet into a coil of wire

electromagnetic (e.m.) spectrum the family of e.m. waves ranging from radio to gamma

electromagnetic (e.m.) waves energy travelling in the form of waves, which require no medium in which to travel

electromotive force (e.m.f.) the energy transferred to each coulomb of charge by a source of electrical energy such as a battery or power supply or the electrical work done in moving unit charge around a complete circuit

electron a very small subatomic particle that is negatively charged and that exists in orbitals round the nucleus of an atom

electrostatic charges +ve or −ve charges that can be present on an insulator; insulators do not allow charges to move so they are static (stay still)

electrostatic induction a method of giving an object an electric charge without making physical contact with another charged object

endoscope a fibre optic device used to image the inside of living bodies

equilibrium when there is no net moment or no net force acting on a body

evaporation the process by which a liquid changes to gas or vapour below its boiling point

exert to make a physical effort such as when applying a force

extension the increase in the length of a spring when a load is attached

fluid a material that flows, such as any liquid or gas

focal length the distance from the centre of the lens to its principal focus

fossil fuel a source of energy such as coal, oil and gas formed from the remains of dead plants and animals over millions of years

frayed cables cables that are unravelled and have worn insulation

free fall an object falling under the influence of gravity alone

frequency the number of waves or vibrations passing a point per second

friction the force that opposes motion when two surfaces rub together

fuse a component designed to melt when a specified current value is exceeded, thus breaking the circuit

galaxy a system of millions or billions of stars

gamma (γ) ray highly penetrating electromagnetic radiation produced when an unstable atom decays

geothermal energy thermal energy produced by nuclear processes in the Earth's core

gradient the ratio of the change in the quantity plotted on the **y**-axis to the corresponding change in the quantity plotted on the **x**-axis; here quantity plotted means, for example, distance/m rather than just distance

gravitational field strength the force in newtons exerted per kilogram of mass by gravity; at the Earth's surface this is 9.8N/kg

gravitational potential energy (g.p.e. or E_p) the energy possessed by an object due to its relative position; for example, its height above the Earth's surface

half-life the average time taken for half the nuclei in a radioactive sample to decay and form a new element

Hooke's Law the extension of an object is proportional to the load producing it, provided that the limit of proportionality is not exceeded

hydroelectric energy electrical energy produced using the gravitational potential energy of water stored in reservoirs in mountainous regions to turn turbines and drive generators

image optical reproduction of an object using lenses or mirrors (see real and virtual)

impulse the impulse acting on a body is equal to the product of the force acting on the body and the time for which it acts

incident ray a ray of light arriving at or striking a surface

induce to give rise to or cause something to happen by induction

induction see electromagnetic and electrostatic induction

inelastic collision a collision in which some of the kinetic energy is transferred into another form such as sound and thermal energy

infrared radiation the portion of the electromagnetic spectrum between microwaves and visible light that is sometimes known as thermal radiation

infrasound low-frequency sound, lower than 20Hz (the normal limit of human hearing)

insulator a material that does not transfer thermal energy or allow charges to pass through it easily

interact to act in a manner that causes objects to have an effect on each other

interaction see interact

internal energy the total kinetic and potential energy of the particles within an object

inversely proportional as one quantity increases, the other quantity decreases so that their product is constant

ionisation the process by which a particle (atom or molecule) becomes electrically charged by losing or gaining electrons

ionising radiation charged particles or high-energy light rays that ionise the material through which they travel

isotopes atoms of an element that have the same atomic number but different nucleon number (the same number of protons but a different number of neutrons)

kilogram (kg) the base unit of mass

kilowatt-hour (kWh) a unit of electrical energy. A 1 kilowatt fire uses 1kWh of energy to run for 1 hour

kinetic energy (k.e. or E_k) the energy of an object due to its motion

lagging insulating material

lamina a flat object of constant thickness

laser a device that produces a concentrated narrow beam of single-frequency light

Lenz's Law the magnetic field generated by an induced current opposes the change in field that caused the current

light-dependent resistor (LDR) a resistor whose resistance varies according to the amount of light falling on it

light-emitting diode (LED) a diode that glows when current passes through it

light-year a measurement of distance used for astronomical distances. One light-year is the distance travelled by light in one year approximately equal to 9.5×10^{15}m

limit of proportionality the point beyond which the extension is no longer proportional to the load

linear in a straight line

load a force that causes a spring to extend

longitudinal wave the particles of the medium through which the wave travels move backwards and forwards along the same line as the direction of travel

loudness how we perceive the amplitude of a sound wave

luminous gives out light

magnetic field a region in space around a magnet or electric current in which a magnet will feel a force

magnetic material material that is attracted to or can be made into a magnet; steel and iron are examples of magnetic materials

magnified enlarged; for example, a magnified image is larger than the object

magnitude the size of a quantity

mass the amount of matter in an object; its base unit is the kilogram (kg)

mass number see nucleon number

matter an object that has a mass and occupies space

mean value an average value

medium a material that waves can travel through, such as air, water or glass

melting point the temperature at which a solid melts to become a liquid at normal pressure

meniscus the curved surface of a liquid as seen, for example, within a measuring cylinder

metre (m) the base unit of length

model a mental or physical representation that cannot be observed directly; usually used as an aid to understanding

moment the turning effect of a force about a pivot; the product of force and perpendicular distance from the pivot

momentum the product of mass and velocity of a body; it is a measure of the quantity of motion in a body

moon a natural satellite of a planet

monochromatic radiation of a single wavelength, such as laser light

negligible small enough to be ignored

nebula a giant cloud of gas dust in space

neutral having no overall positive or negative charge

neutron an electrically neutral particle found in the nucleus of an atom

neutron star a celestial object of very small radius and very high density

Newton's 1st Law an object will remain at rest or move at a steady speed in a straight line unless acted upon by an unbalanced force

Newton's 2nd Law an object will accelerate in the direction of an unbalanced force

normal a construction line drawn at right angles where a light ray strikes a surface such as a mirror or glass block

nuclear energy the energy stored in the nucleus of an atom

nuclear fission the process by which energy is released by the splitting of a large heavy nucleus into two or more lighter nuclei

nuclear fusion the process by which energy is released by the joining of two small light nuclei to form a new heavier nucleus

nucleon a particle such as a proton or neutron found in the nucleus of an atom

nucleon number (A) (also known as mass number) the number of protons and neutrons found in the nucleus of an atom

nucleus the very small and densely concentrated centre of an atom made up of protons and neutrons

nuclide a 'species' of a nucleus characterised by its atomic and mass numbers

Ohm's Law the current in a metal conductor is directly proportional to the potential difference across it provided the temperature remains the same

orbit the path of a satellite or planet around a celestial body or an electron around the nucleus of an atom

orbital speed the average speed of a planet calculated by dividing the length of the orbit by the time taken to complete one orbit

oscillation a repetitive motion, such as a pendulum swinging back and forth

parallax error the apparent change in position of a measurement caused by viewing the measurement at an angle less than or greater than 90 degrees to the scale

parallel circuit a circuit in which current has more than one path

penetrating passing through or into something

period the time taken for one complete cycle of oscillation, vibration or passage of a wave

periscope an optical device for viewing objects otherwise out of sight

perpendicular at right angles or 90 degrees

pitch how high or low a musical note sounds; is related to frequency: the higher the frequency the higher the pitch

pivot the fixed point about which a lever turns

potential difference (p.d.) defined as the work done by unit charge passing through a conductor or the difference in electrical energy between two points of a circuit measured across the terminals of an electrical component such as a bulb; often referred to as voltage

potential divider usually consists of two or more resistors arranged in series across a power supply; designed to deliberately split the voltage in a circuit

potential energy the energy stored in a body due to its position, electric charge, or the arrangement of the particles within it e.g. a raised weight, a charged battery, a coiled spring

power the rate at which energy is transferred or work is done

precise how close repeated measurements of the same quantity are to each other; precise measurements do not necessarily indicate accuracy

pressure the force acting per unit area at right angles to the surface

primary coil the input coil to a transformer

principal axis the line passing through the centre of a lens at right angles (perpendicular) to its surface

principal focus the point at which rays of light parallel to the principal axis converge after passing through a converging lens

propagation direction of travel

proportional when a change in one quantity is accompanied by a consistent change in the other

proton a positively charged particle found in the nucleus of an atom

proton number (**Z**) (also known as atomic number) the number of protons in the nucleus of an atom

protostar a very young star

radial moving or directed along the radius of a circle

radiation the transfer of energy by electromagnetic waves

radioactive decay the natural and random change of an unstable nucleus when it emits radiation

random a spontaneous event that cannot be predicted; for example, random decay means that it is not possible to predict when a particular nucleus will decay (but, statistically, it is possible to determine how many nuclei will decay in a given time)

range the difference between the minimum and maximum reading of an instrument; or the maximum distance a particle can travel

rarefaction a region of a sound wave in which the particles are further apart

ray a narrow beam of light

real image an optical image that can be formed on a screen

rectification the process of converting a.c. into d.c. with the use of one or more diodes

red giant a stage of the life cycle of a star when the star becomes unstable and starts to expand

redshift the apparent change in wavelength of light, due to the Doppler effect, from distant galaxies that are moving away from us

reflection the change in direction when a ray of light or sound wave bounces off a surface

refraction the change in direction of a light ray when passing from one material into another

refractive index the ratio of speed of light in a vacuum to that in a particular material; a material that has a large refractive index will refract light more than a material with a lower index

relay an electromagnetic switch

repulsion a force that causes objects to separate and move in opposite directions

resistance a measure of how difficult it is for current to pass through a circuit or part of a circuit; measured in ohms (Ω)

resistor a component in an electrical circuit that resists current

resultant force the net force acting on a body when two or more forces are unbalanced; effectively the replacement of all forces acting on an object with one equivalent force

ripple a small, uniform wave on the surface of water

Sankey diagram a diagram summarising the energy transfers in a process

satellite an object in orbit around another object

scintillations flashes of light

second (**s**) the base unit of time

secondary coil the output coil of a transformer

sensitivity response to change; a sensitive instrument gives a large reading for a small change in the quantity being measured

series circuit a circuit in which current has one path

short circuit a low-resistance connection between two points, causing a large current to flow

SI an internationally agreed system of units based on the metric system

slip rings used to allow the passage of current to and from a coil in an a.c. generator

Snell's Law the ratio of sin i to sin r is a constant and is equal to the refractive index of the second medium with respect to the first

soft magnetic materials materials that, once magnetised, can easily be demagnetised

solar cell a device that converts energy from the Sun into electricity

Solar System the region of the Universe that contains our Sun, the Earth and Moon, seven other planets and their moons and satellites, as well as asteroids and comets

solenoid a coil of wire that becomes magnetised when a current is present in the coil

sound wave a longitudinal wave that carries sound energy from place to place

specific heat capacity (**s.h.c.**) the energy needed to raise the temperature of one kilogram of a substance by one degree Celsius

spectrum colours of light separated out in the order of their wavelengths

speed the distance travelled by an object per second

speed of light in a vacuum is 3×10^8 m/s

split ring used to allow the passage of current to and from a coil in a d.c. motor; also reverses the direction of the current every half turn

star a luminous celestial body comprising of gas held together by gravitational force

spring constant a measure of the stiffness of a spring defined as the force per unit extension

static electricity electric charge held by a charged insulator

stationary standing still

stellar of or relating to the stars

sterilise to kill bacteria and clean

streamlined smoothed and somewhat rounded in order to reduce air resistance

supernova a large explosion that takes place at the end of a star's life cycle

temperature a measure of how hot a body is

terminal velocity the maximum velocity reached by an object moving through a fluid such as air; reached when the force due to its weight is equal to the force due to air resistance

thermal energy the internal energy a body has because of the motion of its particles

thermocouple a thermometer made from two metal wires joined at the ends to form junctions

time period the time taken for one complete cycle of oscillation, vibration, passage of a wave, or orbit

total internal reflection all light is reflected back from a surface between materials; this happens as a result of the angle of incidence being greater than the critical angle

transducer any device or component that converts one form of energy into another

transformer a device used to change the voltage of an a.c. electricity supply

transmission lines power cables used to carry electricity from power stations to consumers

transverse wave a wave in which the vibrations or oscillations are at right angles to the direction of travel

turbine a machine similar to a fan with blades that rotate when air, steam or water passes through; often used to generate electricity

ultrasound sound waves with frequencies greater than 20 000 Hz, which cannot be heard by the human ear

ultraviolet radiation the portion of the electromagnetic spectrum between visible light and X-rays, which can cause tanning of the skin

uniform constant

variable resistor a component whose resistance can be manually altered

vector a quantity with both magnitude (size) and direction

velocity the speed of an object in a particular direction

virtual image an image that cannot be formed on a screen

voltage a measure of the energy converted per unit charge passing through a component; also a measure of the amount of energy transferred to electrical form per unit charge by an electrical power supply, like a battery; measured in volts (V)

voltmeter a meter used for measuring the voltage (p.d.) between two points

wavefront the set of points connected in space by a wave or vibration at the same instant; wavefronts generally form a continuous line or surface; for example the lines formed by ripples on a pond

wavelength the distance between two adjacent identical points on a wave

weight the downward force due to gravity acting on an object's mass

white dwarf a small very dense star

work done the product of force and distance in the direction of the force

Glossary for examination terminology

When answering an examination question it is important to understand what you are being asked. This glossary is intended as a guide only. The meaning of a term will always depend on context.

Calculate work out from given facts, figures or information

Comment give an informed opinion

Compare identify/comment on similarities and/or differences

Deduce conclude from available information

Define give precise meaning

Describe state the points of a topic/give characteristics and main features

Determine establish an answer using the information available

Explain set out purposes or reasons/make the relationships between things evident/provide why and/or how and support with relevant evidence

Give produce an answer from a given source or recall/memory

Identify name/select/recognise

Justify support a case with evidence/argument

Predict suggest what may happen based on available information

Sketch make a simple freehand drawing showing the key features, taking care over proportions

State express in clear terms

Suggest apply knowledge and understanding to situations where there are a range of valid responses in order to make proposals/put forward considerations

Index